In *The Emotional Life of Babies*, Dr. Marion Rose shares her amazing ability to perceive the world through a baby's eyes. She offers a gentle invitation for parents to put aside preconceived ideas about babies and learn to interpret cues that are often overlooked or misunderstood. With deep compassion, she explains how parents' own childhood experiences can cause them to misinterpret what their babies are trying to tell them. Parents who follow her advice will enhance their baby's emotional development and strengthen attachment.

– Aletha Solter, PhD, founder of Aware Parenting

Marion's work has completely transformed my family and my life – through individual sessions, groups, courses, her articles, her podcast, and having the absolute honour and pleasure of becoming her friend. Her depth of knowledge about Aware Parenting, together with her extraordinary compassion, have evolved parenting to be so powerfully healing, so deeply connecting and so joyful. I learn profound new things from her in every conversation we have, and I see through our work together how she has transformed so many other families too. I recommend her work so highly. I feel truly blessed to have come across her work 17 years ago and to be still learning more from her every day.

This powerful book is going to transform our understanding of babies and how to meet their needs. The clarity about the theory of Aware Parenting and the deep compassion that Marion's work always brings, is beautifully woven in with stories, reflections, guidance, her own experiences of deeply embodying this approach, together with the baby's perspective. The pace and structure of the book is skilfully arranged so that even the most exhausted parent can understand and then implement all the key concepts.

I have read a lot of books about parenting and this is the first time that I have found a book that offers information about attachment and trauma, together with a compassionate invitation and a process to observe your baby and decide for yourself what works for you and your family. It is so empowering, not just because it allows parents to deeply understand this information and implement it, but also because of the deeply connected and attuned relationships that it supports between parents and their children. I wish I had had this book when my babies were little and I highly recommend it for all parents.

– Joss Goulden, Aware Parenting instructor

The Aware Parenting model and Marion's work in particular have not only informed my practice as a Clinical Psychologist working with parents, but also my own parenting. Practicing Aware Parenting with newborns can enrich attachment and enjoyment of the newborn and infant period as well as significantly reduce anxiety in new parents and allow them to focus on following cues and enjoying their new relationship. Aware Parenting from birth then supports the natural progression to Aware Parenting with older children, therefore fostering an ongoing emotionally healthy parent-child attachment. Marion's work – including *The Emotional Life of Babies* – is in line with the plethora of research on infant attachment and long term child psychological well-being and I will forever be grateful for her contribution to Aware Parenting.

– Dr Jessica Klug, Clinical Psychologist, Aware Parenting instructor

In *The Emotional Life of Babies*, Marion shares her love, experience, passion and deep knowledge of Aware Parenting for babies. This book is a culmination of Marion's own personal journey and profound evolution of her life's work. Underpinned by evidence-based research, it provides parents with an abundance of information, anecdotes, advice and stories on how to support the emotional life of babies. Marion is the centrepiece for Aware Parenting in the Southern Hemisphere, holding the position of Regional Co-ordinator for Australia and New Zealand. As a community we have all benefited hugely from her wisdom and expertise. I wish I had this resource when I first became a mother. I will be sharing this far and wide. This book is a gift to the world.

– Georgie Bancroft PhD, Psychologist, Aware Parenting instructor, Hand In Hand Parenting Instructor.

Marion has been in the field of developmental psychology for more than 30 years, studying the mother-infant relationship in her PhD, as well as exploring the experience of the infant through various psychotherapy modalities. There is no-one I have come across who understands babies and infants more deeply than Marion. She is a world leader in this field and every parent needs this information. As a therapist and as a parent her work has been life changing. *The Emotional Life of Babies* will help any parent understand their baby's needs and how to meet them. A divinely insightful book I wish I had when I was first a parent. A must read for all parents, grandparents, therapists, childcare workers or anyone who will be spending time with a baby. This book will change your life.

– Shelley Clarke, Aware Parenting instructor,
Marion Method Mentor, CranioSacral Therapist

Aware Parenting offers an intuitive approach to learning about your baby centred on respect, connection and curiosity. Getting to know your baby can be such a rewarding experience. Babies have beautiful teachings to share, such as slowing down, being more mindful, noticing the subtleties around us and living an embodied life.

In the last decade of working alongside parents and babies, I have witnessed the ease and delight of parenting when there is an understanding that babies have feelings. By recognising that babies are completely aware, parents are offered gifts of presence, deep connection and joy in the parenting journey.

This rich connection with your baby can be a balm to some of the challenges experienced in the early parenting journey. Time and time again, I have observed obstacles navigated with ease when parents focus on understanding their baby's emotional needs. This awareness can have a profound and positive impact on the pregnancy, birth experience, feeding and sleep journey and the rite of passage into parenthood.

Marion offers her extensive experience and knowledge with empathy, compassion and warmth. This book is a beautiful invitation to learn about the innate wisdom of your baby and enjoy the gifts that it will bring.

> – Carly Facius, Registered Midwife, International Board Certified Lactation Consultant, Master Primary Maternity Care,
> Aware Parenting instructor

I'm not even sure where to begin acknowledging how radically my life changed 17 years ago after I booked a session with Marion. How do I thank someone who helped me regain sanity, showed me a more beautiful way to raise children, reaffirmed my deeper knowing about compassionate living, introduced me to the wonders of Aware Parenting and who gave my family the gift of sound sleep? (And that was in the first session alone!) Marion's sweet guidance opened up an entirely new world for my wee family and I am still noticing profound results in my teenage children, and in myself, on a daily basis.

Before meeting Marion, I knew there must be a more gentle, baby respecting, caregiver-honouring, developmental psychology-aligned version of sleep guidance but had yet to discover it. Thank you, Marion, for opening the path to that way, that deeper connection, that better relating, that more harmonious parenting and so much more.

> – Chiara Rossetti, Aware Parenting instructor and Field Project Certified Facilitator

What stands out to me as a health practitioner in this field is that Marion also uniquely focuses on the well-being of the care-giver. I often find that the stresses of the care-giver have such a profound impact on the baby and yet this is often largely ignored. The baby IS the extension of the care-giver. So how the care-giver speaks to themselves will echo in the baby.

The Emotional Life of Babies so eloquently discusses Aware Parenting and how it applies to babies and their care-givers. It provides real-life examples to assist the reader to have a better grasp of the key concepts of Aware Parenting applied in the real world. Marion writes in such a beautiful way that keeps the reader engaged, encouraged and inspired to provide the best care for both themselves and their little ones.

– Dr Clare Molino, Registered Chiropractor, Osteopath

My Aware Parenting sessions with Marion, along with her body of work and the community I've found as a result of meeting her, helped me change the trajectory of my parenting (and my life) in the most profound, connected, healing and deeply beautiful ways…13 years on, I'm still as grateful as ever.

– Emma Mason, Aware Parenting instructor

I am so incredibly grateful to Marion for so many reasons. It was her essay at the back of a Calmbirth booklet that introduced me to Aware Parenting. Over the past decade she has supported my journey as an Aware Parenting instructor. Marion has also walked next to me as I grew my own business, providing unconditional loving support to everything I do. Marion's passion is so evident in all the amazing contributions she makes to the world. From *The Aware Parenting Podcast*, her online courses, her 1:1 mentoring and her beautiful books that are filled with so much compassion. As a massive bookworm, I'm so excited to be able to sit down and read all her books.

In *The Emotional Life of Babies*, I loved the moments of self-compassion woven beautifully throughout the book, inviting readers to really tune in with what resonates for them and to place down any 'emotional sticks'. I also really enjoyed the emphasis Marion placed on parents really observing their baby. Often, parents tend to rely on the outside opinion of others, when there is no one-size-fits-all approach. The invitations to always check in with ourselves and our babies, I believe, can really connect parents to their babies in even greater and deeply loving ways, which also has the ability to further empower us not just as parents, but also as human beings.

– Stephanie Heartfield of Spirited Hearts, Aware Parenting instructor, Counsellor, Early Childhood Educator

What Marion Rose has brought to Aware Parenting and to my own personal journey is difficult to put into words. Marion's extensive knowledge in relation to the mother-baby connection has been refined over 33 years of observation, study and deeply personal experiences with thousands of clients all over the world and her own parenting journey. After learning about Aware Parenting from Aletha Solter PhD, she began to create online courses offering this incredible knowledge in a way that parents could easily understand and begin to implement the philosophy and techniques immediately in their lives. Her online courses are fun, interactive and invite you to explore your own re-parenting journey and childhood, as well as your parenting journey with your child.

It was through her Love Being a Mother Course that I was first introduced to her world and Aware Parenting. This was an incredibly pivotal point in my life. At this time, I was a first-time mother with a child who hadn't slept for three years. I knew nothing about listening to feelings or healing trauma through crying and play. After a difficult separation from her father and zero sleep, I was at the lowest point in my parenting journey.

I can say with all my heart that Marion coming into my world literally saved my life and saved my relationship with my daughter. I would not be here today without her. Her presence, wisdom and unwavering love and support has been the light that I was desperately wanting, to escape the intense darkness I was experiencing. Fast forward more than eight years and I am honoured to call her my mentor, colleague and dear friend. I have spent the past eight years listening and learning from her and have been able to deeply connect with my own soul's calling and share her wisdom with the world. What Marion has brought to my life and to the lives of many, many people around the world, is priceless. There are no words to describe my deepest respect, love and gratitude for her.

– Nic Wilson, Aware Parenting instructor, Marion Method Mentor

Marion's wealth of experience, wisdom and compassion for babies has been the guiding light in our parenting journey. Her empathetic approach, combined with her extensive knowledge, has profoundly reshaped our lives – mine, our baby's, and our entire family's, in unimaginable ways. The practical and tangible practices Marion provides continue to be an invaluable source of support, forever ingraining a sense of profound gratitude within us. I passionately wish that every expectant and new parent is bestowed with this vital and transformative book.

– Sarah Mason, Postpartum Care Provider,
Aware Parenting instructor

While reading *The Emotional Life of Babies*, I constantly thought, "How different would my child be if I had this knowledge when he was a baby? How different would our world be if we allowed our babies and children to express their feelings freely?"

An amazing book, which gives us great insight into how healing it is for our babies to do what parents dread the most: crying. Marion Rose explains in detail how parents can distinguish the reasons why a baby cries, and then either meet the need that is behind the cry, or give the baby the time, space, and presence for them to express all the feelings that make them uncomfortable.

Reading the baby's perspective on every situation, and how our methods of stopping the crying affect them and cause their dissociation from their feelings was illuminating.

Marion also offers moments of compassion and self-reflection after every new piece of information, inviting the readers to let go of any possible guilt for their past practices, and constantly mentions how important it is for parents, especially mothers, to receive support in order to be able to be present for their babies.

A book that must be in the bookcase of every parent and every specialist who works with children.

Thank you, Marion. The world definitely needs more space for crying.

– Eirini Anagnostopoulou, Parenting Coach

The Emotional Life of Babies is a gem for parents looking to deepen their understanding and foster a loving and safe environment in which to welcome and enable babies to communicate their needs and feelings. Marion provides practical tips and techniques for parents to implement, touching on attachment and responsiveness. One of my most profound takeaways from this book is the emphasis of self-compassion for parents, recognising that one's own emotional well-being influences their child's emotional growth.

– Brittany

Marion has been an invaluable presence in my life over the past decade. From her parenting articles to her amazing personal consultations and the incredible groups she facilitates. Through her I have learned so much about my daughter's emotions and actions and how to deal with them lovingly, consciously and effectively. And through that, I have learned more about how to deal with my own emotions lovingly, consciously and effectively.

Her impact has been far reaching – she has helped me grow into the person I want to be (or rather, come back to the core of who I am), develop myself as a business entrepreneur, strengthen my relationship with my husband, and open my eyes to an amazing way to parent. I have had a number of personal development and business coaches, and none of them have provided the richness, the depth nor the loving compassion or insight that Marion has given me.

My, and my family's life is much richer and more connected as a result and I can't thank you enough Marion!

– Helena Mooney, Parenting with Play, Aware Parenting instructor, Hand in Hand Instructor

I took Marion's sleep course when I was struggling with sleep. My son was doing the crocodile death roll every night in bed – he was so restless and wakeful. After completing Marion's course our sleep completely changed. And to be honest my connection and relationship with my children deepened.

I then took what I learnt from Marion into my workplace working with families and babies and that is where I have seen the magic of 'melty baby' happen again and again. We discuss how the mums feel when their bub has big feelings and big episodes of crying…and every single time they have the same answer – it makes them think they are not good enough, they are doing something wrong and cannot seem to fix their baby. They then become frustrated and disempowered and lose all confidence in their ability to parent.

But, when I then talk to them about how their little one has big feelings just like them, and the importance of 'being with' them through these feelings, it's like something inside them clicks and they understand. It's like a language is spoken and the mums just seem to get it.

We then take the next step and work together listening to their babies' cries.. and I kid you not the babies seem to melt into their mums' arms once they get their big feelings (cries) out!! MELTY BABY… And the mums are just ecstatic. They feel empowered and you can just see their confidence grow and their bond with their baby is magical. No longer trying to 'fix' something that never needed to be fixed at all.

– Kimberley Cousins, Registered Nurse specialising in perinatal mental health, Aware Parenting instructor in training

I have been privileged to receive Marion's expert guidance over many years through private and group mentoring. Going through her flagship Marion Method courses (Inner Loving Presence Process, Conversations with Life and the Willingness Practice) has changed my inner and outer dialogue in ways that mean my own compassionate wise and supportive self is the only voice in my head. I am constantly whispering words of kindness where prior had only been criticism and ridicule.

Her unwavering commitment, compassion and brilliance meant I could grow my understanding and acceptance of my child's and my own earliest experiences *in utero* and the first days, months and years of life that set up patterns of behaviour. Marion's work in intelligently unraveling the emotional lives of babies meant I could navigate the often complex and sometimes troubling behaviours as well as transmute emotional stumbling blocks in ways that left me feeling that I belong to a world that makes sense.

Now, I am increasingly able to graciously meet my child's physiological and developmental needs while deeply honouring my own genuine needs, feelings and desires. I also help others through my own work as an Aware Parenting instructor. Working with Marion has, hands down, been the most important journey of my life. Her work is for anyone who has ever had a baby, ever will have a baby or ever was a baby themselves.

– Devon Harris, Aware Parenting instructor

I was recommended by a friend to Marion's work when my first baby was 10 months old. I was practicing Classical Attachment Parenting and I couldn't understand why my baby wasn't sleeping. He wasn't having his naps during the day any more and was sleeping very poorly during the night. I was exhausted. Through Marion's work, I was able to identify that he had a breastfeeding control pattern. When I started to apply what I learnt from Marion about listening to his feelings, everything shifted, and he (and I) started to sleep much better. With Marion, I've also learnt how to be compassionate with myself, especially while learning how to parent my baby with much more awareness to his (and my own) emotions.

Marion also supported me with my second baby, who had developed a thumb-sucking control pattern. Through receiving one-to-one support from her, Marion helped me to understand the reasons behind my baby's control pattern. Marion supported me and my partner in reflecting back what we could do for ourselves to enable more emotional capacity so our daughter would feel emotionally safer to express her feelings to us. We've applied what Marion taught us and very soon we could notice a difference in our daughter as she started expressing her feelings much more. We also started to feel much more compassionate to our own feelings whenever she would suck her thumb.

Marion's work is also so beautiful in supporting mothers to be more compassionate with themselves and this is definitely for me, one of the most unique things that I've learnt from her approach. Learning a new way to parent our children can be hard to take in as we might find ourselves feeling guilty about how we used to do it before. Marion has this beautiful talent of offering all this information while holding the parents with so much love and compassion, that melts the guilt away. It's very hard to find someone with the ability to do this, and I see so many instructors like me, who work close to Marion, who are all learning this beautiful Aware Parenting way from her. Thank you Marion, your beautiful work and dedication impacts so many families around the world in finding much more connection and compassion in their homes.

– Rafa Guadalupe, Aware Parenting instructor

I am so glad Marion is here in this life with us, sharing her wisdom and love. I am grateful for all Marion's shared experiences and stories, particularly of herself as a baby. For her deep empathy, understanding and insight (for both babies and mothers). For her countless hours of dedication, research, practice and contribution.

I am grateful for Marion's big picture lens and willingness to tirelessly and generously share information and resources and create processes and practices to contribute to Life's evolution. I am blessed to have personally and deeply experienced Marion's knowledge, wisdom, compassion, listening and love through many of her courses and offerings; one on one mentoring – in both Aware Parenting and Marion Method spaces, countless articles and recordings and her first wonderful book with Lael Stone.

Over the years Marion's work has touched me deeply and invited much introspection, healing, clarity and expansion. Thank you Marion for lovingly holding what is possible and continuing to inspire and shine the light for me (us) on the road less travelled. What a beautiful ripple effect I know this book will create for babies, mothers and families, for all of time.

– Anne Smith, Aware Parenting instructor, Marion Method Mentor

I found Marion and Aware Parenting in 2012 when my son was eight weeks old. He had never really cried, and I thought that was a good thing! We had a very traumatic birth and I didn't really consider how it might have impacted him. He had all kinds of physical symptoms from colic to food intolerance to waking all night to constant restlessness. If he ever started to cry, I rocked or breastfed him; I thought he was crying only from hunger not from built up feelings.

Once I heard about this compassionate listening to crying, the next time he started crying I held him and was just present and listened. He cried his heart out while I held him and said, "I hear you. I love you," for around 30 minutes. Then he stopped and slept longer than he'd ever napped and woke up smiling and happy (he previously always woke starting to cry and I usually fed him). For the next week he was a different baby – way more calm in his body, present, sleeping well, and no more colic. Incredible! And then every few days or so, another big release and he was rebalanced again!

Marion also saved my sanity again when he was two years old and waking every hour through the night to breastfeed. A loving gentle reminder to let him express his feelings even if it was the middle of the night and all it took was one night of waking and crying in my arms while I listened and he then slept through the night! It's incredible how far a bit of empathy and listening and compassion can go, and I tell you, one sleepless night of listening was far better than years of waking hourly to breastfeed!!

Now 11 years old, I can still tell when my boy needs a good cry. He will seem restless, hyperactive, angry, impatient, forgetful, agitated and unfocused. If we can get some decent connected empathy in, or if he has a good cry or laugh, he is immediately relaxed and calm again. I can sincerely say that without Aware Parenting my son would have an ADHD or ASD diagnosis for what I've come to realise for him are actually built-up feelings needing to be released.

If only all of us were raised with this awareness I wonder how many of us as adults would be far more calm, relaxed, embodied and self-aware! Thank you Marion, for all you bring to this world. You are a voice for babies that every parent can benefit from hearing.

– Elle

I was introduced to Aware Parenting and Marion's work after a pretty rough start. My baby was born with a cephal haematoma and we further found he had an infection so spent the first week in special care. From this experience with no sleep to him coming home the first three months he was averaging six to eight hours of broken sleep in a 24-hour period and basically when he wasn't sleeping, he was crying/screaming. Exhausted is an understatement. This spiralled my mental health out of control.

I was searching for any remedy to help him sleep and spent (I would hate to know how much) money on sleep schedules, sleep apps, white noise machines and advice from anything I could find, however this only made things worse as I couldn't get my baby to 'fit the mould' of these programs or schedules and his cries just triggered me into panic attacks. Eventually I got admitted to an amazing Perinatal Mental health unit at a private hospital where I was cared for by some amazing staff, and two notable staff who introduced me to Aware Parenting. I bought *Raising Resilient and Compassionate Children* and have listened to most of the episodes of *The Aware Parenting Podcast* and can easily credit my comeback to Marion's work resonating so closely with me.

I have a background in early childhood education, youth out of home care and more recently family violence. I have worked with trauma so much, yet did not consider this for my own baby. After listening to and reading Marion's work and other recommendations and implementing the practices I am so enjoying the bond I have with my baby, we are both getting a lot more sleep and I really look forward to seeing him grow into a compassionate and resilient person.

– Thalia Ellis

I have been a fan of Marion's work for a couple of years now. The work she does around children/toddlers/babies and their emotions is amazing. I have also loved the work she has guided me in doing in healing my own childhood stuff and to love being a mother – and let's not forget the stuff she's put together on letting go of guilt. It's like she just knows what mothers need for all aspects of it. I am so grateful for her work and our family is indebted to her for the connection we all feel from using the tools she has provided us with. Whether her work is delivered via an online course, podcast, YouTube clip, book or social media, she is ALWAYS giving back.

– Alishya

Thank you Marion Rose, for being one of the most important Mother voices in my life. Putting on *The Aware Parenting Podcast*, reading your posts and articles, or watching a video from your Making Friends with Children's Feelings Course always makes me feel inspired, loved and supported. Your wisdom has been and is a crucial part of becoming my own Inner Loving Mother and the Mother I want to be to my daughter.

— Kia Linnéa

You have been incredibly helpful on my journey... Just over two years ago, when I came across Aware Parenting and when I joined the Facebook group, you were the first one to respond to my post asking for help. You were so kind and reassuring and you gave me such wonderful advice. I actually keep going back to your words when reassuring others who are at the beginning of their journey of becoming Aware Parents. Since then, I've listened to your Podcast, read your book (co-authored with Lael Stone), joined your Aware Parenting Instructor Mentoring Course... You are such an inspiration... Kind and loving, generous with your love and wisdom. I love learning from you.

— Lucia Gaston, Aware Parenting instructor in training, Dramatherapist, Forest School Practitioner and Play Ranger, Art and Creativity Teacher

Marion's work is truly a gift to the world. Her prolific content through books, podcasts, and courses is a vast vat of deeply insightful knowledge that allows a person to examine their life to find more beauty, more kindness, more nurturance. To work with her 1:1 has been to shift the deepest and darkest ancestral paradigms that have been passed down to me, and that have shaped my thinking, so that I can raise my beautiful daughter in a newly imagined paradigm that is filled with magic, not only for her but also for me. The work is bittersweet as it reveals layers of deeply grooved shame, guilt, and pain – and with Marion the work is so sacred as she is both witness and guide through transformative moments.

— Natalie Gyte

Marion's work on Aware Parenting through her book, podcast and other resources has transformed my parenting journey. I spend every night listening to her podcast as I put my son to bed and I feel more calm, confident and supported in my parenting and role as a mother. Aware Parenting has been just as much a transformational journey for me as it has for my son and gives me more compassion and guidance to be the parent I want to be each and every day. I now see his emotions and tantrums as necessary instead of inconvenient or something to be fixed and am improving on my ability to hold space for him. Marion's work truly is priceless.

– Simone Blake, Physiotherapist

I've come to deeply trust Aware Parenting through seeing the difference between how my daughter is now as a three month old baby, and how my son was as a baby – he is almost three years old. We've practiced Aware Parenting, starting with crying-in-arms, from my daughter's birth and she already sleeps through the night at 10 weeks, has had no digestive issues and seems so present – really looking into our eyes and smiling, playing with her hands. Everyone comments on how "aware she is", which I find ironic!

With my son we got to Aware Parenting more actively when he was around 18 months old. I see now how my desperation to stop his crying any way I could – walking, jiggling, feeding – led to him not being able to have the release that my daughter has had by us simply holding her as she cries, and how much of a difference it has had in her body. My son seemed to suffer with reflux early on and certainly didn't sleep through the night – this is the starkest difference. It's hard to accept as a parent, but as a result of my inability to be with his crying, my belief that I had to make it stop however I could, lack of awareness that babies have feelings too, I believe he was also less present, less aware, less able to simply observe and engage in the way that my daughter can, and it was hard for him to relax his body enough to fall asleep and stay asleep. What I love about Aware Parenting is that it's never too late, there is always healing to be done and we've been working through his feelings release as a toddler ever since.

Marion's dedicated Aware Parenting support has been the ultimate gift to our family. A gift to me and my own personal growth, particularly the awareness I have now of my own control patterns and their impact in my own life. And what a gift to our children and their futures! If you have the opportunity to work with Marion you must grab it with both hands!!

– Helen Attia Tolken, Feelings Inc.

I have been interested in Aware Parenting for two years now, but it never caught me so much as when I started to listen to *The Aware Parenting Podcast*, by Marion Rose PhD and Lael Stone. Immediately after the first episode, I felt like I had found gold. I devoured all episodes, often multiple times, and I still do every time there is a new one. I read all books by the founder of Aware Parenting, Aletha Solter, the lovely book of Marion and Lael, and I followed multiple Dutch webinars. I am so grateful and stunned by how much Aware Parenting has changed me. It so profoundly improved my connection to my two lovely children, to my parents, to friends and colleagues, bottom line, the world. And I see how my boys do things so differently, their words and insights already outgrow little me. My journey has not ended yet, the inner work is sometimes really hard, but I found my divine mother within me (thank you Marion) and she is always there to support and love me.

– Josine van Buul

Aware Parenting came into our lives when our daughter was eight months old. I generally enjoyed pregnancy very much. Birth was 26 hours of labour and ended in an emergency C-section. It was very hard first months for all of us. Not enough milk as I lost lots of blood, recovering from birth, frequent night waking, lots of crying and trying to find the need to stop the crying. We were tired and felt helpless a lot. The crying stopped when I breastfed her, so I thought that I had found the need and fed our daughter a lot.

When I started reading *The Aware Baby* by Aletha Solter and let my baby cry in my arms, the night waking changed from 5-10 times to 1-2 times a night within a few days, and our daughter became much more clear and satisfied. Being with the crying was always the easiest and hardest hour of the day. Easy, because my body could rest, and I was not trying to keep her from crying. Hard, because it was challenging to see my baby 'suffer' and I had to be with my inner child as well and tell her that there is nothing to do than just be there with compassion. Since then, Aware Parenting has become our 'daily bread'. Playing, crying, raging, laughing, being with myself and my daughter.

I love the way that Marion is continuing the work of Aletha Solter and how she adds her style – her gentle, compassionate way of talking, writing, being with herself and others. I learn most from honest people – which I find Marion is. I am inspired how willingly she shares her story.

She helped me with the interviews with Aletha on YouTube, her videos, her charts with important Aware Parenting understandings, the answers she gives in the Facebook group, and how she wants to heal from her wounds and how she also wants other people to heal. To me, Marion is someone who is healing, and passing on the healing to her surroundings very actively – like a 'healing-spreader'.

I am sooo thankful for the work of Marion (and all the other Aware Parenting instructors), as I understand so much about the psyche of humans. I am becoming more compassionate with myself, my husband and our daughters (we have two now) and I think it has improved our lives very very much. I'm also willing to spread the healing.

– Rebecca Thums

Aware Parenting, explained by Marion Rose, has helped us ALL sleep better, feel our feelings, play more and ultimately, love being parents to our two wonderful toddlers. Marion holds a beautiful mirror and helps us see that we have the power within us to create stronger connections, form closer attachments and honour the needs of both parent and baby/child. Marion's insights have the potential to change parenting lineages for generations to come, she certainly has mine, and for that, we will be forever grateful.

– Charlotte Abelson, Occupational Therapist

I so loved this book. It wrapped a warm blanket of compassion and reassurance around me to make me feel so acknowledged as a parent in following my gut feeling and trusting my baby and my own intuition. The information makes it all sound so logical and led to more 'aha-moments' than I've ever had when reading a parenting book. On top of that, it offered a deep feeling of connection with all the people who shared their stories in the book, including Marion's own story, because each time it resonated so much with our own. At times it felt like Marion was personally writing about our little boy. That's what made it even more touching and powerful. *The Emotional Life of Babies* is incredible.

– Sarah Pannekoeke

I found Aware Parenting when my daughter was 9 months old. I had attachment-parented after reading *The Continuum Concept* during pregnancy. I breastfed on demand, practiced baby-wearing and co-sleeping which seemed so wonderful and natural and brought ease to my life at the beginning. However, my little one was becoming increasingly pent up. I noticed it was harder and harder for her to fall asleep, and she would wake often. Where she had been such an easy going delight, she seemed uncomfortable in her skin and discontented. Then she started being aggressive towards the other baby whose family we were living with at the time. This was horrifying to me. Something had to give.

I remembered reading about letting babies release feelings in a supported way so I I did a Google search and found Aletha Solter's work, and she described my baby so well, I ordered *The Aware Baby* book straight away. The book spoke to me on a deep level. It fitted with attachment parenting, which I so resonated with, yet also brought in a new level of respect towards babies and trust in their smart and innate ways of working trauma and troubles out of their nervous systems. The first time I tentatively placed a *Loving Limit* around breastfeeding on my little one was so very hard, I questioned myself to the core. It was like I had released a floodgate and my little one tantrummed for hours, rolling around on the bed, scratching at me, screaming and crying. I felt like this tiny baby was so mad at me – her mama who had only thought about nourishing her with all of herself since conception for the last 18 months. I felt awful but I stayed with it as I believed Aletha. It took about a week of big tantrums almost every day, sometimes lasting over an hour, but I started to notice things shifting.

It was deeply transformative for my little one. She was no longer aggressive, she returned to her bright bubbly happy self. Witnessing this deep, embodied transformation in her has meant I have seen firsthand what this kind of release can do for a baby, flowing on to the family unit as a whole.

The next layer in my Aware Parenting journey was when I found Marion's work (The Marion Method), in particular her willingness work. At the time I was trying to night-wean and the process was feeling so, so gut wrenching. My little one would scream and paw at my breast for hours and I felt so awful denying her something which I could easily give her. While I knew in my heart that listening to tears was healing and I had experienced this countless times with my babe, she was still deeply attached to the breast, no matter how much I tried to listen. I felt there was some other patterning going on that I couldn't quite put my finger on. One day, I read one of Marion's posts about willingness, and how sometimes we may WANT something but not be willing for it, and so life never gives us that thing. It sparked something deep and dormant within me.

I realised that while I really wanted to night wean my daughter, a part of me that had experienced love being withdrawn as a child was so, so scared of losing her love. There was a part of me that was scared that if I did not give her what she wanted, namely, the breast, then she would stop loving me. As I listened to this little girl's terror at love being withdrawn, rivers of tears poured out of me in deep, heaving sobs. I couldn't believe the emotion that was hiding in my subconscious waiting to be lovingly heard! I knew I had to explore Marion's work. Through listening to myself and providing myself with the reparative experience of being loved unconditionally and loveable no matter what, (an ongoing process as grief and healing are not linear) the fear of losing the love of my daughter was lessened and I was able to claim on a much more embodied level my desire to night wean. This was the missing piece to being able to listen in a present and grounded way to my daughter's grief around losing her booby time which allowed us to work gently towards night weaning. And this allowed my daughter to sleep peacefully through the night for the first time, albeit wrapped in my arms, giving this mama bear a whole new lease on life and rediscovery post-matrescence.

I am so grateful for Marion's work. While I can agree cognitively with all the principles of Aware Parenting, sometimes there is a gap between being able to put them into practice in real life. For me, it has been through discovering Marion's tools, especially the re-parenting practices, that I can truly embody Aware Parenting. For without listening to my own hurts, it is hard to parent in the way I truly desire, despite my best intentions. This is an ongoing, transformative and wonderfully rich process.

– Marisa Taylor, Aware Parenting instructor

Incredible! I honestly heard Marion's voice reading to me the whole way through. I will be recommending this to any new parent I work with. Thank you, Marion, for your amazing work.

– Sahara Norton, Midwife, International Board Certified Lactation Consultant

Published in Australia by
Loving Being Publishing
PO Box 256, Doreen, VIC 3754
marion@marionrose.net
www.marionrose.net

First published in Australia 2023
Copyright © Marion Rose 2023

All rights reserved. No part of this publication may be reproduced, stored in a retrieval system, or transmitted, in any form or by any means without the prior written permission of the publisher, nor be otherwise circulated in any form of binding or cover other than that in which it is published and without a similar condition being imposed on the subsequent purchaser.

National Library of Australia Cataloguing-in-Publication entry

 A catalogue record for this book is available from the National Library of Australia

ISBN: 978-0-6458575-0-4 (paperback)
ISBN: 978-0-6458575-2-8 (hardback)
ISBN: 978-0-6458575-3-5 (epub)

Cover photography by Michael Rose
Cover layout and design by Jelena Mirkovic
Illustration by Lana Rose
Typesetting by Sophie White Design (sophiewhite.com.au)

Printed by Ingram Spark

Disclaimer: All care has been taken in the preparation of the information herein, but no responsibility can be accepted by the publisher or author for any damages resulting from the misinterpretation of this work. All contact details given in this book were current at the time of publication, but are subject to change.

The advice given in this book is based on the experience of the individuals. Professionals should be consulted for individual problems. The author and publisher shall not be responsible for any person with regard to any loss or damage caused directly or indirectly by the information in this book.

Today, and every day, I acknowledge the Traditional Custodians of this land where I live and work, which include the Arakwal people, the Minjungbal people, the Widjabul people and the Bundjalung people. I pay my respects to elders past, present and emerging. I acknowledge and recognise them as the original storytellers and wisdom keepers.

THE EMOTIONAL
Life of Babies

Find closeness, presence, and sleep
for you and your baby with this
compassionate approach to crying

MARION ROSE, PHD

For my lovely Mum.
This book is dedicated to you.

ABOUT THE AUTHOR

My passion for understanding babies began when I was a teenager and I started to realise that my premature birth and experiences in an incubator as a newborn baby had been having a huge effect on my life.

After a degree in psychology, I did a PhD on postnatal depression and the mother-infant relationship at The Winnicott Research Unit, Cambridge University, where I learnt to observe babies. At the same time, I also read *The Continuum Concept* by Jean Liedloff, about the Yequana people. Concurrently, I trained as a Psychosynthesis Psychotherapist at The Institute of Psyschosynthesis in London, while also having weekly psychotherapy throughout my twenties. I became passionate about pre- and peri-natal psychology, experiencing modalities such as rebirthing and Holotropic Breathwork. I was a Post-Doctoral Fellow at Exeter University, studying the cognitive capabilities of babies, and then taught M.A. students about The Therapeutic Relationship while working in a private practice as a psychotherapist.

This combination of intellectual rigour, scientific observation, therapeutic practice, decolonisation, deep compassion and inner work has carried through my life.

At 30, I moved to Australia, and dived in deeper to the topic of birth – training in both HypnoBirthing, and later, Calm Birth, using each of these when I gave birth to my daughter and then my son. I came across Aware Parenting when I was pregnant with my daughter, my first child, in 2001.

I became an Aware Parenting instructor in 2005, travelled around Australia sharing workshops, and then started creating online courses in 2014. I've mentored thousands of parents, created tens of online courses, co-created *The Aware Parenting Podcast* with Lael Stone and went on to become the solo host from episode 124, which at the time of publication of this book, has two and a half million downloads. I also co-authored the book *Raising Resilient and Compassionate Children* with Lael. I am a Level 2 Aware Parenting instructor and the Regional Coordinator for Australia and New Zealand. I mentor people to become Aware Parenting instructors.

I've also created my own work, The Marion Method, which is primarily a form of reparenting and reculturing that can be used for our own inner work while practicing Aware Parenting, and I also mentor people to become Marion Method Mentors.

I've been longing to be an author for many years and am so delighted that this book you are reading now exists. There are several more by me being published in 2023.

I'm grateful to be doing this work. Aware Parenting and The Marion Method are an important part of a bigger collective and cultural change, which I believe to be so necessary at this time.

AUTHOR'S NOTE

This book is an educational resource focusing on the emotional needs of babies; it is not intended to be a substitute for medical advice or treatment. Many of the behaviours and symptoms discussed can be an indication of serious emotional or physical problems. Readers are advised to consult with a competent health care provider whenever babies display behavioural or emotional issues, a sudden change in sleep, eating or crying patterns, or when pain or illness are suspected. Furthermore, some of the suggested practices in this book may not be suitable under all conditions or with babies suffering from certain physical or emotional challenges.

If you are ever concerned when your baby is crying, or if your baby's crying is suddenly high pitched, please seek advice from your health care provider. As outlined in this book, one of the reasons that babies cry is when they are in physical pain, so please trust yourself if you are ever worried.

I ask that you don't do anything just because you read it in this book; rather, I invite you to always view yourself as your own authority in parenting – and to first listen in to whether what you read resonates with you, and if you do, to try it out – and observe your baby's behaviour afterwards. You are the researcher here. I will be talking about this process of you claiming your authority as a parent in more detail in the following pages.

Most of all, please listen to yourself. If you are concerned, please listen to that concern. You know your baby the most. I invite you to deeply trust your perceptions and intuitions.

Note about breastfeeding and bottlefeeding and welcoming all those who care for children

The book tends to concentrate more on breastfeeding rather than bottlefeeding, but the majority of the information is relevant if you are bottlefeeding. Please translate what you read to fit your own unique situation. You are so welcome here, however you feed your baby!

Similarly, most of the parents I work with are mothers, but anyone who cares for babies is also welcome here, whatever your relationship and role to the baby in your life.

CONTENTS

About the author	26
Author's note	27
Introduction	37

1 Listening to yourself, observing your baby — 45
- My first invitation to you — 45
- My second invitation to you — 48
- Seeing yourself on the Aware Parenting spectrum — 50
- Emotional support for ourselves is essential — 52
- Seeing through a baby's eyes — 53

2 The two types of uncomfortable feelings — 55
- Needs-feelings and healing-feelings — 56
- Needs-feelings — 57
- Important note about checking for physical discomfort — 60
- Checklist if you think your baby might be feeling physically uncomfortable — 61
- Sucking and movement are not needs — 66
- Healing-feelings — 68
- The history of understanding babies' needs and feelings — 69
- Changing our beliefs about babies — 74
- Stress, trauma and healing — the fight/flight/freeze response, or hyperarousal and dissociation — 78
- Sources of stress for babies and how they heal — 81
- Returning again to healing-feelings — 103
- Healing from stress and trauma — 105
- Being heard and understood: a feelings perspective and a nervous system perspective — 107
- How do we differentiate between the two types of feelings? — 115
- Possible longer-term effects of understanding needs-feelings and healing-feelings — 121
- Summary — 123

3	**Why don't all babies cry? Understanding dissociation and suppression**	**127**
	What is happening when a baby rarely or never cries?	128
	Is your baby telling you that they don't like something?	130
	How we can tell the difference between when a baby is expressing needs-feelings or healing-feelings	131
	Common ways of distracting babies from their healing-feelings	133
	Distracting babies more and more of the time	147
	Important note about physical discomfort and trusting yourself	150
	Differentiating true relaxation from dissociation	151
	The concepts of 'soothing' and 'self-soothing' don't exist in Aware Parenting	155
	Differentiating between mouthing, teething and a control pattern of thumb-sucking	156
	What difference does it make anyway, listening to their feelings?	159
4	**Deepening your understanding through observation and reflection**	**169**
	Being a researcher	169
	Noticing how we might be distracting babies from their feelings	177
	Becoming more present	177
	How can we tell if a baby is relatively free from pent-up uncomfortable feelings?	178
5	**Starting to be with healing-feelings**	**179**
	The first time I was present with my daughter's healing-feelings	179
	Aware Parenting the second time around	183
	Starting to listen to your baby's healing-feelings	187
	What might you observe when your baby has feelings to express to you?	189
	Suggestions for when you're starting crying-in-arms with a pre-crawling baby	190
	Once a baby becomes mobile – from crying-in-arms to the *crying dance*	*196*
	What about holding a mobile baby?	204

Big feelings are normal	207
When you're not able to listen with full presence	209
What do you really want for you and your baby with Aware Parenting?	212

6 Differentiating between needs-feelings (especially hunger) and healing-feelings — 215

Differentiating between hunger and healing-feelings	215
My journey of differentiating hunger from healing-feelings with my son	216
If your baby's healing-feelings are being suppressed through breastfeeding	225
A breastfeeding control pattern can lead to a baby crying more easily with their other parent	228
If your baby is dissociating from their healing-feelings in other ways	229
Map of indications that your baby probably has healing-feelings to express	237

7 The relationship between sleep, needs and feelings — 239

The three things babies, children and adults need for peaceful sleep	240
Waking soon after crying-in-arms	258
What happens during the day affects what happens at night	261
Listening before sleep or listening during the night?	265
Helping your baby to sleep for longer stretches at night	266
Attachment play before sleep	273
Different sleep perceptions and concepts compared to other parenting paradigms	274
Toddlers who move all around the bed	277
Family co-sleeping and waking	280
An invitation to reframe sleep	281

8 Why listening to babies' feelings can be so hard and how we can help it be easier — 285

The three key areas we can focus on	287

9 Attachment play with babies	**293**
Contingency play	294
Separation games	295
Why tickling isn't recommended	297
Offering a baby your loving presence (non-directive child-centred play)	297
10 Aware Parenting and Elimination Communication	**303**
11 Frequently Asked Questions	**311**
General information and preparation	311
How can I know if my baby is benefitting from crying-in-arms?	311
I'm pregnant. What can I do to prepare for practicing Aware Parenting?	312
What kind of inner work will help me with Aware Parenting?	316
How will I be able to listen to my baby's feelings when I also have another child?	317
Closeness and presence	318
Is swaddling helpful?	318
Do I have to carry my baby in a carrier to practice Aware Parenting?	319
When I put my baby in the baby carrier, she starts to cry. I think she doesn't like it.	320
Is it okay for my baby to fall asleep in the carrier or will it create a control pattern for movement?	322
If I sit still with my baby, he will start to grunt and then start to cry.	323
My partner scoops up the baby and he isn't present at all in his body with her. What can I do?	323
My baby has a soft toy bunny to go to sleep with.	324
My breastfed baby cries whenever her dad holds her. Does she need me or is she expressing feelings to him?	325
My five month old baby never cries with me. Does that have something to do with breastfeeding and what can I do to help her express her feelings?	329

THE EMOTIONAL LIFE OF BABIES

Crying-in-arms	330
Sometimes I get worried when my baby daughter is crying in my arms. What can I do?	330
What can I do to feel more comfortable with crying-in-arms?	331
When do I listen to crying?	332
Is the crying still helpful if I stop her crying before she has finished crying in my arms?	333
Does my baby son need to finish a whole cry or a whole chunk of feelings?	333
When my daughter shows signs of having feelings but she avoids eye contact, shall I just move on or should I continue trying to help her feel safe to let those feelings out?	334
How can I hold my baby when he is crying so that I don't restrict his feelings but I'm holding him safely?	334
Do I always need to hold my baby in my arms for crying to be healing? At what age does this change?	335
I can clearly see that my baby really needs to cry. What can I do help her do that?	335
When can I first start listening to crying-in-arms?	336
Is it okay for me to cry when my baby is crying in my arms?	336
My baby has bigger feelings than other babies and is so intense when he's crying.	337
I hardly ever reach the end of a crying cycle, as my baby cries for more than an hour.	338
Is it harmful if I do crying-in-arms while not being emotionally present?	339
Sleep	339
My baby is just fussy because his last nap was so short. I don't know if he has feelings to tell me.	339
How will my baby fall asleep? After breastfeeding and awake time, should I just hold him still in my arms?	339
My baby will sleep for hours in the carrier but only for short periods when I put her in the bassinet. What can I do?	340
If my baby does crying-in arms, this prolongs his awake time. Should I stop him from crying so he doesn't get overwhelmed and can sleep?	340

Do I have to listen to my baby's feelings before sleep?	341
How do I know that my baby really isn't waking up hungry?	341
I've started to listen to my baby's feelings in the night. Do I need the light on so he can see me?	342
I want to 'night wean' my baby because she is waking up so much at night.	342
I've started to wean my 18 month old baby at night but she is crying for two hours in the middle of the night.	343

Illness and physical discomfort — 343

How can I tell if my baby is in physical pain? I worry about him.	343
What about colic?	344
I would love to hear what the Aware Parenting perspective is on breastfeeding as 'soothing' for teething babies.	346
What about sniffly noses, coughs and colds?	348
What happens if my baby cries more when I touch his head?	348
My baby has a medical condition. Is it safe for her to heal through crying-in-arms?	349

Nappy changes — 350

How can nappy changes with my daughter be easier?	350
My baby always cries during nappy changes. I think he's remembering a medical procedure he had when he was lying down.	350

I'm listening to their feelings. Why is this thing still happening? — 351

I'm listening to my baby daughter's feelings, so why am I still seeing these things happening?	351

Feeding — 352

Quite often I don't know whether my baby is hungry or she has feelings to tell me. How can I tell the difference?	352
I'm finding it difficult to understand when our baby has feelings to tell us.	353
Is breastfeeding 'for comfort' okay?	354
My baby has started biting me when he feeds. What can I do?	355
My baby twirls my hair or pinches my skin when she's feeding. I really don't like it.	356

My baby is always 'cluster feeding'. He had a really long birth and ventouse and always cries in the car seat.	*356*
My baby 'cluster feeds' every evening for hours and she is constantly spitting up milk. What is going on?	*357*
If my baby is crying or falling asleep while breastfeeding, how can I tell the difference between a tongue tie and healing-feelings?	*357*
How long should a nine-month-old baby go between feedings?	*358*
I've been trying to discern between hunger and healing-feelings but never get to give my son a full feed.	*359*
Thumb-sucking	359
I've done everything I can to listen to my baby's feelings. Why is she sucking her thumb?	*359*
Do I pull my baby's thumb out of his mouth to help him cry?	*360*
Dummy / pacifier	361
Now I understand that a dummy is helping my daughter dissociate, I want to help her not have one anymore. Do I just stop giving it to her?	*361*
Why is a dummy different to thumb-sucking in Aware Parenting?	*362*
Out and about and travelling	363
When we are busy, my baby doesn't cry. What's going on?	*363*
What happens if my baby needs to cry when I'm out and about with him?	*363*
We went on a plane and my baby didn't need to cry – she slept as long as I fed her, patted her, and held the dummy in her mouth.	*364*
My baby daughter cries in the car seat. What can I do?	*365*
Other people	370
How can I respond to other people who don't understand this way of parenting and who have judgements or fears?	*370*
Crying at different ages	371
At what age can I start listening to my baby's feelings?	*371*
Our baby is 11 months old and I'm finding it physically difficult to listen to his feelings.	*372*
More than one child	373
How can I listen to my baby daughter crying in my arms if I have more than one child?	*373*

Help with practicing Aware Parenting with a baby and a toddler with only one adult.	*373*
Birth trauma and other forms of trauma	375
How can I help my baby heal from birth trauma?	*375*
My baby was premature. When can I start helping her heal from stress and trauma?	*375*
My baby was adopted. How can I practice Aware Parenting with him?	*378*
My baby has been through major trauma. Can I listen to her feelings to help her heal from it?	*378*

12 Quick reference guide — 379

13 Conclusions — 389

Acknowledgements	394
Glossary	396
Recommended reading and resources	401
Your notes and observations of your baby	403
Diagram of the crying-in-arms position I preferred	407
Ways you can work with me	408
If you enjoyed this book	409
Author contact page	411

Introduction

*Hello and a big warm welcome to you!
I'm so delighted that you're here!*

I wonder whether this is the first time you are learning about Aware Parenting, the parenting philosophy this book is based upon. Or perhaps you know a little about the approach and want to understand more. Maybe you're already familiar with Aware Parenting and want to dive in deeper.

Wherever you are in your Aware Parenting journey, I'm here with open arms. I'm so willing for your reading here to bring you clarity, compassion, and an even more wonderful experience with your baby, as well as whatever else you're looking for in these pages.

I imagine you might already have been bombarded with a million different ideas about babies. In this book, I'll be inviting you to put all the things you think about babies and their needs and feelings to one side for a moment, and to listen in to whether the ideas you read here resonate with you.

My own journey with Aware Parenting began in 2001. I found out about it online when I was pregnant with my first child, immediately deeply resonated with it and have been in love with it ever since. I imagine you will feel my love for this parenting philosophy shining through the pages you read.

There are three main reasons for my passion for Aware Parenting.

Firstly, as a mother, I have seen the huge difference understanding and putting into practice this information has made to my own children since I started practicing it with my baby daughter in 2002.

Secondly, as an Aware Parenting instructor since 2005, I've seen what a huge transformative effect it has on the lives of thousands of babies, children and their parents.

Thirdly, from my own experience of birth trauma as a baby, and all the ways that affected my childhood and teenage years, before I started my healing journey in my early twenties. I wish that that Aware Parenting had existed when I was a baby and that I had been supported to be securely attached and to heal from my early experiences while still in my infancy. I am so delighted every time I see parents supporting their baby to heal from their birth trauma through practicing Aware Parenting so that those babies don't need to experience what I went through when they are children or teenagers.

Aware Parenting was created by Aletha Solter, PhD, whose initial book, *The Aware Baby*, was first published in 1984. The revised edition came out in 2001. If you enjoy reading this book, I recommend reading *The Aware Baby* next (if you haven't already read it)! Whereas *The Emotional Life of Babies* focuses on babies' feelings, *The Aware Baby* explains in depth all the aspects and elements of Aware Parenting with a baby and is filled with research that supports this approach.

As adults, many of us have a deep longing to be heard and understood, as well as to be unconditionally loved exactly as we are. In addition, most of us have lots of ways that we use to suppress or dissociate from our feelings that arise from daily stresses or larger traumas, and yet in this culture we still don't commonly trace these two phenomena back to our own infancy.

In this book, I'm going to show you what you can do to help your baby be more present, more likely to grow up feeling heard, understood and unconditionally loved, and with less need to suppress or dissociate from their feelings.

Babies come into the world wanting to be welcomed and understood. This book offers information so that you can give your baby both of these experiences. Not only that, it will also help you understand the inevitable stresses and mini traumas they have gone through, and how they can heal from those. I'll also show you how unhealed stress and trauma affects how relaxed they are, how they feed, how much eye contact they make, and how they sleep. I'll explain how needs and feelings are deeply connected with a baby's sleep and what you can do to help your baby have restful sleep while also being securely attached. All of these have long-term emotional effects too.

My passion for observing and understanding babies started long before I discovered Aware Parenting. Here's a little of my journey.

I've been on a very long healing path from being in an incubator for five weeks as a premature baby. I've had many years of therapy, have experienced lots of healing modalities, and have connected deeply with all the feelings that I felt in those first days of my life. I began the journey of revisiting those early experiences when I was 22, and in the 33 years since then, I have developed a profound sense of understanding and compassion for the intensity of feelings babies experience.

During my PhD at Cambridge University in the early 1990s, I visited many mothers and videoed them feeding and playing with their babies. Back at the Winnicott Research Unit, I went through the footage millisecond by millisecond, using my training in infant observation to code what I saw.

Since discovering *The Continuum Concept*, a book by Jean Liedloff about her experiences with the Yequana people, in a little secondhand bookshop in Mill Road in Cambridge back in 1992, I have been fascinated by the cultural and historical understanding of parenting. I've learnt how much of what is perceived as 'normal' in industrialised cultures is actually very unusual in the wider picture of human history. I believe that understanding this cultural piece is essential for parents for a number of reasons.

- It helps us see how we've been conditioned to think about babies and offers ways to free ourselves from that conditioning.
- It supports us to provide our babies with experiences that are most helpful for them to thrive physically, emotionally and mentally.
- It offers us compassionate ways to understand why parenting in more biologically and psychologically innate ways is often challenging, because of the culture we live in.
- It invites us to parent in ways that are the biggest fit between what's most optimal for our babies as well as caring for our own needs as parents, living in this particular time and place.

After my PhD, I was a Post-Doctoral Research Fellow at Exeter University in England, this time observing babies to understand their cognitive capabilities. I also trained as a psychotherapist, and had a particular interest in pre- and peri-natal psychology, which looks at the effects of a baby's experience *in utero* and during and after birth.

I found out about Aware Parenting when I was pregnant in 2001, while looking for a style of parenting that would fit with all that I had learnt in the previous 14 years. I was deeply surprised to discover that rather than waiting until adulthood to heal from our experiences early in life, we are born with the innate power to heal.

I knew from pre- and peri-natal psychology and from researchers and clinicians such as Thomas Verny and David Chamberlain that a baby's experience *in utero*, during birth and directly after birth has a profound impact on their later development.

But I had no idea until I came across Aware Parenting that babies could actually heal from any of those experiences right from birth.

I've been passionate about Stan Grof's work since starting training as a psychotherapist in 1992 and I loved that he illustrated how lifelong patterns can be established from a baby's birth experience.

However, until I discovered Aware Parenting, I didn't realise that babies will try to tell us about their experience of birth from birth onwards.

I learned that they have an inherent ability to heal from anything that was stressful or traumatic for them, as long as they are held in the loving arms of an adult with whom they feel safe. Yet so often we can miss those invitations from our babies because in this culture we're not taught to really observe and understand babies and their feelings and what they are communicating to us.

Michel Odent's work, explaining how exquisitely heightened newborn babies' senses are, touched me deeply. I cried when I first read his books in the early nineties, while I thought of baby me in an incubator, with all the bright lights and loud noises and rough touch.

Not until I found Aware Parenting did I realise that babies are constantly trying to communicate their feelings – including in response to how sensitively they are first handled and whether they are separated from their parents after birth. I learned that they can heal from experiences of roughness, overstimulation and separation, right from birth onwards.

My experiences as a mother, practicing Aware Parenting with my daughter and my son (as of 2023, they are 21 and 17 years old respectively) has been the most profound learning journey of all. My daughter's father and I saw straight away the huge effect that helping her heal from stress had on her when we started at three months old – I will share about that experience later in the book – and we learnt so much about Aware Parenting in that first year after she was born.

When our son was born, I had been an Aware Parenting instructor for some time. I could understand babies even more clearly and was more comfortable, competent and confident in practicing all the aspects of Aware Parenting. I helped him heal from his very fast posterior birth – which I also share details about in the book. I wrote down everything that I observed about my babies in a diary, using my earlier experiences as a research psychologist to notice patterns and make conclusions about what I was observing.

I share in this book: those 14 years of research and training before becoming a mother; my own experiences of practicing Aware Parenting with my two babies; 18 years of being an Aware Parenting instructor walking alongside parents; and my own journey of healing from considerable trauma as a baby. It is through weaving together this wealth of embodied knowledge that I share my understandings of babies and their feelings and behaviour with you.

Some of the vital information I will be sharing with you that is still little-known in industrialised cultures, which I collectively name The Disconnected Domination Culture, includes:

- How we can help our babies heal from their experiences, including any stress and trauma they experience *in utero*, during birth, and after birth.
- How we can listen to their feelings from these experiences and give them a deep sense of being heard and understood, and how this can create powerful core beliefs for them – that their feelings matter, that they are understood, that all of their feelings are welcome, that they are safe, and that they are unconditionally loved, however they feel.
- How our perceptions of, and responses to, their feelings affect how much they dissociate from or suppress their feelings, which we can clearly observe when we know what to look for.
- How they don't need to carry painful core beliefs and unexpressed feelings around until they themselves become

parents, with the patterns and feelings bubbling up to be revealed then. Instead, they can express those feelings in our loving arms and heal from stress and trauma while they are still babies themselves.

- How they can then feel much more deeply comfortable, relaxed and present in their bodies, which deeply affects how they connect, concentrate, play, explore, learn, feed and sleep.
- How sleep is profoundly influenced by the way a baby feels. With Aware Parenting, we can help them feel truly relaxed and present – not superficially calm or dissociated – so that they can sleep restfully and restoratively and also be securely attached. They won't need to wake up multiple times at night to try to express the feelings that aren't getting to be expressed and heard during the daytime.
- How Aware Parenting with a baby is a huge, steep learning curve, particularly for those of us who grew up and live within The Disconnected Domination Culture.
- How practicing Aware Parenting brings profound benefits for babies and parents, both in the short and long-term.
- How Aware Parenting helps parents feel even more deeply connected with their babies.

Because Aware Parenting is a form of attachment-style parenting, it is based on the concept that responding in a prompt and attuned way to a baby's needs is vital to secure attachment. Attunement requires us to *understand* what a baby is communicating to us. Because most of us didn't receive prompt and attuned responses when we were babies, and because we live in a culture that doesn't understand babies' needs and feelings, learning to understand what is really going on for them can be a big process for most of us.

*One of the many things I love about Aware Parenting is that the 'proof is in the pudding'. Through practicing Aware Parenting, we can see that promptly meeting a baby's needs and listening to their feelings to support them in healing from daily stress and bigger traumas makes an enormous difference to their sleep, relaxation and general wellbeing. This means that we don't need to wait 20 years to see the results of our parenting.
Our babies will show us. When we know what to look for, we can literally see the foundations of our child's psyche while they are a baby. This book will explain in detail how to really see what is going on for babies, making it easier for you to respond in an attuned way.*

CHAPTER ONE

Listening to yourself, observing your baby

My first invitation to you

I invite you to go through the following process when you read this book.

1. Tune in to your own resonance: first, I invite you to listen in to yourself. Does what you're reading resonate with you? Do you have a big YES in your body as you take in the information?
2. Gain clarity about the philosophy: I invite you to receive as much information as you can, so that you really understand the core philosophy and practices of Aware Parenting. If there's anything you don't understand, I invite you to come back to the book to find that information. (You may want to read and re-read this book!)
3. Do your own research and observations: I invite you to put into practice what you've learnt and observe your baby. Do you see any differences in them? In particular, I suggest observing the amount of eye contact they make, the expression in their eyes and on their face, the amount of tension in their muscles, the extent to which they melt into your hugs, the level of agitation in their vocalisations, the amount they smile, their general level of

happiness, how present they are, how long they concentrate for, how much they move around in their sleep, how tense or relaxed their muscles are when they sleep, and how long they sleep for. This list is at the end of the book, if you want to return to it and make notes.

4. Make your own conclusions: based on your observations (i.e. whether you observe from their behaviour that they feel more, or less, relaxed, connected, calm and present), I invite you to make a decision about whether to continue practicing Aware Parenting. If you decide to continue, is there anything you want to tweak about what you're doing, or do you need any other information as you continue to experiment and observe?

I call this the research triangle of Aware Parenting. It's a triangle consisting of:

*your own resonance, intuition,
sense-making and conclusions;*

*your cognitive
understanding
of the theory and
practice;*
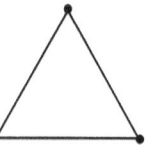
*and the
observations
you make of
your baby.*

*Whenever you feel unsure,
I invite you to come back to this triangle.*

Observing your baby is key to Aware Parenting, and I am going to invite you to do this throughout the book.

Meg shares about her and her partner's experience of listening to themselves and observing their baby while practicing Aware Parenting:

"As first-time parents, we knew we wanted to be gentle, loving and conscious. After a very traumatic birth experience, the first few weeks felt very, very hard. We were bombarded with information about how parenting 'should' be done, especially around sleep. It felt painful and not the right fit for us.

Slowly, piece by piece through Instagram, I found ideas that led me to discover Aware Parenting. The Aware Parenting Podcast *was profound. My heart sang! Holding, connecting, and listening lovingly to our baby made sense, but was not without its challenges as we were asked to look at our own experiences as babies and children. We have listened to tears and sensed at some times that he is telling us about his birth, and I've felt deeply moved as we revisit it together.*

We continue to learn more about Aware Parenting, and to practice more self-love and self-awareness, as our babe grows into toddlerhood. Our family reaps the benefits in confidently parenting from our hearts and with deep connection to our intuition and each other. I feel passionately about our parenting journey being part of a community and global context and hope others can find peace in their parenting and power in motherhood.

He's a very observant, vibrant and gentle being and we can see when this isn't the case and he needs to have a big release of feelings in our arms. Everyone who meets him comments on how he's so relaxed and happy! (Not that I mind much what other people think!) My mother-in-law from interstate listened with interest when I explained how we listen to his feelings and said, 'Now you explain it, it just makes sense!'"

My second invitation to you

I am deeply passionate about parents being compassionate with ourselves.

As you read this information, you might at times feel sadness or grief, overwhelm or confusion. Feelings might bubble up as you reflect on your baby and their experiences, or emotions may emerge that are related to what you yourself experienced as a baby. I invite you to be gentle with yourself, and to listen compassionately to those feelings. If you have someone in your life who is able to listen empathically to you without trying to interrupt, distract or judge you, I invite you to share with them.

You may notice feelings of anger or outrage. Maybe you want to throw the book across the room at times. Again, I invite you to be deeply compassionate with yourself, and explore where those feelings come from. Over the years, I have talked with several people who initially had responses like that when they came across Aware Parenting, but then went on to love it, and even became Aware Parenting instructors themselves.

You might also judge yourself or feel guilty as you read this book, particularly if you haven't known this information before, and if you have responded to your baby in different ways than are written about here. In The Marion Method – which is different to Aware Parenting – I support people in their own reparenting process and talk about putting down the 'emotional sticks'. These are sticks of self-judgement, harshness and 'shoulds' that create what I call 'emotional bruises' of guilt and shame. These aren't inherent feelings but are feelings that are created by harsh ways of thinking[1] that are passed down in this Disconnected Domination Culture (DDC), which is also a Marion Method term. (If you ever need a reminder of which are my terms and which are Aware Parenting ones, you can find them in the Glossary.)

---

1   I'm so grateful to Marshall Rosenberg, PhD and Nonviolent Communication, from whom I learnt so much about guilt and what he called 'The Domination Culture'.

We can learn to stop punishing ourselves by putting down the emotional sticks. So, if you notice yourself feeling guilty or judging yourself, I invite you again and again to connect with the following phrase, "I'm not willing to judge myself." Guilt does not help anyone, and in fact, can often get in the way of us being present with our babies. Have you noticed that if you feel guilty, you actually have less presence to offer your baby?

However, you might find that when you put down that guilt stick, you connect with sadness or mourning instead. Feeling sadness that we didn't then know what we know now, and realising the effects that might have had on our baby, is very different from guilt. We can compassionately be with our sadness and mourning so that those feelings move through us and are released, leaving us feeling clearer about what we might do to repair the effects of our actions in the past.

This process is particularly important because the culture we live in can make offering our babies the most optimal care through practicing Aware Parenting particularly difficult. We are meant to live in community, with plenty of support, and with babies having multiple secure attachment figures. Much of what parents find hard is because of the effects of the culture we live in on our present-day life as well as the effects it had on our needs, feelings and thoughts when we were children – which affects our parenting too. Understanding these cultural effects can help us see clearly, stop judging ourselves, and be compassionate with ourselves instead.

The process of increasingly understanding a baby's needs and feelings and aiming to respond in a prompt and attuned way is a huge one for most of us.
It also invites us on a deep healing, reparenting and de-conditioning journey, where self-compassion is a vital companion.

Seeing yourself on the Aware Parenting spectrum

Another element of listening to yourself is seeing where you sit on the Aware Parenting spectrum, and having deep acceptance and compassion for yourself, whatever position you are on that in any moment.

Each of us is going to be on a different place on that spectrum, depending on many factors, including:

- the way we were parented;
- how much trauma we experienced as babies, children and adults;
- the amount of healing from stress and trauma we've already done;
- the extent to which we can be present in our bodies with our own feelings;
- how much we are suppressing our feelings or dissociating from them;
- the amount of both stress and support we experience in our present-day lives;
- the number of children we have;
- whether we have a partner or wider family connections and support;
- whether our partner has the same beliefs about parenting;
- the amount of societal and financial stresses we're under;
- whether we have already practiced Aware Parenting with previous children.

What do I mean about a spectrum?

Before I say more, I will briefly outline Aware Parenting's three main aspects:

1. attachment-style parenting;
2. non-punitive discipline;
3. preventing stress and trauma as well as supporting babies and children to heal from stress and trauma through cooperating with their natural healing processes which include – for babies – crying-in-arms when all other needs are met.

Given that, let's talk more about the Aware Parenting spectrum for parents of babies. On the far end of one side might be someone who aims to meet their baby's attachment needs as much as possible, finds ways for both parent and child to get their needs met, prevents as much stress as possible and listens to as large a percentage of their baby's crying-in-arms as they can.

On the other end of the spectrum, someone might have a more flexible approach to attachment-style parenting, non-punitive discipline, the prevention of stress and the crying-in-arms parts of Aware Parenting. For example, they might tend to use strollers rather than carry their baby in a carrier, and might have their baby in a cot rather than have their baby close at night. They might only listen to healing-feelings occasionally, for example if they don't seem to be able to stop their baby from crying.

I invite you to be compassionate with yourself, wherever you are on that spectrum. You might even see your position change over time and on different days, depending on how much stress you are experiencing and how many feelings of your own are bubbling up to the surface, as well as how much you understand about Aware Parenting. I also invite you to drop any emotional sticks that say you 'should' be in a different place or that compare you to other people.

Most of all, I will be inviting you to keep on listening in to yourself. If you want to move along the spectrum towards diving in deeper to Aware Parenting, this often requires us to understand more of the nuances of Aware Parenting, have more of our own needs met, reduce the stress in our lives, receive more listening for our own feelings and receive support with putting Aware Parenting intro practice in our own unique family.

> I welcome you with open arms,
> wherever you sit on the spectrum.

In the Disconnected Domination Culture, we've grown up to believe that there's a 'right' and 'wrong' way to do things. We've had our work marked at school, we've been compared with others and have been judged and shamed.

> I am passionate about offering Aware Parenting
> within a context that does none of these things.

I invite you to be a part of a community who welcomes everyone who resonates with this approach, while also being clear about exactly what the Aware Parenting philosophy and practice is. I encourage you to read this information, listen to yourself, observe your baby, and then to practice Aware Parenting in your own unique way in your own particular cultural and family situation.

Emotional support for ourselves is essential

I'm going to say more about getting emotional support here because it really is core to being able to practice Aware Parenting with a baby. It is inevitable that our own feelings from infancy will show up when we are aiming to meet our baby's needs and listen to their feelings. This bubbling up of our emotions can be incredibly challenging. With a huge amount of self-compassion, we can choose to see this as both an opportunity for deep healing for ourselves, as well as an invitation to increase our emotional presence to be able to support our babies in this way.

If you are needing more emotional support, I invite you to reach out to the Aware Parenting community for empathy and/or to find a Listening Partner[2]. This is another parent or any adult who is aiming to understand these ideas and to listen with empathy and without judgement. The classical approach is to regularly meet (in person, on the phone or on a video call) and take turns empathically listening to each other for an equal amount of time. Crying, raging and laughter can often be a part of that process.

For a different sense of support, many parents find that sharing feelings and thoughts with each other through regular voice or text messaging on an app can also make a big difference to their experience of receiving emotional support and the extent to which they're able to meet their baby's needs and listen to their feelings. I term this an empathy buddy or empathy partner as a more fluid form of a mutual support person than a Listening Partner.

You might also consider reaching out to have consultations with Aletha Solter herself, with me, or with another Aware Parenting instructor. You can find a list of Aware Parenting instructors in Australia and New Zealand on my website **www.marionrose.net** and in the rest of the world at Aletha Solter's website **www.awareparenting.com**.

Seeing through a baby's eyes

My own experiences as a baby plus many years of studying infant development have helped me be able to put myself in a baby's shoes (or socks!) and I think this process is vital in Aware Parenting. I invite you to observe your baby as much as you possibly can and to trust

---

[2] This term is from Hand in Hand Parenting, a similar approach to Aware Parenting, and is used with their permission. In Hand in Hand Parenting, the term is used in more specific ways than it generally is in Aware Parenting.

your own intuitive sense of what's going on (eg. if you are thinking of their birth while they are crying in your loving arms, it may be that they are revisiting their birth).

Trusting our intuitive connection with our baby, alongside understanding their cognitive development and what they understand, helps us to imagine how they might feel and helps us be more able to respond to them in an attuned and empathic way, because we actually have a deep sense of what they are likely to be experiencing.

Whenever I see a baby, I put myself in their shoes.

What might they be experiencing?

What might they be perceiving?

What might they be feeling?

What might they be needing?

> *In aiming to really see and understand them, I also aim to be present in my own body, so that I offer deep presence in my holding and touch. Babies thrive on this quality of presence.*

Babies may be small, but they feel deeply. They are easily overwhelmed, because so much is new. A shopping centre, cafe or supermarket can be very overstimulating for a baby. A newborn has no sense of time, so being left alone for a short while can be experienced by them as an eternity where they might feel loneliness or fear. If they feel big feelings on their own, without a loving adult with them, their only option is to dissociate, because they cannot fight or flee. We will be talking more about these topics in later chapters.

CHAPTER TWO

The two types of uncomfortable feelings

Aware Parenting recognises that babies and children are highly sensitive beings who are deeply affected by what they experience *and* that they have innate recovery processes through which they can heal from daily stresses as well as larger traumas. These understandings differentiate Aware Parenting from many other parenting paradigms. This information also leads us to perceive babies' behaviours very differently. You will understand why we don't think that babies 'fight sleep', nor do they have 'sleep regressions'. I'll invite you to see 'cluster feeding', thumb-sucking, dummies, 'self-soothing' and frequent night waking in a very different light too.

To really understand these innate healing processes and their effects on the behaviour of babies, the key is knowing that babies have two types of uncomfortable feelings: needs-feelings and healing-feelings[3].

---

3   These two terms are not official Aware Parenting terms.

Needs-feelings and healing-feelings

The two types of uncomfortable feelings are:

1. Needs-feelings – feelings caused by immediate needs.

Babies express these feelings to communicate an unmet need. Our role here is to meet the need, and then the feelings dissipate. For ease, I call these needs-feelings, but this is not an official Aware Parenting term.

2. Healing-feelings – feelings caused by stress and trauma[4].

Babies express these feelings to heal. Our role here is to lovingly listen to the feelings while holding them in our arms[5]. I call these healing-feelings, which is also not an official Aware Parenting term.

When practicing Aware Parenting with a baby, one of the most important things we are invited to discern between is whether the feelings they are expressing are to communicate a need or are to heal from stress and trauma, so that we can respond promptly and aptly to what they *really* need. To do that, we need to be able to differentiate between needs-feelings and healing-feelings, so we can either:

- meet the need that is causing the needs-feelings, or;
- be present with the healing-feelings.

Let's look more at the two types of uncomfortable feelings.

---

[4] We could also categorise healing as a need, but these terms are used to differentiate healing from other needs.

[5] Once babies are mobile, they need closeness for healing to happen, but might choose to express those feelings without being held in our arms.

Needs-feelings

The first type of uncomfortable feelings is the one that most of us are familiar with, those that are created by unmet needs. In fact, many parenting paradigms *only* recognise this type of uncomfortable feelings.

Babies feel agitated and upset when they experience a need which is not being met, and they communicate this need to us through expressing their feelings – 'needs-feelings'. This communication is often through sounds and vocalisations, movements, 'fussing', and crying. As we get used to observing our baby more, we might see other ways that they communicate their needs before getting to the point of fussing or crying. Some parents observe that their baby makes different vocalisations and different crying sounds depending on whether they're hungry, tired, needing to burp, or have an uncomfortable digestive system, which helps them as the parent to respond promptly and aptly to what their baby needs. This is one of the reasons why observation is so central to practicing Aware Parenting.

Just like babies, as adults we can also experience increasingly strong sensations and feelings the longer a need stays unmet. If we have a need for connection, we might start feeling a little bit lonely. Over time, if those needs still don't get met, we might feel more deeply sad. Similarly, if we're hungry, we might start off with a mild sensation of hunger, which over time grows into feeling really hungry, which might include uncomfortable sensations in our stomach that indicate a sense of something missing – food!

However, despite our similarities, babies are different to us because they rely on us to get their needs met, and many of those needs are required for their survival. So, babies will call out when they need connection, for example, because closeness is such a basic need of theirs.

Aware Parenting is a form of attachment-style parenting and understands the vital importance of attachment needs and the urgency with which babies communicate these needs. Babies need closeness, and a lot of it. The more they get those needs met, the less painful feelings they will feel.

With these needs-feelings, our role is to understand what they are communicating to us as soon as possible, and to respond promptly to meet the need. This means picking them up (if we're not already holding them) and doing whatever they might be asking us to do[6]. Babies thrive when responded to in an attuned way with presence and compassion.

Checklist of needs:

Here is an (incomplete) list of babies' needs:

- Physical closeness;
- Nourishment;
- Physical comfort (eg. temperature, digestion, the sensations and pressure on their skin, etc.);
- Gentle, present and attuned touch;
- Emotional presence;
- Accurate attunement (really understanding what they are feeling and needing);
- Prompt responding to their cues;
- Protection from overstimulation.

We can go through our list of needs, attend to those needs, and observe our baby – are they now calm and contented, or are they still agitated?

---

6   This refers to pre-crawling babies. Once they are mobile, they need us to move close to them when they are calling for us, but don't necessarily need to be picked up. They will let us know whether or not they do, particularly when we know what cues to look for.

When we read their cues accurately and respond promptly, they will feel a deep relaxation which we will be able to sense in the relaxed state of their muscles, the movements they make and the tone of their vocalisations.

If they are still antsy, agitated or crying, it tells us one of three things:

- we haven't yet understood what need they were communicating to us;
- we have understood the need correctly but haven't been able to meet it in that moment, for example if they are suffering from physical discomfort because of illness, allergies, wind / digestive / gut biome issues, or from the birth process;
- they are not crying because of an immediate need (ie. they are expressing healing-feelings not needs-feelings).

This is one of the reasons why it's so important to listen to yourself. If you think that your baby might be suffering from physical pain or discomfort, please get help from a health practitioner before assuming that they are expressing healing-feelings.

If we *haven't* yet understood what is going on for them, we can continue with our detective work, going through the next things on the needs list.

As a form of attachment-style parenting, Aware Parenting invites parents to always respond to our baby's needs as promptly and accurately as we can. This is a core part of developing secure attachment for a baby and bonding for parents.

If we've gone through the list and we are confident that all their needs are met, and that they are physically comfortable and well, and they are still agitated, fussing or crying, we can then interpret that they are expressing the second type of feelings – healing-feelings.

If we continue to learn about Aware Parenting and keep on observing our babies, we can become more accurate and competent at differentiating between when our babies are feeling uncomfortable feelings caused by immediate needs and when they have feelings caused by unhealed stress or trauma that they're trying to express.

Important note about checking for physical discomfort

Babies can feel uncomfortable sensations for all kinds of reasons, including:

- physical tension and pain from their positioning *in utero* or their birth experience;
- physical discomfort from teething or sickness;
- food allergies and intolerances;
- digestive and intestinal issues including from their gut biome;
- other allergies such as to chemical washing powder.

If your baby is crying and:

- their crying is high pitched;
- they seem listless;
- the crying seems directly related to their feeding;
- they had a ventouse or forceps birth;
- you intuitively sense that they are physically uncomfortable despite all you've done to meet their needs,

please seek help from a health professional.

Please never just assume that they just have healing-feelings to express – and always trust your intuition.

The advice in this book is not meant to replace medical advice or treatment. If you think that your baby suffers from birth-related physical pain or structural damage, or any other physical issues, I highly recommend that you consult a qualified health practitioner.

Checklist if you think your baby might be feeling physically uncomfortable

- you may feel called to change your diet if your baby seems to be uncomfortable after breastfeeding. Lactose intolerance can affect some babies. Pesticides, food additives and other environmental toxins can all play a part, so changing to an organic diet can help some babies. I recommend seeking advice from your qualified health practitioner about all of these.
- you might want to explore gut biome issues with a health professional, particularly if your baby was born by Caesarean or if you or they have been on antibiotics;
- if they seem to have trouble latching on, check out with an expert whether they might have a tongue tie;
- if they had a ventouse, forceps or were in challenging positions before or during birth, you might want to look into physical therapies to help release the tension;
- if their skin is red or inflamed, you may consider changing to organic washing powder and/or clothing and bedding and contact your health practitioner.

Breastfeeding: if a baby turns away from the breast, or is agitated on the breast, this can be an indication that they are not hungry, but it can also indicate low milk supply. I invite you to reach out for support from an Aware Parenting instructor who is also a lactation consultant before assuming that a baby has feelings to express.

Aware Parenting is all about deeply observing and understanding a baby, what is really going on for them, and what they most need. Sometimes that is way more than just feeding, burping or changing their nappy.

On the other hand, unexpressed feelings and pent-up stress can lead to tension in the digestive system, which can increase when the baby is being fed. Listening to healing-feelings releases tension and can lead to more comfortable digestion. We will be talking more about the powerful relaxing effects of listening to healing-feelings in the upcoming section. Before that, let's take a little detour into healing-feelings.

Many mothers have told me that listening to crying-in-arms has actually *helped* their baby's digestion. For example, one mother shared that since starting to practice crying-in-arms, her baby just has one easy burp after feeding, compared to the long drawn-out process of burping before learning about Aware Parenting. In our culture, parents tend to be told that crying is *caused* by digestive discomfort, which absolutely can be the case, but healing-crying can actually *relieve* digestive discomfort. If a baby has physical tension or discomfort left over from their birthing experience, or is simply tense from accumulated feelings, healing-crying actually releases physical tension because it's a full-body physiological process. This isn't surprising, given that fight, flight and freeze affect the gut and digestion.

Babies inherently know exactly how to heal
and how to release physical tension,
which they do through specific and particular body
movements while they are crying-in-arms.

Eleanor shares her experience with this:

"A beautiful baby girl in my life was born very early and spent many weeks in the NICU. Her parents adore her and do everything they can to support her needs. But they do not yet have a lot of confidence to listen to healing-feelings. I'm not her parent, so I have been gently introducing some of these ideas to them where they are open to my invitations. I had listened to many short cries with her of just a few minutes, and her parents could see the potential positive effects of this time spent listening to her healing-feelings.

I looked after her one evening, and was able to lovingly listen to her for around 40 minutes as she cried. I held her in my arms and said, "You are here. You made it. It was so hard. I'm so sorry you were alone. You are not alone now. I would love to hear all of your feelings." She really cried so hard! At the end of the 40 minute cry she looked around with interest, blinked as though waking up from a long sleep, then smiled and settled in my arms for a blissful sleep – the longest she'd had to date. I let her mum and dad know about this experience of crying-in-arms.

A few weeks later we were reflecting and her mum said, "She's really so different now, she cries so much less and she's so much happier!" I asked, 'When do you think these changes happened?' and she said, 'About three weeks ago'. This was the exact time I'd listened to her! We discussed the impact this experience of being listened to may have had, and her mum could see how helpful it can be to feel heard after a hard experience. This beautiful baby is so much more alert, aware, open and relaxed when I see her now. That one 40 minutes of listening has made a huge difference."

> I think that all babies growing up in industrialised cultures are likely to have some healing-feelings to express every day for approximately the first year.

These feelings are particularly likely to emerge after a busy day or before sleep.

So, if your baby seems relatively happy for most of the day and is generally upset when they're tired, or when you get home from being out, they are likely to be healing-feelings rather than needs-feelings.

This information can reassure parents – that despite meeting all of their baby's needs, it's common for babies to need to cry in our arms at least once a day. The more you practice Aware Parenting, the more you will be able to differentiate between needs-feelings and healing-feelings clearly and confidently.

And, as Eleanor shared above, any listening to healing-feelings that we do will make a difference to how our baby feels. Even one experience of this can help them feel more relaxed and experience being deeply heard.

> **Self-Compassion Moment**
> I also want to remind you to drop any judgement or self-coercion sticks, particularly if you're telling yourself that you 'should' be listening to healing-feelings every day! Any listening will make a difference.

This process of differentiating between the two types of feelings is more complex than we might assume, because of something called dissociation.

Dissociation is a state of consciousness that is called 'freeze' in some other paradigms. Later in the chapter, I'll be talking more about the fight/flight/freeze response and how it applies to Aware Parenting.

Why isn't it simple to understand the difference between needs-feelings and healing-feelings? Well, because we might think that our baby is communicating a need and we might feed them, jiggle them, give them a dummy, or do other things to stop them crying and they may indeed stop crying. If we think that the stopping crying proves that they were expressing a need and now that need is met, we might miss what is really going on for them.

If we look more closely, and we know what to look for, we may realise that we're not seeing the true indication of a need being met, which is relaxed presence.

Presence, relaxed muscles, calm movement and relaxed eye contact communicate that a need has been met and that the baby is connected with the sensations in their body. In contrast, if their muscles are tense, their movements are agitated and they are avoiding eye contact, perhaps gazing off into space or having a glazed look, they may be mildly dissociated. Their facial expression may show tension and painful feelings rather than a sense of ease and relaxation. For example, perhaps they are frowning and the muscles around their eyes and eyebrows are tense. This tells us that rather than being deeply fulfilled from having their needs met, they may be in a mild state of dissociation.

Learning to observe your baby and knowing what to look for so that you can differentiate between *relaxed presence* and *dissociation* is an essential part of Aware Parenting.

Parents may sometimes think that they have met their baby's needs when the baby wasn't actually fussing or crying to communicate an unmet need but was trying to heal through expressing healing-feelings. The stopping of the crying at those times is a suppressing of feelings, not a meeting of needs.

> ### Self-Compassion Moment
> Here's a self-compassion moment! I want to remind you of my earlier invitation. If this information resonates with you, I invite you to put down any guilt sticks you might be tempted to pick up and be compassionate with yourself instead. You might say to yourself, "I'm not willing to judge myself for what I didn't know and I am willing to be compassionate with myself." I also want to let you know that whatever you've done in the past, it's never too late to put this new information into practice and to offer your baby opportunities to heal from past experiences.

Sucking and movement are not needs

In Aware Parenting, sucking is perceived to be a reflex, not a need. Aletha Solter wrote: *"The sucking urge is very strong to ensure survival through adequate food intake. Infants with a weak sucking instinct would not have survived in prehistoric times. But the fact that infants will eagerly suck on anything does not imply that they need to do this for emotional health."* (*The Aware Baby*, pages 75-76). In other words, sucking is for meeting the need for milk. The sucking reflex – like the rooting reflex – is for survival. Understanding the inherent reasons for rooting and sucking is an important part of helping parents understand what is really going on for their baby when they are rooting or sucking and are not hungry. Rooting is not caused by hunger and so does not necessarily indicate that a baby is hungry. Likewise, sucking is not a need separate from the need for nourishment.

With Aware Parenting, we don't believe that babies cry due to a need to suck (when they aren't hungry). Instead of interpreting that babies cry because they aren't getting to suck on something, we perceive that sucking is a common way that babies dissociate from their feelings, which is why dummies and thumb-sucking both suppress feelings and create a mild form of dissociation – more on that later.

In Aware Parenting, we also don't believe that babies cry due to a need for repetitive movement. Babies do enjoy gentle movement, but unlike with physical closeness, they don't cry because of a lack of movement. Rather, it is often our gentle and still presence, as we hold our baby in our arms, that helps them connect with any healing-feelings they need to express. Movement often creates dissociation which actually bypasses a baby's healing-feelings that they are trying to express to us.

Self-Compassion Moment

If you have encouraged your baby to suck on a dummy or their thumb, or you've done lots of movement to stop them from crying, and if this information resonates with you, I am here to remind you to put down any guilt sticks and to let you know that it is never too late to start differentiating between the two types of uncomfortable feelings and to put into practice what I will be sharing about later. I wonder if you find it helpful to know that I often used to hold my baby daughter and bounce on a fit ball to stop her from crying in the first three months of her life!

Through a baby's eyes

"Darkness, and now light. So bright, so different to how it used to be. Looking around, seeing shapes. More brightness there, more darkness there. Movement, ahhh, they come. Touch, closeness, warmth. Cuddle in. Ahhh ... relief, softness, touch. Home. This is known."

A baby's words

"Please see me. Please understand me. I am so vulnerable. I need you for everything and I depend on you coming to me and understanding what I need. I need your holding so much. There is so much air and

space around me and I'm not used to it. Everything is so loud and so bright. It's so much. All I know is how things were, and everything is new. I love it when you are really present in your body, so you know how I feel in my body when you gently pick me up and I can feel your presence in my body. I feel you holding me. I see you seeing me. I feel a relief as wide as my world when you understand what is really going on for me. Everything falls into place when I have a need and you know what it is and you meet that need for me. Please be gentle and present with me. Please see me. Please understand me. You are everything in my world and my world is so big for me right now."

Healing-feelings

Healing-feelings are far less well-known than needs-feelings, particularly in relation to babies. Many parenting paradigms do not recognise that babies have healing-feelings.

Remember the third aspect of Aware Parenting – that babies are highly sensitive and are deeply affected by what they experience. All babies experience stress every day, most experience mini-traumas from time to time, and some babies experience more severe trauma, including birth trauma. They feel feelings as a result of these stresses and traumas. Those feelings might include overwhelm or confusion, fear or terror, frustration or powerlessness and sadness or grief.

However, babies also come into the world with the inbuilt ability to heal from daily stresses, mini-traumas and bigger traumas, through crying in our loving arms when all their needs are met.

Self-Compassion Moment

How do you feel and what do you think when you read this?

This information is often surprising to us, given that most of us have often only been told about needs-feelings.

To put this in context, I'm going to share about our history of understanding and responding to babies.

The history of understanding babies' needs and feelings

In industrialised countries, it wasn't until the resurgence of attachment-style parenting in the 1970s that we remembered that babies had needs, including attachment needs. In contrast, if we look at many Indigenous cultures, we see that babies often have their attachment needs met. They often experience a lot of closeness. Cots and prams don't exist. Babies often co-sleep and are carried in carriers that vary depending on the cultural traditions and beliefs and the climate. As toddlers, they are often carried on the hip of an older child or another member of the community.

The practice of having babies sleep separately from their parents first started with the Romans. Prams were invented in the 1800s by the upper classes in England. We can see that a disconnection from babies and their attachment needs spread from the industrialised countries around the world, until cots and prams were common, and co-sleeping and baby carrying became perceived as inferior or lower class. Judgement of more traditional ways of being close with babies also spread.

Attachment research beginning in the 1950s by John Bowlby, Mary Ainsworth and others showed how important close and ongoing connection is for babies and children. In the 1970s, there was an upsurge in returning to more original ways of being with babies, as baby carrying and co-sleeping began to edge back into society. Yet, they were often perceived as 'alternative'. Over the past couple of decades, co-sleeping and baby carrying are becoming more and more common in industrialised cultures.

In the present day, cultural beliefs that co-sleeping and baby carrying are 'inferior,' 'weird' – or even dangerous – still exist, and parents are still commonly shamed or judged if they co-sleep or carry their baby. In The Marion Method, I talk about how 'shame and judgement sticks' are one of the ways that the cultural conditioning of The Disconnected Domination Culture (The DDC) gets passed down. The first priority of The DDC is to disconnect babies from their parents, and shaming or judging parents for co-sleeping or carrying their baby is a very effective way of doing that.

On the other hand, since parents who aim to meet their baby's attachment needs through co-sleeping or carrying their babies have often needed to fight to have these practices acknowledged and valued, it's understandable that this can get in the way of being open to learning about healing-feelings. The fight for acknowledgement that babies actually have attachment needs has been a huge one, and has emerged after centuries of denying babies' needs. I so deeply acknowledge and appreciate all those who have fought for the recognition of babies' attachment needs.

However, in their dedication to this information about attachment needs, there has often been an assumption that *all* uncomfortable feelings and *all* crying is a communication of needs-feelings, and thus that if a baby is crying, even in loving arms, it means that the baby has an immediate need.

For this reason, there has been a common perception that even if we have checked that we have met all of their needs, and our baby is still crying in our arms, that this indicates the baby still has more unmet needs. The practice of listening to a baby cry in arms to release healing-feelings has therefore often been considered equivalent in the baby's experience to the practice of leaving babies to cry alone (known as controlled crying or cry-it-out).

This belief has also led many parents to think that they are doing something wrong, that they are missing something, or that they are failing as a parent, if they've done everything they can to meet their baby's needs, and their baby is still crying in their arms.

Aware Parenting shines a very different light on this.

I wonder if you are seeing why the following three things, which are core to this book and Aware Parenting, are so vital:

- Acknowledging that there are two types of uncomfortable feelings – needs-feelings and healing-feelings;
- Being able to differentiate between when a baby is communicating a needs-feeling or a healing-feeling;
- Being able to observe the differences between dissociation (when we either don't meet a baby's needs or we distract a baby from healing-feelings) and the relaxed presence that comes about when either their needs are met or they release a chunk of healing-feelings through crying-in-arms.

When we can understand and clearly see these three things, we receive absolute reassurance that a baby has a completely different experience when crying-in-arms if all their needs are met, compared to if they are crying when they are on their own.

If, when we were a baby, we didn't experience the relief and relaxation that comes from fully crying-in-arms to express our own healing-feelings (which most of us haven't), we don't have an embodied experience of that process and those sensations. Without that body knowing, it is very easy to assume that a baby feels the same feelings when they're crying in our loving arms with all their needs met, as they would if they were left alone to cry.

It is often only when we've experienced holding our baby and listening to their healing-feelings when all their needs are met, and we witness the profound relaxation they clearly show us afterwards, that we have reassurance that this is a completely different experience for a baby compared to them going through controlled crying or 'cry-it-out'.

Without having seen that deep presence, eye contact and relaxation in their muscles after expressing their healing-feelings in our loving arms, the whole idea of healing-feelings can seem strange at first. Yet, after a few times of seeing that deep relaxation, the peaceful presence, their smiles and true calmness, we receive deep reassurance that this is so very helpful for them.

Have you ever observed this difference in your baby? If not, and you are experimenting with crying-in-arms, I invite you to observe if you can clearly see these differences.

After expressing healing-feelings through crying-in-arms, a baby is likely to feel more relaxed in their body, be present, make more eye contact, and sleep more restfully. In contrast, after controlled crying, they would be likely to feel more tension in their muscles, make less eye contact, and need to sleep with the help of some kind of suppression or dissociation in place, all of which we will talk about later.

Self-Compassion Moment

We are always doing what we think is most helpful at the time, and there is so much conflicting information available about babies. That's why I will be inviting you to keep on listening in to yourself and to what resonates with you. I will also be repeatedly inviting you to be deeply compassionate with yourself and to drop any guilt or self-judgement sticks.

If you've been at the receiving end of judgements towards your choices with your baby, such as with co-sleeping or baby carrying, I'm sending you so much love and compassion. I wonder if you find it helpful to remember that cultural conditioning is powerful, and when you present a new way (as you may have done with co-sleeping and baby carrying – which is actually a very, very old way, given that cots and prams are very recent in human history), this can be very challenging to people's conditioning, and you have been at the receiving end of their conditioning.

The Disconnected Domination Culture[7] doesn't want disconnection to be removed, because it is the disconnection that gives way to domination. In other words, although you might experience judgement from others as personal, it's part of a system trying to keep itself in place.

Any person judging you for keeping your baby close was once a baby longing for closeness.

---

7   Remember that this is a term from The Marion Method.

Changing our beliefs about babies

If you have ever judged people for co-sleeping or carrying their baby, I wonder whether it resonates with you that this judgement might have been a thought you were taught to believe when you were younger, from being around people who had also been conditioned by Disconnected Domination Culture (DDC) ways of thinking? If so, are you willing to be deeply compassionate with yourself as you understand that you needed to think in these same ways as them in order to be safe, to belong or be loved?

Do you see things differently if you think about those judgements as a way that The DDC keeps people believing in the disconnection that it promotes? Might you imagine that you were once a baby longing to be carried, or to have closeness at night, before you learnt these ways of thinking?

The wonderful thing is that we can change our beliefs at any point in our lives. Parenting is one of the most important times to revisit our beliefs about human nature, so that we can choose what is true for us, rather than perpetuate old beliefs that were passed down to us which may not resonate with us at all.

Self-Compassion Moment

I wonder if you felt uncomfortable feelings when reading about the concept that babies have healing-feelings to express through crying-in-arms? Perhaps you had the thought that it's the same as controlled crying or cry-it-out? If so, does it resonate with you that these feelings might be coming from the pain you've felt seeing babies left alone to cry, or even your own experiences being left alone to cry as a baby? Or perhaps you've fought to stand up for babies' attachment needs in your community or family, and taking on the idea that crying can be healing is a huge thing to process?

If so, I'm sending you lots of compassion and such appreciation for all the ways you deeply value the needs of babies.

And I would love to ask you ... Are you open to the possibility that we can meet all of a baby's immediate needs, and that they will still have feelings to express, just like children, teens, adults and elders do?

I so support you in whatever thoughts and perceptions most resonate with you.

If you have given your baby a dummy or blanket or soft toy to stop crying or to go to sleep with in a cot, are you open to different ways of seeing babies and their needs and feelings? Is it possible for you to believe that babies need lots of closeness and that they have feelings to express to us from experiences of daily stress and larger trauma, and that you can have sound sleep as well as support your baby to be securely attached?

Co-sleeping and baby carrying are both based on the understanding of a baby's attachment needs, and the knowledge (backed up by research) that the more those attachment needs are met, the less a baby will feel painful feelings. Because Aware Parenting is a style of attachment parenting, the aim is to meet our baby's needs as much as we can.

However, alongside this, I believe that it's vital that we are compassionate with ourselves, knowing that attachment-style parenting is meant to exist within a wider culture of community, where at any time, a baby might be being carried by their parents, grandparents, aunties and uncles, older siblings or other family or community members. A baby having multiple secure attachments is by far the norm in the majority of human history, compared to the pattern of one or two secure attachments for a baby which exists in today's nuclear families.

> Practicing attachment-style parenting within The Disconnected Domination Culture is inherently going to be more difficult, because one or two adults looking after one or more children is not how we are meant to live.

This is one of the reasons why I talk about the spectrum of Aware Parenting, to invite you to listen in compassionately to both your baby and yourself, and to find ways of getting both of your needs met as much as possible *within* the society that you live in.

If meeting attachment needs was known and practiced in many traditional cultures, what about healing-feelings? Were these understood? Are they perceived now in Indigenous cultures? Over the years, I have talked to people with Indigenous backgrounds who told me that their cultures *did* indeed believe in healing-feelings and did listen to babies' feelings in this way. From them I learnt that one of the reasons we might not have heard about this in more industrialised countries is because it wasn't safe for people in many Indigenous cultures to share their deeper beliefs and practices with colonisers. However, it's possible that healing-feelings were not generally understood in the past and that parents have only started practicing crying-in-arms relatively recently.

> *Self-Compassion Moment*
>
> As you continue reading, I invite you to keep on listening in to yourself and to what does and doesn't resonate, and to be deeply compassionate with yourself. I always support you in staying true to what you experience as most aligned with your values.

Talking of the effects of the culture, being with our baby's healing-feelings is also inevitably going to be hard at times, because in this culture, most of us don't have the kind of physical and emotional support that we really need. This is another reason for acceptance of where you are on the Aware Parenting spectrum at any time, and compassion for yourself practicing something which the dominant culture is set up to work against.

Danielle, a paediatric physiotherapist, reflects on her journey of thinking about babies from an Aware Parenting perspective and what changed for her when she understood the two types of feelings:

"With my daughter, Eliza, I had not found Aware Parenting (and was likely not yet ready for this way of thinking) but I attempted to parent in a gentle way with some Montessori inspiration. She had a long and difficult birth. She cried ... a lot. I worked hard to meet her needs and constantly fed and rocked her to stop the crying. She ended up very plump! Although we had a deep bond I was frustrated by motherhood and at times resentful of her. She woke frequently in her cot and we resorted to sleep training methods which seemed to only give results for a short time.

I found Aware Parenting when my son, Joey, was born. It was a healing birth. I listened to his crying and it never lasted long. I think that because he was heard he didn't feel the need to continue to cry as Eliza had. It was much easier to listen rather than rock and jiggle and constantly search for a reason for the tears. We bed share and both get a good sleep this way. Mothering in this way feels easier and seems to come more naturally, and my baby seems more content."

When we understand how much babies are affected by what they experience, we can do whatever we can to lessen the amount of stress and trauma they experience, while also holding in mind that they have natural processes to heal from any stress and trauma that they *do* experience. *And* that *whatever* we do to meet their needs, *all* babies have feelings to express to us and *all* babies experience at least some stress, approximately every day for their first year.

Stress, trauma and healing – the fight/flight/freeze response, or hyperarousal and dissociation

To understand how babies heal from stress and trauma, we first need to know about how stress and trauma operate. Aletha Solter, in *Healing Your Traumatized Child*, defines a traumatic event as: "…anything that causes physical or emotional pain or that threatens a child's wellbeing…. Anything that the child interprets as threatening can be traumatic, even when it does not pose a real danger." (p.21) She also offers this definition of trauma: "…trauma results when children's attempts to defend themselves or escape are unsuccessful or when they give up and dissociate." (p.36) In other words, if a baby moves into the fight/flight response but isn't able to successfully fight or flee from whatever is stressful, they experience trauma.

When babies experience something stressful or threatening, some automatically move into the fight/flight response, which is a survival response. They might try to fight, such as through pushing away an unwanted intervention by kicking with their feet. Before they are able to crawl, they have limited options to flee, but they will do what they can, such as through turning their head away. Once they *can* crawl or walk, they will move away from something they experience as stressful by crawling or running away.

> We can see that both making noise and using body movements are a core part of the fight/flight response. I invite you to hold this in mind when listening to the sounds of your baby's crying and observing the vigorous movement that happens when they are crying-in-arms to heal from stress and trauma.

The term hyperarousal is used to describe the fight/flight response. This is mediated by the sympathetic nervous system, which increases both a baby's heart rate and the blood flow to their arms and legs, to support enough energy for fighting or fleeing.

However, since babies are so vulnerable, they are often both easily stressed and unable to successfully prevent or get away from the stressful events that do occur and so they move into a state which is often referred to as freeze or dissociation. Some babies don't even try to defend themselves or escape, and they move directly into a state of dissociation.

Dissociation is marked by quietness, stillness and numbness.

Dissociation is mediated by the parasympathetic nervous system, which reduces heart rate and blood pressure. In addition, endogenous opioids numb physical pain and "...reduce emotions of fear and anger, sometimes even producing narcotic-like euphoria. Dopamine, which plays a role in addictive behaviors, is also involved in dissociation. The high levels of both endorphins and dopamine may help to explain why dissociative states can be both pleasurable and addictive." (Aletha Solter, pages 25-26 of *Healing Your Traumatized Child*)

Understanding dissociation, and differentiating it from relaxed presence, is key to understanding babies and their behaviour.

Many of the practices that our culture teaches parents actually make babies dissociate from feelings caused by stressful or traumatic events. In contrast, Aware Parenting invites parents to support their babies to express those emotions in healthy ways, heal from stress and trauma, and return to the homeostatic state of relaxed presence.

When a baby is dissociated, that tells us that the effects of stress and/or trauma are still affecting their body.

After a stressful or traumatic event, a baby's body is innately wired to move out of the fight/flight/freeze response and back to homeostasis, which is the calm relaxation I've been talking about. However, babies are less likely to move back into that relaxed state if:

- they didn't experience feeling protected or supported during the event;
- they weren't able to prevent the stressful thing happening through fighting or fleeing;
- they moved into dissociation and went numb while it was happening.

Immediately after the stressful or traumatic event, babies will often try to heal from the experience through crying in the arms[8] of an adult with whom they feel safe. This is the natural and healthy expression of healing-feelings.

This combination of crying and vigorous movement helps release the energy that was mobilised to get away from the threatening event. If a baby doesn't get to cry-in-arms, the unexpressed crying, feelings and muscle tension remain in their bodies. With each stressful event, more and more tension *accumulates*, leading to many of the things that parents find challenging – agitation, screeching, wriggling, feeding challenges, taking a long time to go to sleep and waking up frequently. These symptoms can indicate that babies haven't had the opportunity to heal from those stressful or traumatic events. As those feelings accumulate, babies may be in a state of hyperarousal or dissociation for an increasing amount of time.

---

8 Once babies are crawling, they need closeness but not necessarily to be held in our arms for their crying to be healing.

Even if the stressful or traumatic event happened a while ago, babies still have the capacity to heal from its effects when there is the balance of attention of feeling emotionally safe in the present while revisiting the past experience and crying, raging and moving vigorously.

They can also heal through laughter and play (without tickling), which we will return to more in the chapter on *attachment play*.

I want to remind you that in our modern culture, it is common for babies to experience several stressful experiences every day, even if we do everything we can to meet their needs and to protect them from stress and trauma.

Sources of stress for babies and how they heal

In utero

Babies are deeply affected by what they experience in the womb. Research over the past several decades has shown clearly that babies are sentient, feeling, learning beings while *in utero*. Researchers such as Thomas Verny have observed babies in the womb trying to kick away an amniocentesis needle – this is an example of the fight/flight response in action.

When a mother is highly stressed for long periods, her state of hyperarousal can affect her unborn baby. Mothers have shared with me that they were very stressed during pregnancy and saw their baby sucking their thumb on the screen of an ultrasound scan. They later observed their baby thumb-sucking after they were born. We'll talk more about the Aware Parenting way of understanding thumb-sucking later in the book.

> *Self-Compassion Moment*
>
> I'm here to remind you to refrain from self-judgement if you experienced lots of stress during pregnancy and/or if your baby sucks their thumb.

When we understand that babies experience stress *in utero*, this can inspire us to receive more support, nourishment and empathy during pregnancy. Is there anything we can do to reduce the stress we're experiencing? Are we willing to do anything differently? Are we willing to rest more? Various forms of bodywork can be deeply nourishing for mothers during pregnancy, and knowing that her own nourishment will influence her baby can be a powerful inspiration for mothers-to-be. If you've found yourself crying more easily during pregnancy, you'll have experienced your own natural ability to heal from stress through crying with loving support. I also recommend talking to your baby during your pregnancy. It can create even more connection which can then continue after birth. There are many beautiful ways we can support pregnant women to have a less stressful pregnancy, and again I want to bring in the cultural piece here. In a healthy culture, mothers would be given plenty of support and protected from stress wherever possible, as a way of caring for both her and the unborn baby.

During birth

Babies feel a huge amount of sensations and feelings during birth, even if the birthing process is calm and blissful for the mother and also if they experience a planned Caesarean. If we put ourselves in the position of the baby and imagine the physical experience of moving through the birth canal, we can get an idea of the titanic forces they experience during a vaginal birth. Stan Grof's work expresses this so clearly. Lots of fear experienced by the mother or the people supporting her can affect the baby, as can interventions, such as speeding up the process, or a Caesarean. Artificial induction can create faster and more intense contractions or surges – these not only can be more painful for the mother, they can also be more stressful for the baby. The experience of forceps and ventouse can be shocking and painful for babies. All of these physical experiences have emotional counterparts for babies. Babies feel during birth *and* they can also heal from their birthing experiences.

The culture we live in has a powerful effect on birthing practices and beliefs. Understanding that can help women reconnect with their power during birth. We can do whatever possible to prepare for birth, physically and emotionally, including understanding the cycle of interventions, healing from any past fears, and from our own experiences of being born, and connecting with our own power and agency during birth. Working with a birthing professional who understands birth biodynamics can be deeply helpful. Having a supportive team in place can make a huge difference, including having people who advocate for you and your baby and remind the birthing team that their voices, their words and the birthing environment make a difference for you and your baby. Talking to your baby about what is happening and giving them empathy for what they might be experiencing and feeling is another way of giving them that experience of empathic understanding, even if they don't understand the words.

> I'm here to remind you that whatever your baby experienced during their birth, they have the inbuilt capacity to heal from it with your support.

Greer, a Soul Healing Coach and Birth-keeper, shares about her family's experience with Aware Parenting straight after their son's birth. I felt so moved when I first heard her share this story in a workshop I facilitated. Imagine if all babies had their *in utero* and birth-related feelings acknowledged and heard soon after their birth!

"My partner and I were lucky enough to be introduced to Aware Parenting during my pregnancy. Our midwife had heard us mention that one of our most important values as parents was ensuring that our child knew that all of his emotions were welcome in our home and that he would be safe and loved when expressing them. We had our first opportunity to embody this the moment our little Tully was born. After a 24-hour labour he arrived naturally at home and as he took his first breaths he immediately began releasing some huge emotions. It was so obvious to us even in all our joy and hormone bliss that our little boy was releasing more than some big feelings; Intuitively it felt like a deeper trauma. He cried solidly and with his whole body for at least 20 minutes. We sat with him in my arms in the birth pool while we spoke with him amidst kisses between his dad and me. Most of this time was spent simply holding him still, looking into his eyes, hand on his chest, welcoming his emotions and anchoring him into safety with our loving presence.

At first his body, arms and legs were jolting, his whole being expressing a story that he needed to have heard and seen. I intuitively knew the story. Over the course of his release his little body began to soften, his eyes that had been mostly closed began to open and he began to explore with his hands. By the end, he was beautifully calm and we were able to move to the couch to start our breastfeeding journey.

I had a lot of opposition in those early years to crying-in-arms from those around me, telling me it seemed cruel not to stop him crying with jiggling, bouncing, shushing etc. But to us, it seemed like the most normal thing in the world to not try and make our little boy stop feeling what clearly needed to be felt! The way his body always went into the deepest calm and often straight to sleep afterwards was all the proof we needed. It still is. We will be forever grateful to Aware Parenting for showing us a way that recognised the importance and beauty of crying."

Self-Compassion Moment

I invite you to connect in to yourself and your thoughts and feelings after reading about baby Tully's experience.

What are you thinking? How do you feel?

I invite you to be deeply compassionate with yourself in this moment. Reading stories like this can help us connect with all kinds of feelings. I want to remind you to pause whenever you feel called to and particularly whenever you notice feelings bubbling up in you. Are you willing to tend to your own emotions and reach out for empathy and listening if you need that? I welcome all of your feelings as you read this. Perhaps you might like to imagine me listening to your feelings while you read my words.

Here, I share the origin of my fascination for understanding the effects of birth.

As a baby, I was born at 30 weeks and was in an incubator for the first five weeks of my life, and this experience sowed the seed of a passion in me. From my teens onwards, I wanted to understand what babies experience during and after birth. I remember the first time I consciously realised that our birth deeply influences us. I was about 14 and was having dinner in the kitchen in my home in England on a dark wintry night, and my parents were listening to a man on the radio talking about remembering his birth during hypnotherapy. I was spellbound. In my twenties, while training as a psychotherapist, I became passionate about pre- and peri-natal psychology, and immersed myself in the research which showed the profound influence of birth and before and after. I went to several rebirthing and Holotropic Breathwork workshops and sessions.

When I was pregnant in 2001, I came across Aware Parenting, and learnt that we don't need to wait until adulthood to express the feelings from our time in utero and during and after birth; that was another lightbulb moment. I am so grateful that I had this information before my children were born, and that their dad and I could listen to their feelings related to their births while they were still babies. And I love to remind parents that it's never too late to listen to feelings!

Babies and children have so much innate wisdom. They know how to heal. The more we free ourselves from our cultural conditioning about babies, and the more we have our own unexpressed feelings heard by empathic listeners, the more we are able to lovingly hold our babies in our arms when they have feelings to tell us and to cooperate with their natural healing processes.

We *can* heal from our birth experiences as adults, as my experience shows:

I first started reconnecting with the feelings from my early experiences when I was in my late teens. When I was 18, I got really drunk on New Year's Eve and I cried and cried. The grief I felt was huge and deep. I cried for hours, not knowing why I felt so much sadness. It wasn't until a few years later that I realised that the new year was helping me connect with my birth experience, that first beginning. The year before, at 17, I'd experienced a panic attack for the first time, and I'd run out of my family home in full flight mode, not understanding then about the fight/flight/freeze response and why I was desperate to flee.

It wasn't until I started therapy a few years later that I put the pieces together and realised that the terror and the grief that had poured out when I was 17 and 18 were from my experiences in the incubator, where I experienced grief about the profound lack of closeness and connection that I innately needed, and terror from that and all the powerlessness of the medical interventions. These feelings were coming up nearly two decades later as I started to contemplate leaving home – reminding me of the original separation when I was born.

Over time, with years and years of inner work, I was able to feel more feelings, and dive in deeper to the core of the experience that I had as a baby. Grief, disappointment, fear, terror, powerlessness, rage, overwhelm and confusion have been feelings I've become increasingly able to be present with in my body and have then released.

I uncovered feelings of deep grief and isolation, being alone for so long when every cell of my being cried out to be held.

I revisited terror and powerlessness, having no agency or ability to bring about change. No way to stop the medical procedures, no way to fight or to flee.

I reconnected with overwhelm from being amongst bright lights and machine noises for all those weeks, unable to find peace or solace.

I felt the excruciating pain of nobody having any clue about what I was experiencing. No-one understood the depth of feelings I had felt. I uncovered the deep dissociation I had required, freeze being my only option when fight and flight were not possible in the little plastic box.

Then there were all the beliefs that I acquired from this experience, such as, 'I have to do things myself'. And I'm celebrating all the ways that I adapted to that, and how I even thrived at times with this core belief. However, in more recent years, through my Inner Loving Presence Process work, which is part of The Marion Method, I've become more and more comfortable with receiving support. Little baby Marion knows that she is not on her own any more and doesn't need to do everything herself. In fact, in front of me now is a piece of paper with words from my Inner Loving Mother and my Inner Loving Father (also part of The Marion Method work) to little baby me.

It says:

"We will hold you for as long as you want to be held. We are not willing for you to be hurt again. We are here to listen to ALL of your feelings."

Every morning when I first wake up, I connect in with my Inner Loving Mother and Inner Loving Father and after welcoming little baby Marion into the world, they say those phrases to her, and I breathe out a sigh of receiving and relief. The reparenting process has been profound and deep, as I now cherish and care for my body, feelings and needs. My inner dialogue is now deeply nourishing and compassionate. There has been huge healing in 33 years. My Mum and I are deeply connected now, her at 91 and me at 55.

However, this has been a long and arduous journey, and the effects of that unhealed trauma led to many painful experiences in the first three decades of my life, including a profound sense of aloneness and something wrong with me-ness, and a deep longing for closeness that was the fabric of my life for so long. That is why I am so willing for more people to understand what babies experience, and to know how to help them heal from early stressful and traumatic experiences while they are still babies.

I recognise in babies who have been through traumatic births, separation and medical procedures, similar feelings and states to those I experienced. The look in their eyes that shows their fear or terror. The tension in their muscles indicating all the feelings they're holding within. The particular quality of dissociation that they have needed to be in to survive. I wish every baby who has gone through a stressful or traumatic birth could experience the deep understanding and healing that comes through experiencing Aware Parenting. Healing from birth trauma while still a baby is completely possible and makes a profound difference to the trajectory of their life. I'm sending you so much love if you experienced pre- or peri-natal trauma, and I'm sending you and your little one so much love if they did.

Imagine supporting our babies to heal from their birth *while they are still babies!*

Imagine giving that experience to your baby now, whatever they have experienced so far, so that they don't need to wait decades to do that healing, or to experience those feelings showing up when they're leaving home, separating from a partner, giving birth or becoming a parent. Yet, being with our baby in this way requires so much from us, and invites us on our own deep healing journey.

In the following story, Kata explains her experience of how situations in the present can help our babies revisit their birth experiences so that they can heal from them:

"Since birth, whenever I was changing his nappy, my son would squirm, seem to be uncomfortable, worried or even scared, and he would continuously kick my stomach as he was laying in front of me. I tried all kinds of things, e.g. setting a warm light, keeping him warm, cuddling, putting him on his tummy or on his side instead of on his back, talking to him gently, etc. Nothing seemed to make him more comfortable. In the meanwhile, he would literally search for my tummy with his little legs whenever I stood in front of him, and push his toes forcefully into my body. He also started to refuse shirts or pullovers to be pulled over his head, or hats in general (and this was wintertime).

It then occurred to me that these may be his birth movements and that the position with me in front of him was enabling his birth trauma to come up... he was 'stuck' for several hours after the full opening of my cervix. He had so much pressure on his head and was unable to move (as I could just not 'let him outside into the world' due to emotional trauma on my side, until I expressed that fear to my midwife and husband) and then I still needed to push forcefully for quite a long time. It was very painful (and loud), I guess for him, as well.

So I got so calm and decided to 'stand my ground', for him to be able to push against my tummy with his feet. I did not move away anymore. I looked into his eyes and he immediately started crying intensely, strongly pushing against my tummy with his feet. I stayed with him and held him, and then as he pushed himself towards the edge of the table (into the wall), I gently cupped the top of his head with my hands, too. This brought about very intense crying and sweating as he pushed his head into my hands with all his might. I could see how he moved deeper and deeper into those layers of emotions and expressed them while I was with him. I saw the fear and the panic and it felt like we were back there right at his birth. This lasted for about 30 minutes. I stayed with him for as long as he needed it.

Afterwards, with a sigh, he became so calm. I could literally sense the shift of energy in both of us. It felt really connected and clear, and he looked right in my eyes. I remember that changing his nappy or massaging him became so much more relaxing for both of us afterwards, and he never ever had a problem with hats or shirts anymore!"

I wonder if you noticed how Kata started off thinking that her baby was expressing a need, and then realised that her son was trying to heal, and once she realised that, was able to support him to heal in the way he had been trying to do. This is one of the reasons why understanding the difference between needs-feelings and healing-feelings is so important.

Gwen shares a similar experience of supporting her baby daughter heal from her birth experience, and also observes the long-term effects of doing so:

"My daughter had a tricky birth that eventually ended in a Caesarean. We were in the hospital for five days, where she was given a 'Gentle Chiropractic' adjustment and it was lovely watching her little body shift as it needed to. Once we were home, after a couple of days, she was lying on her change table, looking into my eyes and she started to cry. I knew she was fed and changed and so I listened to her. At one point, she started to push one little foot into my hand and cried harder. I kept my hand there and she kept pushing and crying, with

eye contact, for as long as she needed to. This experience happened a couple more times and from then on, she was a placid, easy going baby and child, who slept easily and was cooperative and laughed a lot. I was very grateful to have come across the understandings about emotional release and connection a few years before becoming a parent. Being regularly listened to without judgement or advice really helped me to relax around my daughter's feelings and just be present while she did what she needed to do.

I can't help wondering if children who receive diagnoses for 'bouncing off the walls' around age four are still valiantly trying to release birth trauma and we, with best intentions, are shutting that down and dragging it out. I'm excited that more and more parents are coming to this way of parenting that makes life a little easier for everyone and has long term positive repercussions. My daughter is 22 now and calls me a few days a week on her way to work to chat and talk things through, which she has always done. There was no 'teenage rebellion' and she listens to her friends and is so incredibly thoughtful. That's just her, of course, but I didn't add obstacles to her staying that way, thanks to these understandings about human needs and feelings."

Directly after birth

Babies are exquisitely sensitive directly after birth. They come from an environment where sounds and light were muted, they were carried in an environment of warm amniotic fluid and containment, and where they were receiving all their nourishment at a consistent rate. When they come out into the world, everything is different. The more we keep that environment similar to the one in the womb, the less overwhelm they will experience. That means having muted sounds and light if possible, talking in soft and loving voices, touching their skin with gentleness, presence and care, holding them within loving arms, having skin to skin contact, and putting only soft fabric or clothing against their skin.

If babies are taken away after birth, or there are loud noises, if they are put onto hard and cold scales, or are suctioned, they will have feelings to tell us. They will also pick up on the feelings of those in the room. *And* they can heal from these experiences. Letting them know what is going on and telling them in advance may also support them in feeling more connected and less overwhelmed, even if they don't understand the content of the words we say.

Sarah Lou shares how she helped her baby heal from being separated from her for the first ten days of his life:

"My second baby was born suddenly at 36 weeks gestation. He had premature lungs and had to be in an incubator for almost 24 hours a day for the first 10 days of his life. He was rarely awake during this time and didn't cry at all. I think he was using all his energy to stay alive and recover. When he was well enough, we were able to bring him home. Then he started to cry. He slept well and fed well, but when he was awake and not feeding, he would cry. He cried and cried and cried almost constantly for four months.

When I was holding him in my arms it felt to me with all my being that he was expressing all his pain and confusion about his first 10 days. It felt a bit like he was saying through his crying things like, 'Arrrgh! What just happened to me? That was so, so awful. I was all alone. I didn't know where you were'. I had heard about Aware Parenting a few months before but hadn't paid too much attention to it. I remembered reading about how crying could be the process of healing. This was a completely new concept to me but it resonated deeply with what I was seeing in my baby. In the beginning I did try a few methods for distracting/suppressing his crying, such as jiggling and breastfeeding, but nothing even touched it.

> It felt like his feelings and pain were just too big to be suppressed or distracted.

So I just accepted that this was what he needed to heal. In the daytime and nighttime he mostly slept, either in his basket, wrapped to me or next to me. In the evenings he'd be awake for a few hours crying. I'd sit with him in my arms and listen. Sometimes I'd say a few things to him like, 'I'm right here with you, I'm listening, I can hear how awful it was for you, you're with me now,' but mostly I'd just listen and stroke his head and hold him. It became the focus of my evenings for that time; I just accepted that this was what he needed to heal and that his healing was our priority right now. We cancelled a family holiday. I focused on only the essentials for keeping our family functioning day-to-day, and gave time to listen to him crying. Most evenings I'd spend some one to one time with my older son and so give our baby to my husband or a friend to hold for a short time. They both found it difficult to sit with him and listen while he cried, so mostly I would hold him while he cried. This continued for about four months.

And then almost overnight it changed. It seemed like he woke up one day and said, 'I feel much better!' He transformed rapidly into a smiling, laughing happy baby. He had barely smiled before that time, but after that he didn't stop smiling. I would often have comments when we were out about what a happy, smiley baby he was. It used to make me laugh and fill me with delight to think about how different he was from his first four months. He's now three and a half, full of life and generally happy and settled. When he needs to rage or cry now, he does so easily and fully, often without any prompting. He just brings it, does it and it's done! For me, it felt like I was thrust into learning how to hold space for big feelings. I hadn't done it before and had to learn quickly. I now feel deeply comfortable and even joyful holding space for my now three boys' big feelings."

> **Self-Compassion Moment**
>
> How do you feel when you read Sarah Lou's words?
>
> I invite you to be compassionate with any feelings you're feeling, and to drop any emotional sticks such as guilt if you've been tempted to pick them up!

When I read about what Sarah Lou gave her son, I feel so happy that he had this opportunity to heal from the trauma he experienced coming into the world. I know what a huge difference it would have meant for me had I experienced being heard in that way as a baby. I imagine releasing so much of the terror, grief, overwhelm and powerlessness that I only started to express two decades after my birth, holding those feelings in my body for all those years.

The healing process has its own timing. Just because a baby can heal from their early experiences doesn't mean that we are ready to trust and support that process at that time. And sometimes, certain things need to come into place before the healing can happen.

Sami, a pregnancy and postpartum doula, shares about her experience of trusting their timing with her son:

"I discovered Aware Parenting while I was pregnant. I still can't remember just how I stumbled upon The Aware Parenting Podcast, *but I did and felt so connected to it. I went on a deep dive throughout my pregnancy, I read* The Aware Baby *and listened to every single one of the podcast episodes. My bubba and I had a tricky start after his birth, where we needed to navigate interventions and separation. While I was heartbroken that we had to heal from the birth, I was so comforted by having Aware Parenting to lean on. That is until I tried to listen to my bubba's feelings – it turns out he didn't have much to*

express (or so I thought!). After many attempts at creating a safe, calm, and loving space to hold his tears and emotions, I gave up, thinking that Aware Parenting wasn't the right fit for us as a family, or that perhaps I just wasn't cut out for it. Little did I know that my bubba just needed to wait until he was ready to tell us how he felt and I needed to do my own releasing and healing to really be ready to hold space for him.

When my boy was eight weeks old, our city experienced disastrous floods. Houses and roads all around us were being wiped out, friends and family were stranded and we were scared. After a few anxious and worrisome days being stuck inside, wondering how our house would hold up and if our friends and family would be okay, I tried to put my boy down for an afternoon nap. He was full of milk, well rested, warm and dry, every one of his physical needs were met, and yet he cried. He cried so hard and so loud it shocked me. I instantly knew what was happening, understanding the impact of our worries on him, but also of his birth and his eight weeks of life thus far. I knew what he needed, and how I could provide that for him. So we sat together, and I held him and listened while he cried, with the heavy and relentless rain bucketing down outside the window. My partner came in and sat with us, as we assured our boy that we were there, that we were listening, that we loved him and he was safe. The crying lasted about an hour and I was able to stick with him for the whole time. He then fell into the deepest, calmest and most restorative sleep of his young life. I left the room and had a big release myself. We have been using an Aware Parenting approach in our relationship and our parenting ever since and have never looked back."

I invite you to hold in mind both this understanding of timing, as well as the profound interconnectedness between our emotional state and the extent to which a baby is ready and willing to express their healing-feelings to us.

The early days and overstimulation

In the early days, babies can frequently feel overwhelmed, because everything is so new for them. Simply being in a birthing unit, hospital or even being at home can be overwhelming for babies, because they don't have concepts for all the objects that they see, which are thus overstimulating. Their digestive and elimination systems are working in new ways, so the stimulation of feeling hunger and satiation, and of needing to eliminate through weeing and pooing, can all be strong sensations for babies. If babies have been in a Neonatal Unit or Special Care Baby Unit, they will often experience intense overwhelm, not only through the separation from their parents, but also from the bright lights, beeping, and other noises, and also from powerlessness or fear if they have had any medical procedures. Babies who experience this will have a lot of healing-feelings to express to us.

> Having a period of time staying at home, perhaps even in the bedroom and being quiet for a length of time, can really help babies gradually get used to more stimulation, even if they have already had a traumatic birth or have been separated from us. Setting up the environment for us to be supported and for our baby to experience minimal overwhelm can be deeply nourishing for us both, however the birth went.

I did this when my son, Sunny was born. My daughter was four and a half at the time, and we're a non-school family, so I was at home with them for most of the time while their dad was working. I set up the bedroom to be a beautiful space. I had a really comfortable armchair for me and a mini version for my daughter. We both had huge bottles of water and plentiful food to hand. I had loads of activities for my daughter that she could do there. For four months, we were in that space the majority of the time. Having that environment helped me to meet both of their needs as well as listen to their healing-feelings while feeling a sense of support, despite not living in a big community and at times when the father of my children and my friends weren't there to help.

I'm grateful that I was able to do that, and I know that many parents are not in that position or who wouldn't want to do what I did for the length of time that I did. I invite every family to set up a nourishing environment in a way that fits your family set up and life situation.

In many traditional cultures, mothers were and are supported to have plenty of quiet skin-to-skin time, bonding with their baby in the early weeks. Doing what we can to support deep connection in industrialised cultures can make a huge difference for not only mother and baby, but the whole family.

Painful and frightening things can often happen to babies in the early days of their life. My daughter had a traumatic experience as a newborn baby that she kept revisiting and trying to heal from. It took me several months to realise that she was expressing healing-feelings not needs-feelings:

When my daughter was three days old, she had a traumatic experience via a heel-prick test. A nurse visited our home, and tried unsuccessfully three times to get enough blood for the test. My daughter was clearly stressed by the experience. She was born in the summer, and it wasn't until the weather got colder that I realised that she was still being affected by it. Every time I tried to put socks or soft shoes on her, she would cry. Because I was so new to Aware Parenting, I didn't know what to do. At first, I thought it was that she 'just didn't like' having socks put on. As parents we can think that babies are crying because they don't like something, when sometimes it can be that the situation is helping them revisit a past stressful or traumatic event that they are trying to heal from through crying in our arms.

Our daughter's crying then generalised from when we tried to put socks or shoes on her to crying if we went to the beach and her feet touched the sand. Let's hold in mind that when a baby is reminded of a stressful and traumatic event and tries to cry with us, that is healing happening, and that is more helpful for them than if they move into a state of hyperarousal or dissociation at these moments.

For a long time, I just avoided putting on socks and taking her to the beach, not really understanding that we could help her heal rather than avoiding those situations. However, after discussing it in depth with her dad, he decided he wanted to help her heal from the heel prick experience, and the next time we went to the beach, he listened lovingly to her big crying in his arms when her feet touched the sand. After that, those feelings didn't bubble up with socks, shoes or sand, because she'd healed from the experience. She was quite happy to have socks and soft 'barefoot' shoes on and play at the beach.

Overstimulation is one of the key stresses for babies. Anything that's new to a baby can be overstimulating for them. Loud noises, harsh fabrics, new experiences, especially if they are out of the safe haven of our arms, all can be overwhelming for a baby.

From my own experiences both as a baby in an incubator, as well as being highly sensitive, I'm passionate about helping parents understand what their babies experience, and in particular, how easy it is for them to feel overwhelmed. Even before coming across Aware Parenting in 2002, I found Frederick Leboyer's book *Birth Without Violence* in a secondhand bookshop. As I read the words and looked at the pictures, I cried as I recognised how sensitive babies are during and after birth, and how much pain they often experience when this isn't understood, and they are subject to loud noises, bright lights and insensitive touch.

Leboyer said, *"So can we say that a newborn baby doesn't speak? No. It is we who do not listen."*

He also said, *"To protect newborn children from fear, we must reveal the world to them infinitely slowly, and not overwhelm them with more sensations than they can absorb and cope with ... to forge a link between past and present."*

I'm so grateful to have read his book many years before giving birth. It meant that wherever possible, I held and touched my babies with as much presence, gentleness, softness and care as I could.

I always remember learning from Aletha Solter in *The Aware Baby* that we can minimise overwhelm and overstimulation for babies by offering new experiences that are similar in some way to what they have already experienced. Putting ourselves in our baby's shoes can really help us understand what they might experience. To us as adults, being at home, all is known. But to a baby, who has no concepts yet, for whom everything is new, there is so much stimulation, so much to see and hear. As I shared above, setting up an environment at home to support you with your baby can really help with reducing overstimulation. I noticed that for my son, even going into a different room than the bedroom was a lot of visual stimulation for him in those early weeks and months. Going out in a car or public transport, going where there are lots of people, going to a shop, all of these can be highly overwhelming for a baby.

As much as possible, avoiding going to busy places in the early weeks and months, particularly limiting going out in the car or public transport or to places like shopping centres or loud environments, can really help reduce overstimulation.

However, it's so important to value your needs too. If going out will help you feel more energised, present and fulfilled, that will help your baby, so Aware Parenting is always about taking into account both of your needs.

When you do go out, carrying them close to your body in a baby carrier rather than putting them in a pram or stroller can reduce their levels of overwhelm, because they will feel the warm presence of your body, and they will also be able to turn their head in towards you to limit visual overwhelm. Babies will often fall asleep in highly stimulating environments – as a way of preventing overwhelm for themselves.

You may find that they seem to need to feed more in stimulating environments or that you end up jiggling them more or giving them the dummy, breast or bottle more. This happens when a baby is trying to express healing-feelings and we think they're expressing needs-feelings.

As you continue to read this book, you'll understand more about what's really going on during and after outings and how that affects their sleep, and you will have other options for ways you can respond.

If you're feeling overwhelmed when you're out, it's very likely that your baby is feeling very overwhelmed.

For babies who have been separated from their parents after birth or who had any medical interventions, it is even more important that they are held close and protected from overwhelm whenever possible. If a baby has already experienced separation, being disconnected in a pram is likely to also remind them of being separated in the past too, so there will be extra feelings there for them to feel. Carrying them close will protect them from that, while also giving them opportunities at other times to express their feelings and heal from those experiences.

If when you get home after an outing, your baby seems unsettled, or appears to want to feed lots more than usual, or you find yourself jiggling them for hours, or they wake up more often, all of these are probably signs that they are trying to tell you about their feelings of overwhelm, and are wanting to release those from their body so that they feel calm and relaxed enough to sleep.

One of the wonderful things about Aware Parenting is that when a baby does feel overwhelmed and we aren't able to reduce that overstimulation, we know that we can help them release those sensations from their body through listening to their feelings while they cry in our loving arms (when all their immediate needs have been met).

When we get home after being out, we can offer our loving presence by simply holding them in our arms, not jiggling or rocking or distracting, but offering eye contact and saying, "I'm here and listening. Do you want to tell me about how you feel and how that was for you?" Babies are deeply sensitive, *and* they can also heal from overwhelm through expressing and releasing their feelings in our loving arms. This can lead to them feeling relaxed in their bodies, feeding with calmness and presence, and falling into a relaxed sleep, even after a busy day.

Self-Compassion Moment

Here's another opportunity for self-compassion if you didn't have this information when your baby was a newborn. I invite you to drop any guilt sticks, and to remember that they can still heal from any overwhelm they felt back then.

I also want to remind you of how important it is for you to also get your own needs met. If going out for a walk with a friend while carrying your baby in a carrier is going to meet your needs for connection, empathy and exercise and help you be more present with your baby afterwards, I so support you to do that. Your needs are vitally important too! Remember that you can also listen to any healing-feelings that they need to express afterwards as a result of the outing.

Through a baby's eyes

"Movement. From soft place to hard place. All unknown. Looking up, fast movement. So fast. What is going on? Fear, overwhelm. Big noise. Big wind. More noise. Warm arms. Oh no! Back to somewhere else. No feeling of presence. Gazing up, so much space, movement, movement. Stop. Now nothing. No eyes, no warm bodies. The movement starts again. Confusion. Overwhelm. So much. Longing, longing."

A baby's words

"When you pick me up and the door opens, all is new for me. When I don't feel your warm arms, all I feel is space and lack. Going in the metal box car is familiar for you, but the way that things speed by is very new for me. I feel overwhelmed. What is going on? Where am I? Where are you? The door opens and the noise is so loud. The movement stops and you pick me up – but there's no touch, I don't feel your warm presence, and again, when you start pushing me along, all I want is your loving arms. There's so much movement as you push me along. And then suddenly, I don't see anything. Did you put a cloth over the pram? Now I can't see you either. Are you still there? I hope you are! I miss you. I want you. Home is in your arms. My body still feels movement. Oh now we've stopped. Oh now I can see you again. Will you pick me up? Please. Please. I long for you. I love being held by you. When I'm in your arms I am home again."

Unmet past needs

When we don't understand what a baby is communicating to us, this can be stressful for them, because they have a strong need to be understood. Offering them our loving presence so we can really observe them and be attuned to what they need makes a huge difference to them. And we are all learning, because most of us didn't grow up seeing babies have their needs met. I'm here to remind you that it would be very different if we had!

Continuing to learn all you can about babies and their needs and their cues will help, as will continuing to observe your baby, so that you understand them even more deeply. Each baby is so unique and has subtly different ways of communicating their needs. And again, I want to remind you that they can heal from times where we don't understand what they need or we don't have what is required to meet their needs in the moment. I wonder if you find that reassuring to know?

Returning again to healing-feelings

I've shared with you that all babies have healing-feelings, and that these feelings are different from needs-feelings. I want to remind you that with needs-feelings, our role is to understand the need and to meet it as promptly as we can, and when we do, that feeling will go away because the need is now met.

> When a baby has healing-feelings to express but we think that babies only have needs-feelings, we will try to meet their apparent needs when actually they are inviting us to listen to their feelings.

At these times, they may stop crying when we feed them, rock them, jiggle them, change position, or sing to them, but this isn't because we've met their needs, even though we might interpret it that way. It's because we've suppressed their feelings.

Self-Compassion Moment

Again, I invite you to drop any emotional sticks here. We don't know what we don't know. In the early months with my daughter, I wasn't able to see what was really going on for her, despite being trained in infant observation and psychotherapy! Many times, I thought I was doing things to meet her needs when in fact I was suppressing the healing-feelings she was trying to express.

> However, we can all increase our understanding of our baby's cues with information, experience and practice.

We will start being able to see that when we suppress our baby's feelings, they may look mildly dissociated, with a glazed look and tense muscles. In comparison, if we've truly met their needs, they will be relaxed both in their eye contact and in their muscles.

When we don't understand that there are two types of feelings and we keep distracting our babies away from their healing-feelings, those unexpressed feelings accumulate in their bodies, leading to increasing agitation, which means they find it harder to go to sleep and to sleep as long as they need.

Healing-feelings are caused by stress or trauma. However much we aim to meet a baby's needs, healing-feelings don't leave, because they are not needs-feelings. They are not caused by present moment needs and so cannot be got rid of through meeting needs. The way to help our babies release those feelings from their bodies is to listen to them. This is their innate healing process in operation. They are literally trying to tell us about their experiences and the feelings they felt when they went through those stressful or traumatic experiences.

> With healing-feelings, our role is to be deeply present, hold our baby in our arms[9], without jiggling or rocking, offering our warm voice and eye contact, and to listen to those feelings.

---

9   This is for babies who are not yet crawling. 'Healing crying' changes when babies become mobile, as I explain later in the book.

> *Self-Compassion Moment*
>
> I wonder how you feel when you read this?
>
> What are you thinking as you read this?
>
> I wonder what comes up for you when you imagine holding your baby in your arms when you're sure that all their needs are met, and deeply listening to them?
>
> Remember what I said earlier about how understandable it is for us to feel big feelings when we think about our babies expressing their feelings to us?
>
> I wonder if you feel scared or confused, or even outraged? Perhaps incredulous or discombobulated or numb?
>
> Whatever you are feeling right now, I'm sending you so much love.
>
> Perhaps you're feeling worried or concerned, thinking that a baby would feel scared or overwhelmed if they cried in this way?
>
> Perhaps you feel fear or sadness, and you have a sense that you're tapping into your own experiences of being left alone to cry as a baby?
>
> Perhaps you feel outraged, and you think that this isn't true and that all feelings are caused by here and now needs?
>
> Again, I want to remind you to keep on staying connected with yourself and keep on reminding yourself that you get to choose what you believe and what you do with your baby. I so deeply support you to keep on listening to yourself.

Healing from stress and trauma

How does this work? How do babies heal from stress and trauma through crying in our loving arms when all of their needs are met?

Babies feel real feelings. They feel fear and they feel overwhelm. They feel confusion and they feel frustration. They feel terror and they feel rage. These and more are all feelings that babies feel. And just like us, they need those feelings to be heard. They want to be understood. Just as we want to be understood by our friends, parents or partner, babies want to be deeply understood by us.

In my own experience of healing from the trauma I experienced as a baby, born at 30 weeks' gestation and being in an incubator for five weeks, I have revisited the deep and profound pain of not being understood. Nobody knew what I was feeling. Nobody understood that when I was alone in the incubator, I felt both deeply lonely and extremely terrified. Nobody understood that experiencing all the lights and noises, I felt completely overwhelmed. Nobody understood that, with all the tubes and tape, I felt powerless and uncomfortable. No-one understood at the time, and no-one understood for decades, until I met people who did know about what babies feel. Feeling the pain of not being understood was excruciating for me, yet I wasn't able to express those feelings until many years later, when I felt the emotional safety and supportive outer and inner presence to do so.

Understanding how painful it is for babies to not be understood is partly what has called me to write this book. I don't want any baby to experience the pain that I did and to be alone with their feelings.

And, I want to remind you that it is never too late for us to understand what our baby is experiencing and might have experienced in the past, and it is never too late to give them a sense of being deeply understood. All the overwhelm, loneliness, terror and pain can be healed from. It really is possible!

Babies want to be heard and understood. They have real feelings, and just like we want the people in our lives to hear and understand how we feel, babies want that too.

My own experiences as an adult have helped me understand the painful ongoing effects of not being heard as a baby can be, if we don't get to express those feelings in our infancy or childhood. Despite lots of healing, I sometimes still find challenges in being heard, even now, more than half a century later and with decades of healing under my belt. Old feelings of frustration and profound powerlessness can bubble up for me at these times. Listening to our baby's feelings when they are still a baby can make a huge difference for how they feel when they are adults.

Being heard and understood: a feelings perspective and a nervous system perspective

From a feelings perspective, babies have feelings that they want to have heard and understood. Those feelings are too much for them to continue feeling and expressing if we are not present with them hearing those feelings – we will talk more later about what happens if we aren't with them or aren't really present with them.

When we do hear those feelings, while holding them and giving them our loving presence and empathy, they feel relieved. They experience being heard and understood. Their feelings are honoured and validated.

This can set up deep beliefs that their feelings matter, their emotions are listened to, and that their feelings will always be heard, and those core beliefs can reverberate throughout the rest of their lives.

From a nervous system perspective, we can observe the process of *hyperarousal*, or the fight/flight/freeze response. When a baby experiences something as a threat, as all of what I listed above are for a baby, they will go into a fight or flight response. This is the way their nervous system is designed to operate, for survival. We might see this when a baby who is going to receive an intervention tries to push away or kick away with their hand or foot, or when they turn away from something harsh or unwanted.

Babies innately know how to come back into homeostasis from that state of *hyperarousal*, through crying in our arms (or with our loving support, once they are mobile).

> *However, because babies have very little capacity to fight or flee, they will often go into freeze mode; as I shared before, in Aware Parenting – as in other paradigms – we call this dissociation. During dissociation, there is a numbing of painful emotions, without any reduction in stress levels.*

How can we tell a baby is dissociated? They often become very still, and their eyes may glaze over.

I remember when I first saw the freeze response in animals. We have rabbits and dogs in our family, and many years ago, one of the dogs went up close to the rabbits' enclosure. The rabbits simply froze. I had an 'aha' moment back then, realising what was going on.

> *In this culture, where we are not taught to see the difference between relaxed presence and dissociation, parents often think their baby is relaxed when in actual fact, their little one is mildly dissociated. In dissociation, their eyes might look wide-eyed but glazed over. They might be staring. They might be doing something at the same time – eg. urgently sucking on something, but with the rest of their body still, or they might simply be very still. There is often a muscular tension, in readiness to fight or flee if possible.*

If we look at this behaviour from a survival perspective, it makes sense, doesn't it? If a baby is all alone and there is a threat from an animal, for example, the freeze makes it seem as if they are dead, just like our rabbits when the dog came close. Animals rarely eat other creatures that are already dead. The freeze response is also adaptive because it numbs sensations, so if they were to be hurt, they wouldn't feel it as much. This is how any initial big feelings that a baby feels - terror, overwhelm, powerlessness or rage - become numbed.

> Dissociation is a relief in a highly stressful situation. However, it is meant to be a short-term solution to that stress. Hence, there are long-term consequences if a baby stays in that state.

Since we are on the topic of the fight/flight/freeze response, it can also be helpful to differentiate a parent's perception of their baby being alert, when the infant is actually in a state of *hyperarousal*. Here, we might see them with a wide-eyed, shocked or wary expression on their face, indicating they are feeling fear or terror. Or, they might always be busy, not sleep very restfully, and in a state of *hypervigilance*. In comparison to these two states, healthy alertness can be discerned because babies show openness and spaciousness while also being relaxed.

> *Our amazing bodies are 'designed' for survival through the fight/flight/freeze response. In addition, they have inbuilt mechanisms to return to healthy homeostasis after a threatening experience, even if no fighting or fleeing actually occurred.*

For babies, this return to calm happens through crying, raging and vigorous movement in compassionate arms[10], along with vigorous movement. A baby needs to be in the presence of our loving arms for healing to happen, because the warm and relaxed connection is the signal that they are safe now.

This combination of feeling safe in the present while revisiting the past and expressing the pent-up feelings is what creates the healing. In Aware Parenting this is called the balance of attention and it is central to healing from stress and trauma, not only in babies, but also in children and adults too.

When babies cry in loving arms[11], they are expressing feelings from past experiences. They also move vigorously, which is how they release the tension that was mobilised in their body to fight or flee from the stressful experience. They may kick (releasing the tension mobilised to flee), their arms will flail around (releasing the energy mobilised to fight), and they will often move their heads from side to side. Loud crying and raging would have been an instinctive survival mechanism to signal a need for help from the parents.

This combination of movement and sound releases the physical tension that has accumulated from being ready to fight or to flee.

This recovery process of crying, raging and physical movement is particularly important for babies who dissociated during the stressful or traumatic experience.

This is because moving from a state of dissociation, to expressing the

---

10 Again, if they are mobile, they might cry with us close or touching but not in our arms.
11 Before they are crawling, or with closeness and connection once they are mobile.

feelings and the fight/flight energy, not only helps them feel relieved, it also helps them feel powerful. When they kick during the crying or lash out with their hand and get to feel that pressure and contact of our body, they feel their powerfulness. This also then becomes a reparative experience for them, as they move from powerlessness to embodied power. You may remember Kata sharing about her son healing from his birth experience through that kicking motion and how she supported him with that by providing him the physical connection to push against.

Their movements will also be a revisiting of their specific past experiences. So, for example, if they are expressing feelings from, and healing from, their birthing experience, they will often repeat what happened back then. They will get in positions that replicate their birth. The crying will often intensify if we provide our hand for their feet to kick against or we put gentle pressure on their head. They may repeatedly get into positions where they seem to invite this kind of contact. We may see them again and again arching their backs if they were born vaginally, as they replicate what happened during their birth.

This is the innate wisdom of their healing and recovery process in action.

If we lovingly support them in this healing process, they will express a chunk of feelings to us, and will also release the physical tension in their bodies from a particular past experience.

Given the opportunity – ie. if we are able to stay with the feelings and not distract them – that process will come to a natural conclusion, where they finish the crying and move into a state of deep calm and relaxation.

Feyza, who is a doula and breastfeeding counsellor who works with infant mental health as well as pregnancy and birth biomechanics, shares about her experience with her babies moving during healing-crying:

"It can feel overwhelming to hold and support a baby who wants to twist and turn and arch their back. I remember feeling overwhelmed when my first baby wanted to move so much while crying with me, I thought she didn't want to be in my arms and I'd put her down. It was all very confusing at the time, heartbreaking when I think about it all now. I would put her down, wanting her to be happier because she would be 'free' from my arms, but I wouldn't be able to make sense of why she wouldn't smile, and instead she would either have a frozen face or start whining or start fussing again. I didn't understand why I couldn't make her happy when she was in my arms, or when she wasn't!

Bodywork was the scaffold I needed to connect with my baby. Now that I have my third baby and am more comfortable in holding her the way she wants to be held, it feels much better. She used to arch her back a lot (which is a sign of body tension) but because I let her arch and unarch, twist and untwist her body, I find now she doesn't arch her back anymore. Babies have incredible healing capacity. So I love that you say that crying lets them unwind their bodies.

My third baby did a lot of physically turning around in my arms while crying. I attribute it to the fact that I had a lot of tension in my body during my pregnancy with her, and could barely ever feel her turn in my womb, she was almost always stuck in one position. I imagine that while she was crying and turning around, she was releasing all the physical and emotional tension of being stuck."

The confusion that Feyza felt is common when parents don't know about healing-feelings. If their baby is crying in their arms, they often think that the baby is communicating that they don't like being held, rather than that the parent's warm presence is helping them express their healing-feelings.

Movement is a central part of healing-crying. Babies' bodies know exactly how to heal from the physical experiences they had *in utero* and during birth. When we understand this, we can support their big emotional and physiological releases in nuanced and subtle ways, like a partner dance.

I have often been with a mother who is talking about the birth experience and the baby starts crying at a particularly relevant part of the retelling, or moves into a position similar to that during that part of the birth story. Babies are so wise!

Feyza continues, this time sharing her experience of helping her daughter heal from birth trauma at six months old:

"I started listening to my second daughter's tears when she was almost five months old. When she was six months old, we were at a friend's house on a day when I felt particularly relaxed (the power of community!) and my baby woke up from her nap. As I took her into my arms, she immediately started crying very intensely. Her tears started flowing, so even though I was visiting a friend, I knew this was a time I needed to dedicate to her.

Then, something magical happened. I noticed she positioned her body in the exact way she was stuck during labour, so I followed her cues and decided to support her body in the way she preferred. Her head was turned sideways and her body was shifted to the right. She started making straining sounds, similar to ones we make while pushing our babies out. Interestingly, she was born by Caesarean. Due to the sounds she was making, I understood then that she had put just as much effort to be born vaginally as I had during our labour experience six months before. This went on for more than an hour, where she continued to cry with non-stop tears. Afterwards, she pushed her feet against my abdomen, as if to be born out, then brought herself to my arms, and her crying ceased. I knew at that moment that she had re-enacted her birth experience and released her birth trauma.

I had a habit of caressing her elbow because she had eczema there, and I noticed immediately after her crying ended that her eczema was gone. I view this as a profound spiritual experience and feel very grateful for the healing she experienced in my loving arms."

We can think of the tears that a baby is expressing as like frozen ice that has melted into water. Our warmth and love helps the freeze response melt into tears which then flow away like a mountain stream returning to the sea.

In contrast, if we keep distracting our baby from their feelings, those feelings might be like an underground river that is constantly bubbling to the surface. Throughout the day, the emotions might be coming up as whining, agitation, incessant vocalisations or an apparent need to feed for hours on end – often called 'cluster feeding' in other paradigms.

Emily experienced this agitation of the underground river of unexpressed healing-feelings with her five month old:

"My son was getting more and more agitated, to the point that he was making this kind of moaning and burbling sound all day long. His Dad and I were starting to go a bit crazy. We were doing all the things we thought we could to make him happy, and he just clearly wasn't, so we were starting to get frustrated and resentful too. Then, we found out about Aware Parenting, and started listening to his feelings. The more feelings we listened to, the less of the moaning and burbling there was. It really helped our sanity return! We realised we hadn't been doing everything that we could after all!"

> *Self-Compassion Moment*
>
> How do you feel, reading this? I'm sending you lots of love to any and all feelings you might be feeling.
>
> I'm here to let you know that whatever you did with your baby in the past, all babies and children will keep on inviting us to support them in their healing, and at any time, when we are ready and willing, we can say yes to that invitation.

How do we differentiate between the two types of feelings?

This is the million-dollar question and the one that is often the hardest for parents, particularly in terms of distinguishing between when a baby is hungry and when they are trying to express healing-feelings. That's so natural, isn't it – given that most of us have not had an embodied experience of being at the receiving end of this kind of presence and listening ourselves. The majority of us have never even witnessed other parents making this kind of differentiation.

We can differentiate between the two by observing:

- When they are upset / crying;
- How they are crying or expressing the upset;
- What happens after we've responded to them.

When they are crying

Babies cry when they are tired. As I share in the chapter on sleep, this isn't because tiredness is painful. Rather, this crying when tired is a natural part of their innate relaxation and healing response, so that a baby can feel more deeply relaxed and sleep more restfully. If your baby tends to cry when they are tired, this indicates that those feelings are likely to be healing-feelings.

If a younger baby isn't crying and they are happily playing on the ground and we pick them up and offer them our loving presence and they start crying, it's likely that our loving presence is helping them experience being safe to feel and express their emotions. Some parents can think that their baby doesn't want to be with them because the little one starts crying when they pick them up and hold them in their arms, but nothing could be further than the truth. The closeness and presence is helping them express healing-feelings.

If they are not yet mobile and are crying in your arms and when you put them down, they stop crying, that's also likely to be healing-feelings.

If they start crying when you gaze into their eyes, that's likely to be healing-feelings, because they are feeling the emotional safety of your loving presence.

If you have a busy day with your baby, and they start crying, that's likely to be healing-crying, as they express their feelings from their day.

If they tend to cry in the evenings, that is likely to be healing-feelings, because the combination of tiredness plus another day of stimulation leads to the healing-feelings being released.

If they seem to need to feed all evening, this is likely to indicate that they are trying to cry to heal so that they feel relaxed and can sleep more restfully.

How they are crying

Some parents find that they can discern between different sounds of crying, and that through clear observation, they can tell when a cry indicates hunger, discomfort, or healing-feelings.

If a baby is happy and alert and being held and suddenly starts crying, this can indicate that they are tapping into healing-feelings. Of course, we make this conclusion after checking that there isn't anything painful happening to them.

Some parents also find they can read their baby's cues before they get to the point of crying – and, if our response is to rock, jiggle, or offer a dummy, those actions are suppressing feelings rather than meeting needs because being moved and sucking aren't inherent needs.

What happens *after* we've responded to them

If we are jiggling and rocking them and we stop the movement and they start crying, that's likely to be healing-crying, because movement is not a need that leads to crying. Our calm and still loving presence is likely to be helping them connect with their body and healing-feelings.

If we take a dummy away from them and we are holding them and they start crying, that's likely to be healing-feelings, because having a dummy isn't a need in Aware Parenting.

If we're feeding them and they're coming on and off the breast or bottle (and they don't have a tongue tie) or they suck intermittently, or they fall asleep soon after starting feeding, or they're agitated and crying while feeding, it's likely that they weren't hungry but have feelings to express. I talk more about this in Chapter Six.

Let's explore this 'what we observe after we've responded to them' part in more detail, because this is a clear way that we can know that we have understood which type of feeling it was.

How do we know that we've accurately understood which type of feeling it was?

If we have truly attended to the source of the feelings, whether it be needs-feelings or healing-feelings, we will generally see a baby relaxed in their body, able to make eye contact, and spaciously engaged with us and their world.

To be able to see this clear difference, we will often need to practice observing a baby and making sense of what we see.

We've been taught to think that a baby has their needs met when they stop crying, but may not notice if the baby has become still, or that their eyes have glazed over, or that they aren't really connected, don't interact and aren't very alert. These signs can indicate that rather than feeling calm and present, they are actually mildly dissociated.

As I've been sharing, not seeing this has led to the belief that there is only one type of feeling – needs-feelings – because dissociation can look like calmness if we don't know to look for these signs.

Nathalie, a peri-natal coach and lactation consultant, shared her experience of seeing the difference in her baby son when she started to listen to his feelings in her loving arms, and how that increased her confidence to be with his healing-feelings for longer periods:

"I discovered Aware Parenting through a synchronicity when my son was four months old. I had done something that had quite clearly led him to feel angry, and as I picked him up, I put him to the breast with the aim of calming him down. As he sucked quite actively with what seemed like a residue of anger, I remember turning to my husband and telling him that I didn't like how I had responded to this situation. I decided that in the future I'd prefer to listen to him express his anger to me rather than try and stop it at all costs.

A few days later, I was listening to a parenting podcast that I enjoy, and Spotify suggested The Aware Parenting Podcast. *Within a few episodes, I had a true felt sense that Aware Parenting provided the tools to feel more comfortable with listening to feelings, not at all presented as a lifeless list of tasks, but rather a nuanced and delicate approach.*

What I appreciated, first and foremost, was the empathy and compassion that radiated out from the philosophy for where parents are on their journey with feelings. I had thought for a long time that I would aim to listen to my child's feelings, but I realised in that moment that it wasn't always as simple as saying it. It took feeling it too.

Little by little, my husband and I started to observe our son differently and we started to notice when he appeared more tense, and deciphered needs from feelings. [needs-feelings from healing-feelings.]

This process didn't happen overnight at all; it was a very gradual process and we appreciated through what we learned about Aware Parenting that it never suggested to rush through or challenge our own intuition. In fact, it always suggested that we remain connected to it.

At first I felt comfortable listening to my son cry in my arms without 'doing' anything (rocking, walking, patting, shushing) for only a few minutes, and as I began to see the beneficial effects on him, it became easier to trust that we were indeed helping him while we listened to his feelings. He would fall into restful sleep, gaze into our eyes more and seem genuinely more comfortable in himself throughout the day.

My son is now two years old and I think that the fact that we listened to many of his tears has contributed to the fact that he is overall very calm, connected, and cooperative, all while feeling comfortable to assert his will as well!

People regularly comment on how calm he is, and I often respond saying that he also has big emotional releases with us (often around bedtime), because I so truly believe that the two are connected. In our case, our son rarely has big releases in public so it could be misleading from the outside to only ever see the enjoyable effects of Aware Parenting without hearing about the expression of feelings.

Just last night, after a few days of a family reunion with many people around and way more stimulation than he's used to, I suspected he might have some accumulated tension from this. While I was getting him into his pyjamas a bit later than usual, he instantly began to cry so strongly, so much so that I connected it with feelings because he is usually able to tell me in a more collected way if he wants things done in a specific way, in which case I try to give him as much autonomy as I can depending on the circumstances.

I decided to continue to get him into his pyjamas using gentle hands, all while telling him that I was listening to him (it seemed that in this situation, this action was the 'balance of attention' that Marion talks about which was allowing him to release his feelings). I told him that I was not willing to force him, but he was so tired, that as his mommy I thought it was best if I got his pyjamas on so he could quickly rest his body.

I was right next to him and he cried deeply for about 20 minutes, and at the end, he started to laugh about something and then he curled up in my arms and we gazed into each other's eyes so deeply. It was such a profound moment of connection.

His releases don't always end with quite a moment, although they almost always end with a softening of his body and a big hug together.

I feel so grateful to be able to experience these moments of connection with him and to be able to truly feel at peace with listening to my son's feelings. I now see them as a good thing!

I'd like to specify that I don't always have the energy to listen to feelings, that depending on the day, I obviously have my own things going on internally, and one of the things I appreciate about Aware Parenting is that it recognises that reality in parents, and it deeply trusts that we will make space when we are able to listen to feelings. I also have a Listening Partner[12] with whom I speak weekly, and this helps me to express my own feelings, so I can better listen to my son's. I am now pregnant with our second child and I look forward to using these tools with him or her."

---

12 This is a term from Hand in Hand Parenting that is used by some people in the Aware Parenting community, but isn't used by Aletha Solter.

Possible longer-term effects of understanding needs-feelings and healing-feelings

When we respond to a baby's needs promptly and fairly accurately, it is likely that they will internalise those responses.

That means if our baby tells us that they want to be close, and we meet that need for closeness, then they are likely to learn that:

a. Their need for closeness is valuable;
b. If they signal that they want closeness, they will get that need met;
c. Their need for closeness is heard and understood;
d. Expressing their needs leads to them getting their needs met;
e. Their needs are welcomed.

You can imagine how that might affect the rest of their life.

They are likely to stay connected with their need for closeness, and will value it. They will be confident that it's an important need and that they will get that need met.

Imagine how that will be for them when they are a child, a teenager, an adult, in a relationship, and a parent!

And that's just one need!

Responding relatively accurately to our baby's needs:

- For closeness;
- For nourishment;
- To be heard;
- For protection;
- To be physically comfortable;
- To play;
- To learn;

- To explore the world;
- To be valued;
- To express uncomfortable feelings;
- and so on,

all influence how they respond to those needs in themselves.

And the key is "relatively accurately!"

This isn't about trying to be perfect, nor about being accurate all the time!

This is about us doing what we can to respond to our baby's needs and feelings accurately *most* of the time. They learn from what generally happens!

So, if we *generally* respond accurately to when they need closeness, when they are hungry, when they are uncomfortable, when they need to express healing-feelings to us, and so on, then they internalise those responses.

They are likely to then know when they need closeness, when they are hungry, when they are uncomfortable, when they need to express uncomfortable feelings to us, and so on!

They are likely to know the difference between:

- Hunger and tiredness;
- Upset feelings and hunger;
- Upset feelings and boredom.

They will be connected with their own needs and will value their own needs.

They will also thus understand, recognise and value the needs of others – which will affect their relationship with us, with their friends when they get older, and with their partner and own children when they become an adult.

In addition, our words are likely to become their inner voice. For example, we might say to them things like, "Are you hungry sweetheart? Mummy will feed you now." Or, "Are you feeling overwhelmed here? Would you like me to put you in the carrier so that things are are bit quieter?"

How do you want your baby to respond to their feelings? Giving them empathy for their feelings, and listening to their feelings, including their healing-feelings, will mean that they have words for their feelings and will be comfortable to feel and express their uncomfortable feelings.

I hear so often from parents of very young children who have been parented in this way that their little one also responds to the needs and feelings of others in these same ways, staying things like, "I'm here and I'm listening," to their own friends. We have so much power in affecting our child's relationship with their needs and feelings and the needs and feelings of others.

Summary

There are two key questions to ask ourselves in relation to crying:

- If they are 'fussing' or crying, how can we know whether they are needs-feelings or healing-feelings?
- If they have stopped crying, how can we be sure they that we have responded accurately and not just suppressed their feelings?
- If a baby squirms, fusses or cries, we can ask ourselves which of the two types of feelings they are expressing:
  - *Are they communicating a need? (I call these needs-feelings)*
  - *Are they healing from stress and trauma? (I call these healing-feelings)*

1. Needs-feelings – feelings caused by here and now needs.

Our role here is to meet the needs, and then the feelings dissipate because they have done what they were designed to do – alert us to the unmet needs.

If we have truly met a need, our baby is likely to feel more relaxed in their body, and to make eye contact. If our actions have helped them dissociate instead, they are likely to still feel tense in their body, and either avoid eye contact or have a glazed look in their eyes or expressions on their face that communicate confusion, fear or frustration.

2. Healing-feelings – feelings caused by stress and trauma.

Our role here is to listen to their feelings in our loving arms so that the feelings can be released. Their vigorous movement (not ours!) is a part of the releasing of tension from their bodies.

If we listen to a whole chunk of feelings, the baby's crying will come to a natural end. We're likely to notice the release and relief in them through their muscles being more relaxed. If they aren't sleepy, they will probably gaze into our eyes, and if they are tired, they will probably fall into a relaxed sleep without us doing things to 'make' them go to sleep (such as jiggling, rocking or feeding).

If we have listened to some of their feelings but not a whole chunk (which can happen when the crying finishes because they were distracted in some way, including by us) they will feel more relaxed than they did before but will still have some more feelings sitting at the surface to tell us. They may clearly have more relaxed muscles and may make more eye contact, but they may try again later to express the remaining feelings to us.

When we think that babies only have one type of feelings (needs-feelings), we will try to meet their needs at times when they actually need us to listen to their feelings. They may stop crying, but this isn't because we've met their needs. It's because we've suppressed their feelings. When we suppress their feelings, we can usually tell, because they may look dissociated, have a glazed look, and feel tense. If we've truly met their needs, they will make eye contact and be relaxed in their body.

> *Relaxed presence*: relaxed muscles, eye contact, alert relaxed presence.
>
> *Dissociation*: tense muscles, staring eyes or avoiding eye contact.

When we keep distracting our babies away from their healing-feelings, those feelings accumulate in their bodies and lead to increasing agitation, which means they might have a more agitated voice, might push away from contact, find it hard to concentrate and find it harder to go to sleep and sleep as long as they need. They might move into hyperarousal or dissociation when they are in a situation that reminds them of a past situation where they were in fight, flight or freeze and didn't get to express those feelings and return to homeostasis. For example, a baby who was lying down to have a medical procedure and who dissociated at that time might then dissociate when they are lying down having their nappy changed.

The more we observe our baby with this information in mind, the more we will be able to distinguish between when they are truly relaxed and when they are dissociated and we will be even more able to respond in the most attuned way.

Babies have real feelings.
They feel while in the womb.
They feel while they're being born.
They feel after they're born.

They try to tell us about their experiences in utero and during and after their birth.

They do that through trying to cry in our loving arms when all of their needs are met.
Babies who have experienced more trauma will have more feelings to tell us.

These are real feelings.
This is the way that they heal from their experiences in utero and during birth.
This is how they heal from the overwhelm of being a newborn.

All babies have feelings to tell us, however much we meet their needs.
We might miss those feelings, thinking that they have other needs.
We might jiggle them and rock them or give them a dummy or pacifier.
They might keep trying to cry more, especially in the evening.

Those feelings might start waking them up, as they try to tell us about how they feel.
They might start getting more agitated.
They might start feeding more and more.
They might start sleeping for shorter and shorter periods.

However, it is never too late to listen to those feelings.
If your child is two or four or six, they will still try to share those feelings and heal.

They might keep wanting to play tunnels, if their birth was long.
They might cry a lot whenever there is a very small separation, if they were separated after birth.
They might rage and tantrum whenever they feel powerless, if they felt powerless during or after birth.

Babies and children are so wise.
They have real feelings and they know how to heal.
They need us to understand, be present with them, and listen with our ears and open heart.

CHAPTER THREE

Why don't all babies cry? Understanding dissociation and suppression

If *all* babies experience stress, why do *some* babies never or rarely cry?

The lack of crying in some babies often leads to the interpretation that babies only experience one type of uncomfortable feelings (needs-feelings), and that babies who don't cry are communicating that all of their needs are met.

Alternatively, some parents who do know that there are two types of uncomfortable feelings have a baby who never cries. They may then interpret this to mean (as I did for the first three months of my daughter's life), that some babies don't experience any stress or trauma and thus they don't have any healing-feelings to express (and that their baby is one of them.)

Let's look at these two scenarios from an Aware Parenting perspective.

What is happening when a baby rarely or never cries?

From an Aware Parenting perspective, all babies experience at least some stress or trauma, however much we aim to meet all of their needs and protect them from overstimulation and other stresses, and they will try to cry to heal from those healing-feelings.

If we think that a baby is expressing a needs-feeling when they are actually expressing a healing-feeling, and we rock or jiggle or move or sing to them or feed them or give them a dummy, and the baby stops 'fussing' or crying, we might interpret that the need has been met rather than understanding that the baby is dissociating from the feelings.

This confusion can get in the way of us seeing that a baby has some feelings to express to us so they can be heard and heal. We confuse a calm state caused by needs being met with a state of mild dissociation. Rather than having all their needs met, the baby is mildly dissociating from their feelings.

Self-Compassion Moment

Again, I invite you to drop any guilt sticks here. None of us learnt this growing up in The Disconnected Domination Culture, so we are all on a learning journey. And whatever we have done with our baby in the past, it is never too late to be able to see their feelings more clearly and to listen to more of their healing-feelings.

Jacinta shared how she used to think that all cries and uncomfortable feelings were expressing needs, before she came across Aware Parenting:

"My daughter started to wake up a lot at night and then it was harder for her to get to sleep in the daytime too. We just thought it was because she really loved being with us and didn't want to miss out on anything, especially since we have two older children. We just told everyone that she was a really curious baby, so we would walk around showing her things. But over time, this became exhausting as she seemed to want more and more stimulation. If we sat down with her she would start to cry and we thought it meant she was telling us she was bored, so we were on the go almost all the time. We thought it was just her telling us what she wanted and we encouraged ourselves by saying that we were meeting her needs.

Over time, we started feeling more and more frustrated and resentful. She seemed to be so demanding, always wanting us to be on the move. We were doing everything we could to keep her happy, but increasingly she just wasn't content at all. When I learnt about Aware Parenting, I had a huge aha moment! It was a big shift to see that all of that time, we had been interpreting her cries inaccurately. I must admit that I had lots of feelings at first, realising that I hadn't understood her. I also felt really guilty. It took quite a lot, from learning about guilt from Marion, to realise that I could stop feeling guilty and just have my sadness heard at the same time as starting to listen to our daughter's feelings. I just wish that I'd known about the two types of uncomfortable feelings right at the start."

Is your baby telling you that they don't like something?

It is very common for parents to think that their baby doesn't like something, only to discover that their baby was trying to express some healing-feelings. I remember thinking this myself at times when my daughter was a baby. Specifically, about putting on her socks – when in fact, putting socks on her was helping her revisit her experience of a traumatic heel-prick test, as I shared earlier.

>Here are some of the common things that parents say. I wonder if you recognise any of them?

- "My baby doesn't like to be held." – When in fact, being held helps them feel safe to express their feelings.
- "My baby doesn't like me to look at her." – When the eye contact is helping the baby feel the emotional safety, connection and presence to express her feelings.
- "My baby doesn't like me to sit/stand still when I'm holding him." – When the stillness is helping him connect with the sensations of unexpressed healing-feelings.
- "My baby only likes to be held in one position." – When the other positions are offering the connection and presence required for the baby to feel their feelings.
- "My baby doesn't like being carried in a sling." – When the sling is helping the baby revisit their time *in utero* or during birth, and they are trying to express those feelings and heal.
- "My baby doesn't like being in the car-seat." – When the carseat is reminding the baby of their experience *in utero* or during birth, and they are expressing those healing-feelings.

Of course, it is vitally important to be sure that we are reading a baby's cues accurately.

How we can tell the difference between when a baby is expressing needs-feelings or healing-feelings

Here are a few suggestions:

Observing her before and after we take whatever action we take to seemingly meet the need. For example, if you are holding your baby and she starts to cry, and you change position so that she stops crying, how is she then? Does she seem relaxed in her body, does she make eye contact, are her arms relaxed, does she melt in to your body?

Or, does she seem tense, avoid eye contact, have tense fists or seem not really connected?

The latter are the signs that there are healing-feelings bubbling under the surface and that the change in position was distracting her from her feelings rather than meeting her needs.

It's observation that can tell us what is really going on.

If we act to fix the apparent need, but soon afterwards she is upset again, this time in a different scenario, then it is possible that she actually has feelings to express rather than a need that is unmet.

If she has been agitated for hours or all day, then, barring her being sick or physically uncomfortable, then it is likely that she might have some feelings to express.

So this process is always about observation.
But it also invites reflection.

If this situation is reminding her of something from the past that she hasn't expressed fully, what might it be?

For example:

- If she had a long second stage experience during birth, and every time you put her in the car seat or the carrier, she cries, then it is likely that those situations are helping her connect with those feelings and sensations she experienced during her birth.
- If she was born with forceps or ventouse, and she cries every time you put something over her head, then it is likely that she is crying to heal from the original experience.
- If she had a traumatic heel prick test experience and cries every time you put socks on her, then it is likely that she is healing from that.
- If she had surgical procedures where she was lying down, and she cries every time you lie her down for a nappy change, it is likely that she is trying to heal from the trauma of that.

If you can clearly see the link between the present experience and a past experience, that might help give you more clarity about what is going on now.

> *I invite you to think about the times that your baby cries or seems unhappy.*

When do you think they are communicating an immediate need? And what are those needs?

When do you think they are indicating a need to heal? And do you have any ideas about what they might be healing from? (Remember, you don't need to know the answer to this in order for the crying to be healing! While understanding the reason can help us feel more relaxed while they are crying, we can trust that babies know how to heal even when we don't know what they are healing from.)

And of course, observing your baby afterwards can also help confirm whether or not your hypothesis was accurate.

For example, perhaps you think that putting her in the carrier is helping her release feelings related to her birth, and for a few times you keep her in there and listen to her feelings. While she's crying, you might say to her the kinds of things you might have wanted to say to her during her birth. If after that she shows that she is more relaxed, more connected, more at peace, and more aware, that helps confirm your hypothesis. You may also find that after that, you can put her in the carrier and she no longer cries, and is present and happy, because she has released that chunk of feelings.

Another way to be able to 'test' this is by doing more supported crying at other times. The more she gets to release pent-up feelings, the less feelings she will have left to release, and she will increasingly heal from stressful or traumatic experiences, and so what originally helped her connect with those feelings will no longer do that because the feelings have been released.

Common ways of distracting babies from their healing-feelings

There are many ways we can distract a baby from feelings caused by stress or trauma. Here are the most common ones:

Movement

If a baby is upset and we think that they need movement, and we rock or jiggle the baby and the baby stops crying, we could easily interpret this as 'the baby needed movement and now the need is met, they feel calm'.

However, from an Aware Parenting perspective, although babies enjoy gentle movement, this enjoyment is not a need and is not strong enough to cause crying if they are being held and the parent is sitting or standing still.

Instead, when a baby is being rocked or jiggled, they are becoming mildly dissociated. The same is the case if they are being driven in the car or moved in the pram or the baby carrier. You might have felt this state yourself, if you've been in the back seat of a car on a warm day, and you drifted off into a different state of consciousness or even fell asleep. This movement is distracting a baby from their feelings rather than meeting a need. They become relaxed by bypassing feelings and tension in their body.

You might see that while you are rocking or jiggling them, their eyes show that they are somewhat dissociated. You might also notice that there is still tension in their body as they drift off to sleep or when they are asleep – for example, they might be clenching their fists or the muscles around their eyes or mouth. The expression in the eyes and muscle tension are two of the key ways we can distinguish between whether a baby's needs have been met or whether they are dissociating. You might also notice that they tend to wake up when you stop the movement, showing that they weren't deeply relaxed.

> In contrast, when we are still and present while we hold our baby in our arms, they feel that presence, and will either be happy to simply engage with us, or our loving presence will support them to connect with the sensations in their bodies and express any healing-feelings that they have to tell us.

I remember being new to Aware Parenting, and taking turns with the father of my daughter to sit on a big ball and bounce our two-month-old baby to go to sleep, not realising that rather than helping her 'calm down', this was actually preventing her from expressing her healing-feelings. When her dad and I shifted from bouncing her to being deeply still and present in our bodies and offering our loving presence, we saw what a huge difference it made to her to express her healing-feelings with us, and how very different the quality of relaxation was in her body compared to when we used to bounce her!

Rocking and jiggling provide a temporary calm, but when babies get to express their healing-feelings in our loving arms when all their needs are met, they are healing from stress or trauma, releasing tension, and when completed, they can come out the other side of that expression with a much deeper level of relaxation in their bodies which can affect their feeding, general behaviour and sleep. In that experience, we are trusting that with our loving presence, they know how to heal and they know how to feel deeply relaxed.

> In The Disconnected Domination Culture, we are not taught to trust babies. Quite the opposite! Aware Parenting holds an incredibly deep trust in babies and their innate wisdom and invites us on a big journey of getting free from all the ways we've been conditioned to believe otherwise.

Sarah shares her very painful story of experiencing the effects of this kind of conditioning all around her, when her baby cried a lot and she did all she could to stop him from crying using lots of movement:

"I'm quite a perfectionist and control freak, so when pregnant, I prepared like crazy for the perfect birthing experience. I was so focused on this that I forgot about the journey that began once our baby boy was born. We had an amazing, magical home birth.

About a week later, our boy started to cry, and didn't stop for about three months. We tried almost everything, I tried a cow's milk free diet, we went to several doctors, who prescribed medication for his stomach (which I'm not very fond of), we went to a baby psychiatrist, foot reflexologist, lactation consultants, a chiropractor and an osteopath.

He was even hospitalised for an in-depth medical examination. During that hospitalisation they convinced us to take some rest and go home without him, so we could sleep. I still regret that decision. Our boy started throwing up that night, and even had an examination without our presence, and we didn't hear about it until the next morning. I decided not to leave him there alone because my mother-heart broke when I saw how little time the nurses had for those tiny patients and how long they had to cry before help (food, changing, or even help in life threatening situations) would arrive.

Because of the sleep deprivation, exhaustion, and mainly the powerlessness, my husband and I crashed physically and mentally. I was afraid it would get to a point where I would hurt my baby, because I just wanted the crying to stop. I felt guilty for putting him on this earth suffering and not being able to help. My doctor then arranged a psychiatric hospitalisation for me. Luckily I could bring my baby with me. I was only there for one week. It was horrific. The way they treated the babies and mothers there... everything in my body shouted to get out of there (we weren't supposed to be sleeping together, my milk was insufficient for him, breastfeeding was too hard in combination with therapy, the food was (unhealthy) hospital food, I couldn't be with my husband when I needed to be, and babies were 'sleep trained' the old fashioned way).

The baby psychiatrist we had visited sent us to an occupational therapist. Our first appointment was right in the midst of my first week in the psychiatric institution. Although it was far from appreciated, I decided to go. It was a life saver.

We told her all about the attempts to calm our little one, from the rocking firmly up and down, the constant walking or jumping around, the bouncing on a fitness ball, or the driving over cobblestones. She listened patiently and then she suggested to let him cry in our loving arms and to listen to him. He just wanted to tell us what he had experienced so far and how difficult it was for him to adjust to this new world. He was easily overwhelmed, because he was a very alert baby and he wanted to see it all, but he needed to release the tension that this built up.

It made so much sense to us, and we tried the method for the first time that evening. He cried for almost an hour straight but we decided to stay calm and peaceful with him.

When he calmed down, he seemed much more relaxed and he dozed off soon afterwards. The next day our lovely maternity assistant was amazed when she saw us: she had never seen him so relaxed and content.

We had a long conversation with her, and it made us realise that we wanted to take things into our own hands. I wanted to choose the path for me as a mother and not follow others' advice blindly. I found a therapist specialising in mothers and educated in Aware Parenting. She revealed this amazing way of helping children. I started to educate myself in everything on Aware Parenting. I'm now even working on a project to help others finding their way and especially connecting with other parents, because this path can feel quite lonely if you choose another way than the majority in society. I'm exceptionally grateful for this incredible journey my son has taken me on.

Aware Parenting has both changed his life and mine, since I began to understand where my struggles are coming from and began to work with them. I have tried so many therapists before, but none of it seemed to actually work in the long run. Just by immersing myself in Aware Parenting, I noticed a huge shift in my accepting of emotions, thinking and therefore also in my actions. The way I was before, I would have never been able to be so calm around a crying baby. It led to more understanding of how it works scientifically, but also it just felt like coming home for some reason. It's like I found myself again after being lost for more than two decades. And the beauty of it is, that I can also start to understand that whatever happened to me as a child, isn't anybody's fault, it's just partly the result of how other people were raised, detached from their feelings. It brings peace to my mind, I'm much less judgemental and less insecure about being a mom. For our boy, we noticed the change, as I described, after those first three months. He stopped crying all the time and instead became a more content baby. Aware Parenting is here to stay for our family. It works wonders. Literally."

> *Self-Compassion Moment*
>
> If you had an experience similar to Sarah's and couldn't stop your baby from crying, I'm sending you so much love and compassion. I invite you to receive lots of support to share about how hard and painful that was (or is) for you.

If we don't learn about healing-feelings and always rock or jiggle our baby when they have healing-feelings to express, they *can* become toddlers and small children who need to move when they have healing-feelings to express, which can mean they move around a lot and can find it hard to sit still or to feel a deep sense of calm and relaxation in their bodies. We might see this when a toddler moves from one thing to the next, rarely able to sit still, with lots of tension in their muscles. This can be uncomfortable for them, and frustrating and overwhelming for parents. Understanding what is going on and supporting them to release those healing-feelings can bring great relief for both parents and children.

Through a baby's eyes

"Pressure builds and builds. There's been so much. Fuller and fuller. I don't want this. I don't like this. Please listen. Stop! Oh, it's stopped. All this tension still. Tension rises. Ahh, you're here. Warm arms, relief. Listen? Hmmm, what's this. Move, move, move, move ... tension kind of goes but the knot is still there, still waiting. Move, move. Falling to sleep. Knot is still there."

A baby's words

"I know that you want to help me. I see the love in your eyes as you pick me up and hold me. I'm trying to tell you how I feel. I'm trying to release that knot. But instead of the presence and listening and understanding I'm longing for, you start to rock and jiggle me. Faster and faster. I kind of like it, and I can feel some relief, but it's like the surface is relieved but deep inside, I feel this tension still. I long to tell you my feelings. Don't you want to hear? Please listen. Oh the rocking, the rocking, I'm falling asleep. The knot is still there but I'm falling asleep. Maybe you will listen to my feelings when I wake up. I know that you love me and are trying to help me when you jiggle and rock me, but I would love it if you would be still for a while, hold me in your loving arms and your warm presence, look into my eyes and really see what is going on for me. I have real feelings to tell you. When you stop moving, and are present with me, I can feel those feelings and can express them to you. After I let out my feelings in your loving arms, I feel deeply calm and relaxed, which is very different from the kind of calm I feel when you rock or jiggle me."

Sucking

If our baby is crying and we think that they need to suck, we may give them a dummy or pacifier. If the baby then stops crying, we might then interpret that as an indication that they had a need for sucking and that has been met and the baby is now feeling calm.

However, as I shared in the last chapter, we don't see sucking as a need in Aware Parenting. From an Aware Parenting perspective, we see that sucking can often create a mild form of dissociation. This is why babies may also suck their thumb or fingers – to dissociate.

In Aware Parenting, these mild forms of dissociation are called *'control patterns'* because they become common patterns or habitual ways babies repeatedly use to suppress (or mildly dissociate from) their feelings.

We might observe the dissociation when a baby is sucking on a dummy or pacifier – they might have a glazed or staring look on their face, and their body might be very still.

> *Self-Compassion Moment*
>
> I want to remind you to be deeply compassionate with yourself here. If you have done these things, you were doing it because you thought your baby had a need and that you were meeting that need. You were doing it for the most loving of reasons.
>
> And if this Aware Parenting information resonates with you and you would like to listen to the feelings that the dummy was suppressing, it's never too late to start doing that, whatever age your baby is now, or even if they are a child or adult. We all have these innate healing processes available to us, whatever age we are.

Through a baby's eyes

"Tension building more and more. So much. New sights. New sounds. All so new. Beginning to understand things. Noticing rhythms. Understanding when you come and what helps you move to me. Storm building inside me. Tension more and more. Longing to let it all out. So much sensation. You come. Some new sensation comes. Sucking, sucking. Drifting off. Body there but drifting off. Where is this? Where?"

A baby's words

"Day after day, these feelings build in me. I feel more uncomfortable. I long to tell you about my birth and how this is, being out in the world. So much is new to me. I am learning every day. I am so completely dependent on you. I want to do things and I cannot do what I want to do. I need you. Will you listen? Oh, you come. You're here. Joy builds. Thank you! I love you! Will you listen now? Here, I will tell you how I felt when I was being born. I long for you to listen. Oh hang on! What is happening now? What is this in my mouth? It's new and unfamiliar.

Oh, I start sucking. The sucking is a reflex, I don't get to choose it. Oh, I feel different. I'm drifting away. I don't feel that pain any more. Perhaps I don't need to tell you about it after all. Drifting, drifting. Not quite here now. Kind of numb. Kind of pleasant. But I miss you and I miss me. Do my feelings matter? I don't know."

Distraction

If a baby is upset and we think that they are feeling uncomfortable, we might change their position, putting them over our shoulder, or sing them a song or show them things. And again, I want to emphasise that of course Aware Parenting is all about meeting a baby's needs as much as possible, and sometimes a baby might feel physically uncomfortable or may need to burp and moving their position might help.

But Aware Parenting also understands that it can be very easy to distract most babies from their healing-feelings, unless they have experienced severe trauma or they have lots of accumulated feelings that are bubbling up insistently to be heard.

You may remember the stories from the two mothers who couldn't stop their babies from crying. One of those babies had been in an incubator for 10 days. The more trauma a baby has experienced, the more likely they will either keep on trying to cry to heal, or will strongly dissociate.

Let's return to babies who *can* easily be distracted from their healing-feelings. Remember that babies need our loving and relaxed presence to experience the safety and empathy required to express their feelings to us and to heal from stress and trauma. If we keep moving them about, singing to them, or showing them books and toys, that distracts them away from their feelings and can communicate to them that we aren't available to listen.

So again, our role here is to be an emotional detective, to observe our baby to see whether they do have a need, or whether they actually have healing-feelings to tell us.

Feeding[13]

This is sometimes a contentious and controversial topic. So, before I continue, I'd like to say that Aware Parenting, as a form of attachment-style parenting, is passionately supportive of breastfeeding. In fact, I've found that mothers who practice Aware Parenting and breastfeed tend to enjoy the experience even more and often continue breastfeeding for even longer than they may have done without Aware Parenting.

When babies get to regularly express their healing-feelings, they are often even more calm, relaxed and present when feeding and both mother and baby feel that deep connection, compared to a baby or toddler who is desperate to get to the breast to suppress feelings, who moves around a lot when feeding or is mildly dissociated when feeding. Mothers who experience the latter may not feel such a sense of connection with their baby when they are feeding, or may feel exhausted, frustrated or resentful.

Ella-May had an experience like that:

"At my mothers' group, two of the other mothers and I were at our wits' end. Our 18 month old babies were all waking up more and more each night, sometimes even every hour. We were all exhausted. We all decided to give up breastfeeding together because we couldn't go on doing that any more. It was just too much.

---

13 Please note that bottlefeeding can also be a way we as parents can distract a baby from their feelings.

On that weekend, I went to have an in-person session with Marion. In the consultation, she explained about what was going on and why my son was waking up so much. I'd been into Aware Parenting before that, but perhaps a bit half-heartedly. Now, I was really ready to embrace it, because I really didn't want to give up feeding my son but I was desperate to get more sleep! After the session, I went home and instead of breastfeeding him frequently during the evening like usual, I listened to his feelings. He had a really big cry and rage that went on for more than an hour. It was super intense for me and I found it so hard to stay present with all that intensity. But that night, he only woke up three times, so I knew it was helping already.

I listened to more feelings the next day, feeling reassured that this really was helpful for him, and that night he only woke up twice. I kept on going with listening to his big feelings each day, seeing that there really was the light at the end of the tunnel! Hurrah! By the time I went to the next mothers' group, he was only waking up once, and I would feed him back to sleep. That was really manageable for me! I was like a new woman, getting all that lovely sleep!

My mama friends had gone ahead with giving up breastfeeding. I went on to continue feeding him until he was three. I enjoyed it much more after that pivotal weekend. Before fully embracing Aware Parenting, he'd always been so agitated when he was having boobie, hitting me, hitting my boob, twisting around, like I was a human dummy. Sometimes, I hate to admit, I felt quite frustrated and resentful. But when I started to wholeheartedly listen to his feelings, feeding was really different. He was much more present and connected. I could really feel that he was in his body. I enjoyed it, rather than dreading it as I had begun to before. I'm so incredibly grateful for Aware Parenting.

Oh, and one more thing – he had also been hitting other babies at the mothers' group. After that weekend, he hardly ever did that – usually only when I hadn't listened to his feelings for a while. It really made a momentous difference to how he felt, and that affected our whole family and even our mama friendship group too! Thank you so much, Aletha and Marion!"

If a baby is upset and we think they are hungry, then of course we will feed them, either with breastfeeding, bottlefeeding, or food. If the baby stops crying or 'fussing', we might then interpret that we accurately read the cues and that the baby was hungry and isn't now. Or we might think that the baby's feelings have been 'soothed' so that they now no longer feel upset. I'm going to talk more about the idea of 'soothing' later!

From an Aware Parenting perspective, we see things differently. If a baby isn't hungry and we feed them, the sucking during breast or bottlefeeding both create a form of mild dissociation which is biologically useful because it helps a baby be calmer and so less likely to vomit the milk back up again (breast milk also contains amazing calming hormones). And eating of any kind can distract us away from our feelings, whatever age we are (as many of us know in adulthood). The sensations and tastes of eating take us away from the uncomfortable feelings, but those uncomfortable feelings remain hidden away in our bodies.

Feeding a baby is of course a wonderful, necessary, vital thing, and of course it's so important to always feed a baby when they are communicating that they are hungry.

However, if we generally feed our baby when they are trying to express their healing-feelings, this can have longer term effects.

> *Self-Compassion Moment*
>
> Remember, this isn't about judgement. Just as I invite you to not judge yourself, I am not judging you and I am not willing for anyone else to judge you if or when you distract your baby from their feelings.
>
> I'm offering this information because I want people to know about

this way of understanding babies and then to make compassionate choices from that information, not to judge themselves or others.

Disentangling information from judgement can be a big process, particularly in The Disconnected Domination Culture, where we are taught to judge ourselves and others after receiving new information that we didn't have before.

Remember the Aware Parenting spectrum? You might choose to feed your baby to distract them from their feelings most of the time, or multiple times a day, or never, and listen to their feelings once a month, once a week, once a day or every time they have feelings to express. There is no 'right' or 'wrong' here. My invitation to you is to read this information, see if it resonates, observe your baby, and make choices based on what you want to do and are able to do, given your own unique family and personal situation.

In Aware Parenting, there is no judgement if a parent chooses to feed a baby when they actually have healing-feelings to express.

Instead, what each of us is invited to do as parents is to understand the difference between when a baby has immediate needs, such as hunger, and when they have healing-feelings, and then to make our own decisions about how many feelings we can listen to. This will be affected by lots of factors, including how much stress we have in our own lives, how much we are able to be with our own feelings, how much trauma we experienced as babies and children, and how much physical and emotional support we have.

When I first started Aware Parenting with my daughter as a newborn, I'd already read The Aware Baby *and so deeply resonated with everything about Aware Parenting. However, there was so much for me to learn, and there was lots that I couldn't yet see. Despite understanding that babies can heal from stress and trauma through crying in loving arms, I thought that because I could always stop my daughter from crying – through jiggling her on the bouncing ball in our arms, or feeding her for hours every evening, and feeding her as soon as she woke up from every nap and very frequently throughout the day – that that meant she didn't have feelings to express. In talking to other parents who came to Aware Parenting, they share similar stories of the early days; frequent feeding, bouncing and distracting, and believing that meant they were meeting their baby's every need, only to discover through other evidence later on that something quite different was going on.*

I also thought that because she'd had such a calm birth, and because I was carrying her everywhere, co-sleeping, and focusing pretty much entirely on her and her needs, that she wouldn't have any uncomfortable feelings to express. It was only when she was three months old and I started to see some subtle signs of accumulated feelings – she wasn't quite as calm as she had been, she was often regurgitating milk, she was starting to make a bit less eye contact, she was a bit less relaxed in her body – that I realised that she did indeed have healing-feelings to express and that they were accumulating in her body.

I later realised that all babies (in industrialised cultures) have some feelings to tell us every day for about their first year, through crying in loving arms, however much we meet their attachment needs and respond promptly to them.

At three months, her dad and I started to listen to her feelings – generally every evening – and we saw what a huge difference that made – her presence and calmness shone through the room, she was deeply relaxed in her body, she went back to making lots of relaxed eye contact, and she slept more peacefully and for longer periods.

Then, I thought we were definitely listening to all of her feelings.

It was only when she was about 18 months old that I realised that yet again, I hadn't really understood her fully and hadn't been reading her cues as clearly as I had thought, and that many times I was still distracting her from her healing-feelings by feeding her. One of the symptoms of that was that she found it harder and harder to cry with me, while still being able to freely express her feelings to her dad. I saw other signs too, such as her finding it hard to go to sleep in the daytime, despite being relaxed enough to sleep through the night.

Distracting babies more and more of the time

With all of these actions – such as movement, distraction and feeding – if you notice that they seem to be needing them more and more, this is often a key sign that their unexpressed feelings are accumulating.

The more pent-up feelings they have, the more we need to do to suppress those feelings. The more the unexpressed feelings accumulate, we may find that we need to feed them for longer and longer, jiggle or rock them for longer, offer a dummy more, etc. They might be moving from one thing to another, or constantly 'need' entertaining, or are sucking on the dummy for longer and longer.

Are you jiggling and rocking your baby for hours?

Many parents come to Aware Parenting when they are jiggling their baby for hours, walking them up and down the corridor for ages, or taking them in the car for every sleep, and either it becomes unsustainable and they want to find a way that is, or they sense that something else is going on and that their baby is asking for a different response from them.

Are you giving your baby a dummy or pacifier more and more?

If you do give your baby a dummy or pacifier, what do you observe before, during and after? Do they ever spit it out? Do you see an expression on their face when they are sucking on it – perhaps their forehead is scrunched up, their eyes are staring, and their muscles are tense. Are they seeming to need it for longer and longer periods, or for more and more situations?

Does your baby seem to want to feed more and more often?

It's common for babies to seem to want to be fed more and more frequently, despite the fact that their stomachs are gradually getting bigger and can hold more milk. More and more frequent feeding with increasing age is often an indication that a baby's feelings are accumulating. This can particularly be the case during the night. Over the years, I have worked with many parents who had toddlers who were waking up every 45 minutes or hourly to feed. When we understand Aware Parenting, we can see what is often going on here. We'll talk more about it in the chapter on sleep.

Is your baby sucking their thumb or fingers more?

Many of the *control patterns* we have talked about so far are ones that we directly give to babies – movement, a dummy/pacifier, distracting them. However, babies will also find their own ways of distracting themselves from or dissociating from their feelings when they are in an environment that doesn't understand or doesn't have the emotional presence to listen to their feelings caused by stress or trauma, or when we are listening to some of their healing-feelings but at times feel stressed or overwhelmed, or are at times unwittingly distracting them from those feelings. One of the key ways is through sucking their thumb or fingers.

Please note that even if you are listening to a percentage of your baby's healing-feelings, they will still need to suppress whatever percentage you're not able to listen to. This is why babies of parents practicing Aware Parenting can still often end up sucking their thumbs.

Remember we talked about how sucking is a potent way to create dissociation? If your baby is sucking their thumb or fingers more and more as time goes on, and particularly in new or unfamiliar situations or when they're tired, this can be another sign that their feelings and stress levels are accumulating, which means they are needing to do more to disconnect from those feelings.

What do I mean by accumulated feelings? Remember the fight/flight/freeze response? The feelings a baby feels have real physiological correlates. So, when we do things that help them suppress or dissociate, those feelings don't go away – we are simply taking their attention away from those feelings. Over time, the emotions accumulate in their bodies, instead of flowing as they are designed to.

That means more:

- tension in their muscles from the fight/flight response;
- agitated movement;
- attempts to express feelings (such as with whining or screeching);
- dissociation or suppression of feelings.

Important note about physical discomfort and trusting yourself

Please always trust yourself here. If you think that your baby is physically uncomfortable and has an unmet need, keep listening in and do what you might usually do to meet that need. Babies can have physical conditions and somatic discomforts that they communicate to us through movement and crying.

Aware Parenting is all about deeply trusting our gut instinct and observing our babies.

If you have a sense that your baby is feeling physically uncomfortable, please check that out before assuming they have feelings to express to you.

They may have a food intolerance or allergy or gut microbiome issue. They might be teething or getting sick. They might be in physical pain after being in a certain position during birth, or from a ventouse or forceps birth. They might be reacting to polyester clothing or bedding, to the ingredients in clothes washing liquid or powder, to the food you're eating if you're breastfeeding or the food they're eating if they are eating food. They might be being affected by mould, Electro Magnetic Radiation, dirty electricity, or blue light. When we listen to a baby's feelings, it's vitally important that we are feeling confident that they are not expressing a need, which includes a need for feeling physically comfortable.

The more comfortable we become with listening to our baby's feelings when they have healing-feelings, the more clearly we will be able to tell when they are communicating a physical discomfort, because of our familiarity with the sound of a stress-release cry. This is another benefit of listening to their healing-feelings.

Differentiating true relaxation from dissociation

The deep relaxation and presence that babies feel when their needs have been met or their feelings have been heard is very different from how they feel if they are suppressing feelings or dissociating from them.

Quiet doesn't necessarily mean relaxed.

I'm sure you've experienced that yourself. Perhaps you've felt really upset, and really needed to cry, but instead you reached for your phone to scroll Instagram or went to the fridge to reach for some food. During the scrolling or eating, you might not feel upset any more, but do you feel deeply relaxed? Perhaps you notice later on that your shoulders are up near your ears and your thighs are tense. Maybe you get a headache. Or perhaps you're in an interaction with someone and you really want to express your feelings, but you don't feel safe, so you don't say anything. People might assume you are calm, but inside, you're either doing everything you can to suppress your feelings, or you're wildly dissociating and simply feeling numb.

When a baby is expressing a needs-feeling and we then meet that need, we can see this through observing them. They will be willing to make eye contact, they will be happy, they will be willing to connect. They'll melt into our hugs in a relaxed rather than tense way.

If a baby is expressing needs-feelings and we don't meet that need, there are ways to clearly observe the effects of that too.

For example, if a baby is in a cot and is crying, calling out for us to come and we don't come, over time, they might stop calling out. Babies will give up on asking for what they need if that need is repeatedly not met. In that case, we might see that baby sucking their thumb, or clutching on to a soft toy or blanket. They might seem calm, but on closer observation, if we go to them, we will be able to see that they are not truly calm. They might be avoiding eye contact, or have a glazed look in their eyes, or are staring into space. They might be frantically sucking on their thumb or fingers. They might be tightly clutching on to a toy or blanket. Their muscles are likely to be tense. If we do pick them up, they might continue with these behaviours, or they might suddenly start crying.

This is what is often happening with controlled crying or cry-it-out. Babies have simply learnt to suppress or dissociate from their feelings. They are still waking up, being woken by unexpressed feelings, but they have learnt that their cries will not bring anyone, so they suck their thumb or clutch their dummy or pacifier or tense their muscles and move back into suppression or dissociation enough to go back to sleep again.

Self-Compassion Moment

If you have done this with your baby, please put down any guilt sticks you might be tempted to pick up. I also want to remind you that it is never too late to help babies heal from these experiences.

If a baby is expressing healing-feelings and we listen lovingly to those feelings in our arms[14] when we're confident that all their needs are met, we will see a deep level of relaxation once they complete that process.

In fact, we can often feel their muscles becoming more and more relaxed during the crying-in-arms as they literally release the tension from their bodies that was mobilised to fight or flee.

So many parents who have started Aware Parenting with their babies have told me how surprised they were about how relaxed their babies are after crying in their loving arms – they didn't realise it was possible.

If babies have expressed a whole chunk of feelings, they often come out the other side of a crying session and bring a beautiful quality of presence into the whole room.

They often gaze into our eyes. They have a deep quality of relaxation in their bodies which is very different from dissociation. They may often sleep afterwards with their arms above their heads, can be deeply relaxed during sleep, and tend to not move around much in their sleep.

---

14 This is for non-mobile babies. Once they are crawling, they may choose to not be in our arms when crying to heal.

Through a baby's eyes

"Storm building, feelings building, I'm here, you're here with me. Hand holding hand, safety is here. Held. Loved. Feelings build and build. Ahhh, feeling, feeling, all coming out. Tension inside leaves. Feeling. Loud. Expressing. Ahhh ... relief. Your eyes. Your arms. Your touch. Feelings gone. Relief, clearness. I see now. Breathe. Calm. Relief."

A baby's words:

"Oh you're with me, and you're listening. These feelings have been building inside me for so long. They build and build. I cry, I move. The feelings get bigger and bigger. I feel their intensity, and I feel so safe in your arms. I see you with me. I hear your words. I feel your touch. These feelings are safe for me to feel when you're with me. They get really big and loud, and I feel big satisfaction as I feel them and express them to you. You're listening to me. You're with me. The feelings are coming out so fully and freely and I feel so satisfied. I am being me. I am expressing these feelings that I've been trying to tell you about for so long. And you're listening, really listening. You're not trying to keep me quiet. Thank you for being with me. Ahh, as the feelings subside I feel such a sense of relief in my body. I let out a breath, a shudder, a sigh. I feel so deeply relieved. Now I can gaze into your eyes. I see you seeing me. I see you present with me. My heart sings. We are love, together. We are here together. You are here with me! You welcome me and my feelings! You love me unconditionally! I am safe, and I am loved. I am relaxed. I feel all melty and open and happy."

However, if we often interpret our baby's desire to heal through expressing feelings as indicating an unmet need, and we repeatedly rock them or give them a dummy or feed them, they may stop trying to express their feelings and instead will seem to want whatever it was that we gave them when they were upset.

When we interpret a baby's healing-feelings as being needs-feelings and subsequently rock or jiggle them, give them a dummy/pacifier, or feed them when they are not hungry (in an attempt to meet what we think are their needs-feelings), we help the baby to mildly dissociate from those unexpressed healing-feelings. After this, we may think that our method has been effective as we see our baby in what appears to be a relaxed state – however the quality of calm will actually be far more superficial than the level of relaxation talked about above. It isn't as deep as the state they're in after they feel, express, and release a whole chunk of feelings in our loving arms. Their muscles might be tense, they might have their hands in fists, they might avoid eye contact, they might take a long time to go to sleep and wake up frequently at night to try to express the feelings and they might move around a lot in their sleep.

The concepts of 'soothing' and 'self-soothing' don't exist in Aware Parenting

Concepts of 'soothing' and 'self-soothing' are talked about so often in other parenting paradigms, but don't exist in Aware Parenting. I want to remind you that dissociation feels kind of pleasant. It's designed to be like that. There's nothing wrong with it, and our bodies were designed to be able to do it.

> *Self-Compassion Moment*
> I invite you to drop any emotional sticks if you see your baby suppressing feelings or dissociating from them.

Although we're not judging suppression and dissociation, in Aware Parenting we are seeing these behaviours very differently from the idea of 'soothing' and 'self-soothing'. In other paradigms, there is generally a belief that there are no longer-term implications to repeatedly 'soothing' a baby or encouraging them to 'self-soothe'.

However, from an Aware Parenting lens, we perceive that these actions do affect babies over the longer term.

When we are jiggling or rocking or feeding our baby when they are trying to express their healing-feelings, we are distracting them from their feelings, and although dissociation feels mildly pleasant, those feelings don't go away.

Those feelings accumulate and lead to a baby feeling more agitated, which affects how they sleep and how present they are, and has longer term effects which can include how they respond to their own feelings, how they interpret their sensations, what they believe about their feelings and how willing they are to express their feelings to us.

With 'self-soothing,' the difference to 'soothing' is that the baby is finding a *control pattern* that doesn't relate to our physical presence, so they can mildly dissociate from both needs-feelings and healing-feelings without us being there with them.

Again, the dissociation might feel mildly pleasant, but it is likely to also have longer term effects such as an accumulation of feelings, not getting to heal from stress and trauma, feeling more agitated at night and thus waking up more, and may also affect their beliefs about their needs and feelings, their relationship with us and their willingness to express their feelings to us.

Differentiating between mouthing, teething and a *control pattern* of thumb-sucking

Let's look more at thumb-sucking, and how we can differentiate this *control pattern* (mild form of dissociation) from mouthing and teething. There are several reasons for babies to put their hands in their mouths, and I will mention a few here.

One is when babies do a lot of 'mouthing' – because they learn about the world through their senses and putting things in their mouths helps them understand the world more.

Another reason can be if a baby is teething. Putting things in their mouth and feeling the pressure of biting can help relieve the sensations of pressure that the movement of the teeth are creating.

This is very different from thumb-sucking and finger sucking when babies are suppressing their feelings. Sucking itself creates a kind of dissociation, as I've written about earlier in the book, and which is what we are going to be focusing on.

How do we differentiate between mouthing, teething, and thumb-sucking to suppress feelings? There are a few key ways: the look in their eyes, the quality of the action and when a baby is doing it:

- *The baby's eyes.* If they are mouthing, they will probably look quite alert. If they are dissociating, their eyes may have a staring or glazed look.
- The *quality* of the action. Mouthing has an interested quality, because they are actively taking in information from the mouthing. There will also be a variety of mouthing and moving actions. Teething often has more of a biting quality, because they are trying to create counter-pressure to the teething pressure. Dissociation generally has a repetitive and urgent quality to it.
- *When* a baby is doing it. Babies' feelings tend to bubble up when they are tired, which is part of their body's innate wisdom, so they can express their feelings in our loving arms and feel deeply relaxed, thus enhancing their restful sleep. So, if a baby tends to suck their thumb or fingers when they are tired, it's often a sign that they have feelings bubbling which they are suppressing. When a baby is tired, that's not likely to be a time when they are actively exploring the world, such as with mouthing. We can also tell if they do this at other times where they are likely to be feeling uncomfortable feelings – such as in overwhelming situations where there are lots of people, or when having new experiences.

Through a baby's eyes

Mouthing: *"What is this? Picking up things happens now and moving to mouth. Tasting, ahh, soft, smooth. What's this? Oh, different taste, rougher. The world becomes more known."*

Teething: *"Tension up here. Ouch. Ahh, biting happens. Relief comes. Ahhhh ..."*

Dissociation: *"Feelings building, pressure rising. Anyone here to listen? Anyone understand? Anyone? This is too much alone. Where is that? Ahh, here it is. Ahhh ... softness, sucking, some relief. Frantic, frantic, makes the storm stop, but also drifting away happens. Where is here?"*

A baby's words

Mouthing: *"I'm learning all about the world and putting things in my mouth gives me so much information. I can pick things up now, and I love that I have more power in the world. I pick up this thing and put it in my mouth. I feel everything about it – the temperature, the texture, the taste. I'm learning so much. I feel so interested. I love learning about my world and my place in it."*

Teething: *"There's pressure and tension in my mouth. I don't know what it is or what's happening, but I know when I put this toy in my mouth and bite and chew, there's relief. Ahh, sweet relief."*

Dissociation: *"Feelings are building in me. I long to tell you about my experiences. I haven't told you about what my birth was like for me yet, and then there was that time they took me away from you. I long to tell you. Each day is so new and I want you to understand me. I also want to let these feelings out, because each day I feel more and more tense, and it's starting to affect me in other ways. Do you see that? Do you see me? Please see me. Please understand me. Please listen to me. I'm trying to tell you now. I'm feeling it. I'm feeling it all. Oh, what is this? You are putting my hand in my mouth. It's not what I'm used to. It's new. I find myself sucking automatically, because that's just what* *happens. I move away from the feelings. I move away from you. I move away from my body. I'm drifting, drifting. Where am I? Where have the feelings gone? So much sucking, my mouth and tongue sometimes hurts a bit. But now I need to suck. I need to. The feelings are there but not there. Am I here? Where am I?"*

What difference does it make anyway, listening to their feelings?

If our bodies are designed to dissociate from feelings, and if dissociation feels kind of pleasant, what does it matter anyway if we do these things to suppress our babies' feelings or if they are doing those things to themselves?

Let's return to the reason for healing-feelings. Remember how babies want to be understood, and want to be heard, and how they innately know how to heal from stress and trauma?

If we are unable to listen to those feelings over a long period, a few things can happen for babies:

1. They **might** experience not being heard and understood.

These feelings can turn into beliefs that can affect them in later life – that others don't understand them and don't listen to them.

I certainly acquired beliefs like that, and despite many years of healing, they still show up at times. When I first started writing this book in October 2022, a theme of being heard was re-emerging for the next level of healing. I recorded several podcasts, only to find afterwards that my voice could not be heard. When I did Facebook lives, suddenly there was so much noise around me that people were not able to hear me. I bought new microphones and other equipment, and still it kept happening. I saw this as an invitation to feel and express some more of the frustration, deep sadness, powerlessness, and resignation I felt as a baby when I was left alone to cry.

> *Self-Compassion Moment*
>
> I wonder if you recognise any of these beliefs? Perhaps you might have the following thoughts at times: "My anger isn't welcome," "My feelings are too much for people," "I'm too sensitive," "I need to be alone when I'm upset," or, "No-one will listen to me."

Our children's beliefs about their feelings being heard begin in infancy – and it's never too late to start listening to their feelings and supporting them to change their beliefs about being heard, whatever their age.

2. They will have less opportunity to heal from stress and trauma.

In addition to not being heard as much as they need, when we don't listen to healing-feelings they don't get to use their natural healing processes; they don't get to heal from stress and trauma that they've experienced, including that which they experienced during birth and immediately after birth. Although we can heal from stress and trauma that we experienced during and after birth when we are children or even adults, the process is often a lot harder and more complex, because of all the additional feelings, experiences and beliefs that get overlaid and woven in. Birth trauma can have profound effects on our later life, including on what happens when we take action or start new experiences, on our relationships, how safe we feel, and on the amount of fear or terror we experience in our bodies, including if and when we go on to give birth.

> *Self-Compassion Moment*
>
> Are you seeing ways that you haven't healed from your own early experiences in the womb, during your birth, and as a baby? Are you willing to be deeply compassionate with those younger parts of you?

3. They *might* start to believe that it's not safe for them to feel or express their feelings.

When they miss out on the feeling of relief that comes after crying-in-arms, they don't have an embodied experience of feeling their healing-feelings, releasing a whole chunk of these feelings and moving out the other side, feeling relaxed. They might grow up being scared of feeling their feelings, believing that they will be stuck in them forever or that they won't ever come out the other side of them.

> *Self-Compassion Moment*
>
> Do you ever get scared when you're feeling big feelings that you will stay stuck in them forever, or do you worry that they are too big for you? Do you ever worry that your baby might get stuck in feeling really big feelings?

4. They *might* feel agitated and uncomfortable.

The unexpressed feelings accumulate over time and lead to a sense of agitation which is uncomfortable for babies. That agitation also affects many of a baby's behaviours, including sleeping, feeding, learning, playing and concentration.

This agitation often leads to lots of moving around, wriggling and squirming, agitated vocalisations, squealing and high-pitched screaming, back arching and crying when in high chairs and car seats, taking a long time to go to sleep, waking up after one or more sleep cycles, moving around a lot when asleep and not being able to concentrate for very long.

Do you observe any of these in your baby?

5. They learn to interpret and respond to their feelings the way we interpreted and responded to them.

So, they literally perceive the sensations in their bodies differently. This means that in general, they might turn to suppression and dissociation rather than feeling and expressing their feelings as they get older and as those forms of suppression and dissociation morph. Thumb-sucking *can* become nail biting. Eating to suppress feelings *can* continue into childhood and adulthood. Babies who were rocked and jiggled when they were upset *can* become toddlers who move around a lot when upset and who aren't able to sit still.

When I was observing babies as a doctoral student and then post-doctoral Research Fellow, I was amazed to learn how much newborn infants see and understand, and how much they are learning from their experiences. From birth onwards, they are taking in detailed information about each person who interacts with them. They sense the nuances of how we respond to their needs and feelings, and they make both adjustments and conclusions based on what they see.

If we generally misinterpret their healing-feelings as indicating that they are hungry and we feed them, they *might* also learn to interpret the uncomfortable sensation as hunger and will come to then ask to be fed or for food whenever they are upset. Once they have learnt this from us, it becomes harder to differentiate between the two types of feelings, but it is still possible, as we will discuss later in the book. After learning this from us, it will also seem as if they really are hungry whenever they ask to be fed or ask for food, when at times they actually have healing-feelings to express, because that is how they have learnt to interpret those sensations. This is why so many people find it hard to tell when their baby is hungry, and to differentiate hunger from healing-feelings. This is also why many parents believe that babies only have needs-feelings.

If we generally interpret their healing-feelings as indicating that they need movement and we move them, they *may* also learn to interpret that sensation as indicating a need to move and will then start moving whenever they have unexpressed healing-feelings. This can often turn into toddlers who need to move whenever they have unexpressed healing-feelings. In some cases, this might lead to a diagnosis of a disorder, rather than seeing that a child has simply learnt to respond to their feelings the way their feelings were responded to. This interpretation is also why so many adults get really busy when they are upset, or who do exercise, or work really hard. These are all powerful ways we have learnt or found to disconnect from the sensations and feelings in our bodies.

If we generally interpret their feelings as indicating that they need to suck, and we give them a dummy or pacifier, then they will learn to interpret the sensations from healing-feelings to indicate that they need the dummy, and will ask for it. As they get older, this can morph into chewing on clothes, nail biting, tension in the mouth, and so on.

Babies learn quickly from us, and babies also need to do something with whatever percentage of feelings that they're not getting to express, which is why these habitual ways of suppressing or dissociating from feelings, or *control patterns*, are often in place at a very young age, even if we are listening to some of their healing-feelings.

Self-Compassion Moment

Again, I invite you to put down any guilt sticks that you might be tempted to pick up.

I want to emphasise, as I aim to do all the way through this book, that I am not judging anyone here. I'm not judging you and I'm not willing for anyone to be judged for how they respond to their feelings or their baby or child's feelings. Judgement doesn't help in any way.

It's never too late to help babies interpret their sensations accurately, and it's never too late to listen to their feelings.

How do these interpretations happen in the first place? *Control patterns* are often passed down in families.

I wonder if you see that in your family?

For some families, the major *control pattern* might be eating. Most of the family members might have eating as a *control pattern*. That means that when you were a baby, your parent/s probably interpreted your healing-feelings as indicating hunger, just as their healing-feelings were interpreted, and so they would feed you, leading to you having the same interpretation. Perhaps you cried a lot as a baby and they fed you solid food really early, believing that you were very hungry. Perhaps that's one of the stories they tell about you often. That's why Aware Parenting is a big process. We are often attending to intergenerational patterns when we aim to observe and understand our baby and to respond in apt ways to their cues.

Self-Compassion Moment

I invite you to reflect on this if you feel the emotional presence to do so.

What are your parents' *control patterns*?

What are your *control patterns*?

How do you tend to interpret what's going on for your baby if they are agitated or upset?

Do you see any linkages between the three?

How we perceive and respond to our own feelings can influence how we perceive and respond to our baby's feelings.

Do you see any other links?

I'd like to offer some possibilities, and there are many more than these!

If your baby has a dummy or pacifier, do you tend to stop yourself from expressing your feelings to others? Or do you tend to tense up around your mouth or bite your lips when you've got feelings bubbling?

If your baby seems to be hungry all the time, do you tend to eat to suppress your feelings?

If your baby moves around a lot when they're upset, do you tend to get busy or do exercise to suppress feelings?

If your baby wants to be entertained when they're upset, do you tend to entertain yourself with YouTube or a book or social media or online shopping to distract yourself from your feelings?

If your baby sucks their thumb or fingers when they're upset, do you tend to bite your nails or put your hands to your mouth before you've even noticed feelings coming up?

If your baby appears to want to be alone when they're upset, do you tend to want to be on your own when you cry?

So, although suppressing a baby's feelings isn't innately harmful, in the short and long term it can lead to lots of things that are unenjoyable for both them and us and which can have far-reaching implications.

Natalie shares her experience of seeing the effects of accumulated feelings in her first baby, before Aware Parenting, and how she learnt to discern the difference between needs-feelings and healing-feelings in her second baby:

"Practicing Aware Parenting with my second baby from birth has been one of the most challenging yet richest experiences I've had

as a mother. With my first baby, I was unknowingly suppressing his feelings most of the time. Then, when he was eight months old, he began waking up numerous times throughout the night from what I now understand was accumulated feelings. It wasn't until he was 16 months old that my partner and I started practicing Aware Parenting with him and after a few months he finally started sleeping through the night again.

By this stage we had our newborn and I began practicing crying-in-arms. The first few weeks were overwhelming for me, as I made space for him to cry whenever he needed to, which would sometimes be up to six hours a day. I had my own big feelings of outrage and sadness come up around not being listened to in this way when I was a baby, child and adolescent. As I acknowledged and processed this pain, I had more capacity to keep listening to my baby's feelings.

After the first few months of practicing crying-in-arms my baby began to suck his fist a lot less and he started smiling and giggling more each day. I would often mistake his cries as hunger. As I became more reassured that he could go longer between feeds, I began to see that when I was able to let him complete his crying he would then become more relaxed and give clear signals of hunger. Going through this process has taught me to truly tune into my baby and be immensely present with him. What I didn't expect is how it has also taught me to tune into myself and my own feelings and give them the presence they deserve to then be released.

Other things I've noticed with bub is that when he has some accumulated feelings, he will turn his head away and not make eye contact. When I notice this and hold space for him, he has a release of feelings and stares into my eyes during and afterwards. He also starts to smile and laugh with each crying-in-arms release at night – this is new and so adorable. And there is a lot less throw up! His feeds are much more relaxed after a release and because he's calmer when he's eating he's not gulping down too much milk".

> *Self-Compassion Moment*
>
> I invite you to be compassionate with yourself as you take in this information.
>
> Because of our Disconnected Domination Culture conditioning, we might be tempted to pick up guilt sticks if we haven't listened to any or some of our baby's healing-feelings, or if our baby has a dummy, sucks their thumb, or suppresses or dissociates from their feelings in other ways.
>
> Instead of picking up those guilt and self-judgement sticks, I invite you to do something very different. When you read this information, I invite you to be unwilling to pick up those guilt and self-judgement sticks and choose to be deeply compassionate with yourself.
>
> If you notice guilt, you might use The Marion Method, and you could respond with, "I'm not willing to feel guilty. I'm not willing to judge myself. I am willing to be compassionate with myself. I'm celebrating my willingness to learn new things".

Probably none of us were ever held in the loving arms of our parents or grandparents or aunties or uncles, when we were crying to express healing-feelings, with them feeling totally relaxed in their bodies, knowing that we were sharing feelings and healing from our birth experience or daily stresses. So of course we might:

- Not want to believe that babies have feelings to express (because that also means that as babies, we had feelings to express) or;
- Pick up guilt sticks when we see signs of our baby repressing feelings or dissociating, such as through thumb-sucking, a dummy/pacifier, wanting to feed very frequently even as they get older, or waking up lots at night. We grew up in a culture where we were taught to judge ourselves rather than be compassionate with ourselves.

Instead of judging ourselves, we can learn to put down those self-judgement sticks and offer ourselves the same kind of compassion we are offering to our baby.

We can aim to understand what is really going on with our baby without judging ourselves when we are not able to listen to their feelings or when we see them suppressing their feelings. Understanding what's really going on for them and when they are dissociating can make a big difference, even if we're not able to listen to those feelings at that time.

Understanding our baby and responding with empathy, "I see that you're upset and I'm not able to be fully present with your feelings at the moment," is very different from thinking that a baby just needs to be jiggled, rocked, fed or given a dummy and that 'soothing' is a helpful thing with no longer term consequences.

This is also very different from understanding what is going on for them and judging or guilting ourselves.

I LOVE the combination of compassionately understanding a baby AND ourselves! I wonder if you might too?

CHAPTER FOUR

Deepening your understanding through observation and reflection

If what you have read resonates with you so far, would you like to observe and understand your baby's behaviour and feelings even more than you do now? If so, I invite you to have a journal to record your observations. Or perhaps you'd like to do this on your phone, either on an app or in your calendar.

Being a researcher

I made notes in a journal when my children were babies and I found it incredibly helpful. I wrote down when they fed, when they did a wee or a poo, when they slept, when they cried and for how long they cried, and the particular sounds in their crying, what I noticed about their feelings throughout the day and anything that might have been particularly overwhelming for them that we had done that day.

In this way, I started to see patterns. For example, I'd see that when we had busier days, they had more healing-feelings to express. I would see that when we listened to fewer feelings, they were restless in their sleep or woke up more often. I'd notice that the more feelings we listened to, the calmer they were when feeding.

Observing, making notes, and noticing patterns is all part of the process of you being a researcher. When you weave together the theory, your own intuition and the observations you are making, and make sense of them all, this is where deep wisdom emerges. This is where you are embodying Aware Parenting and making it your own. It's where your own practice develops through what you experience and understand. This is an incredibly powerful process that supports deep trust in yourself and in your baby, as well as profound clarity about what is going on for them and what you can do in any moment to respond in the most helpful way.

As yet, there is no published research on practicing Aware Parenting with a baby, but you can research this yourself. Doing that, you can be your own parenting authority. You can receive reassurance that what you are doing is helpful. You can access clear information about your baby and about anything that you need to tweak or change. You don't need to wait twenty years to see the effects of parenting this way on your baby. They will show you the foundation of their psyche and the effects of responding to them in these ways.

If what you have read so far resonates with you and you'd like to start listening to their healing-feelings, you might want to compare the differences you observe in them when you respond in your usual way compared to when you listen to those feelings.

What do you notice about:
- The amount of eye contact they make?
- The length of their attention span?
- The expression in and around their eyes?
- Whether their eyes indicate dissociation or presence?
- Whether their facial expression indicates agitation or relaxed alertness?
- How relaxed or tense their muscles are?
- Whether their arms are relaxed or are in fists?
- How much they melt into your body in a hug or tense up or push away?
- How relaxed they are when they're feeding?
- How alert they are when they're feeding?
- How much they move around when feeding?
- How they are after feeding?
- How much they need to burp?
- Their digestion?
- How interested they are in 'solid foods' (once you've introduced them)?
- How agitated or calm their vocalisations are?
- How long it takes them to go to sleep?
- How long they sleep for?
- How much they move around in their sleep?
- Whether they have their hands above their heads when asleep?
- How often they wake up happy vs. crying?
- How present they are?
- How alert they are?
- How agitated they are?

- How long they can concentrate for?
- How they are in the high chair (if you use one)?
- How they are in the car seat (if you have a car)?
- Anything else?

Here's some other information that I think you might find useful:

I believe that all babies have healing-feelings to express to us every day for about the first year.

The amount and intensity of crying each baby needs to do depends on a couple of things:

- **how highly sensitive they are; and**
- **how much stress and trauma they've experienced in the past and are experiencing on a daily basis.**

Babies will have more healing-feelings to express if they have experienced more stimulation that day – for example, if you've been out to a shopping centre or other busy place.

Some babies might only need to express a small amount of healing-feelings each day, such as 10 minutes. Others may need to express many hours of healing-feelings, particularly if they experienced trauma during birth or after birth, separation, or medical interventions. The more trauma there has been, the more healing-feelings they will have to express.

We don't need to listen to a whole chunk of healing-feelings for it to be helpful for our baby.

Even if we are only able to listen to five minutes to start with, they will still have the experience of being understood and heard and will have released some of the tension from their body.

However, if we stop them before they express a whole chunk of feelings, they might try to express the rest of those feelings soon after.

Even when babies don't understand what we are saying, practicing communicating clearly to them can be helpful for us. For example, if you're feeling overwhelmed yourself, you might say something like,"I see that you're upset, sweetheart. I'm putting these headphones on to help me with my feelings while I'm listening to you. I'm still here with you. You're welcome to keep crying if you need to".

When we first start listening, it might appear that our baby then has even more feelings to tell us.

That's a common experience and can be just like us as adults when we get to know someone who is comfortable with our feelings.

Have you ever experienced getting to know a friend, partner or therapist, and as you feel more and more emotional safety with them, you express more of your feelings to them?

As our babies feel our increasing comfortableness and presence to be with their healing-feelings, they will start to express a larger percentage of those feelings.

Babies can more easily express their healing-feelings when they're tired, so offering them listening in the evenings and before naps and sleep can help that process.

It will be hard for us to listen to our baby's feelings if we're feeling unsure whether all their needs are met. Checking through the list of needs in Chapter 1 (or making your own list) can help us be sure that they really do have healing-feelings to share with us. It's so important that you listen to yourself if you feel unsure and do whatever you can so that you have reassurance that these are not needs-feelings they're expressing, but healing-feelings.

When we first start listening to healing-feelings, it's also very common for us to have big feelings showing up, including fear and concern. This is why it is so essential to receive support from someone who has already been practicing Aware Parenting – whether that's a Listening Partner or an Aware Parenting instructor – so you can express your feelings and receive help to get clear about what you are observing in your baby. Many times, I have supported a parent while they listened to their baby crying in their arms and I listened to the parent's feelings.

This is why it is important that we are making sure that all of a baby's needs are met first, and that we are getting reassurance from observing their behaviour after crying in our arms that expressing their feelings really was helpful for them.

I remember many times in the early days of listening to our daughter's feelings when she was a baby that her dad and I were together with each other, supporting each other with empathy, a hug, or a hand on the other's back. (He is also an Aware Parenting instructor now.)

Without this Aware Parenting information, parents don't often make the connection between their baby's birth and early experiences, and sleeping, feeding and crying. A baby might be waking up often at night, and parents might not realise the correlation between the night-waking and their baby's birth experience, and the feelings they are waking up to try to express.

Parents might be rocking or jiggling their baby for hours in the evening, trying to get them to sleep, not realising that they are inadvertently encouraging their baby to dissociate from their feelings.

Babies might start feeding more and more frequently, even though their baby's stomach is getting bigger and can hold more milk, and their parents might not realise that their baby is trying to communicate their feelings from their birth, or even just from their day.

The more we understand Aware Parenting, the more we know what to observe and what to look for, and the more we start making our own connections, observing the effects of how we are responding to our baby. This gives us more clarity and confidence in what we are doing, because our baby is showing us the effects of how we are responding to them.

Lara shared about the differences she saw in her baby daughter after a week of practicing Aware Parenting:

"Here are some of the changes I have seen in her so far:

- *Much more calm and relaxed when breastfeeding (less pinching, scratching, putting hands in my mouth etc);*
- *Far more interactive when awake, will 'talk' with me across the room when playing;*
- *More responsive to her name being called (more eye contact);*
- *Stronger bond with her dad as he has been listening to her feelings too;*
- *More concentration when playing with a toy or when watching and interpreting a new situation.*

My husband keeps saying 'Wow! She's like a different baby!' But I like to think that this is just her true self shining through".

Stephanie, an Aware Parenting instructor in Australia, shares about her observations of her children as babies:

"I discovered Aware Parenting when I was 32 weeks pregnant with my first child. It immediately resonated with myself and my husband. We started practicing this approach from the moment our son was born. Going into parenthood with the knowledge that babies also cry for

emotional needs, meant we created a deeper attunement with our son.

He is highly sensitive. One thing we noticed from the very beginning was that he had more feelings than other babies (this was especially evident after the birth of our second son, when we reflected back), and would often cry for a few hours every day for many months after his birth. My husband and I would take turns (based on our own needs and willingness) to hold our son lovingly in our arms, listening to all the tears that flowed out, and all the feelings that were being released in those moments.

Some of the signs we could see in him that he had accumulated feelings and was crying for emotional release were: clenched fists, tense facial expression and muscles, or restlessness during sleep.

At any given time, once we had lovingly listened to all of his feelings, we observed remarkable differences in his body language and energy. His fists unclenched and were relaxed, he maintained calm eye contact, he was alert and content. Sometimes, he would smile and giggle, other times he would let out a big sigh, and slowly fall asleep in a relaxed and connected state. This was similar to our experience with our second son. Not being as highly sensitive, his crying was much less. With Aware Parenting, we entered our journey as parents with confidence that we were able to meet not just the physical needs, but also their emotional needs".

Noticing how we might be distracting babies from their feelings

There are many other ways we can subtly distract a baby from their feelings when we think they have needs-feelings and they actually have healing-feelings, i.e. they're crying to heal but we think they're crying to communicate:

- Changing position;
- Distracting through play;
- Distraction through feeding or food;
- Movement;
- Changing activity;
- Going out to where there is lots of activity going on;
- Going in the car;
- Being busy and distracted ourselves.

Did you recognise any of these for yourself and your baby when you were observing and listening?

Becoming more present

When we become more present, which can happen by meeting our needs more, we are more likely to be able to then offer our presence, rather than distracting our baby.

We might ask ourselves in the moment, "Am I willing to move into being deeply present with my baby right now? Am I willing to really deeply connect with them?"

And then, instead of distracting, simply becoming present, and really inviting that kind of connection. Depending on how your baby is feeling, that might lead to play and interaction, or it might lead to crying-in-arms.

How can we tell if a baby is relatively free from pent-up uncomfortable feelings?

Each baby is different, but in general, we might observe the following:

- They're happy to make relaxed eye contact with us;
- Their muscles are relaxed;
- They can concentrate on one thing for long periods;
- They melt into hugs and have a relaxed body;
- They have few *control patterns* or signs of dissociation;
- They frequently smile;
- They make contented vocalisations and sounds;
- They are relaxed when they're sleeping;
- They are aware and present.

Self-Compassion Moment

How are you feeling? What are you wanting to do, having read this chapter? I'm sending you lots of love and want to remind you to listen in to yourself and not to do things because you think you should, but only because they resonate and you have an embodied 'yes' to them!

CHAPTER FIVE

Starting to be with healing-feelings

The first time that we ever listen to our baby's healing-feelings can be a huge experience for a parent. If you've already been through that experience, I'm sending you lots of love. I'd love to share about the first time that my daughter's father and I stopped trying to distract her from her healing-feelings and listened lovingly to them instead.

The first time I was present with my daughter's healing-feelings

As I've already shared at the beginning of the book, I learnt about Aware Parenting when I was pregnant with my daughter back in 2001 and deeply resonated with it, since it corresponded with all that I had learnt in the previous 14 years immersed in developmental psychology and psychotherapy. From her birth onwards, her dad and I practiced the attachment-style parenting aspect of Aware Parenting, always keeping her close, co-sleeping and carrying her in a carrier. We aimed to be deeply present in the ways we held her and touched her, and we talked to her and explained what we were going to be doing, such as before changing her nappy.

However, we didn't start listening to any of our daughter's healing-feelings until she was three months old. Up until then she'd only cried for about a minute (one time when I was getting her changed and it took a moment for me to be able to breastfeed her).

There were two key reasons why we hadn't listened to her feelings.

The first was that I didn't understand that *all* babies have healing-feelings to tell us, however much we aim to meet their needs. I assumed that all of her needs were being met and she didn't have any healing-feelings to share. I didn't realise that all babies have healing-feelings to express most days and that they all feel uncomfortable feelings from daily stresses, however much we aim to meet their needs and protect them from overwhelming and frightening experiences. I assumed that because I was giving her abundant closeness, breastfeeding and being very present and attentive, that she wouldn't feel anything but happy feelings.

The second was related to my own experience as a baby and being in an incubator for the first five weeks of my life. Listening to her feelings when she was the same age I had been when in the incubator, alone and terrified, was too much for that little baby me, despite all the years of therapy and healing from that experience that I had already done.

However, I think there were other factors there too:

- I hadn't ever seen anyone else ever listen to a baby crying-in-arms and I didn't know how to see if a baby needed to express healing-feelings;
- I was wanting to compensate for what I didn't get – and to imagine that she only felt happy feelings;
- I really enjoyed the identity I had of being a mother who had (an apparently) really happy and calm baby;
- I couldn't tell the difference between when she was hungry and when she had healing-feelings to express (despite having read *The Aware Baby* – I clearly hadn't been quite ready to take in that piece of information!);

- I wasn't able to discern the difference between true relaxation and mild dissociation.

(Reading these last two might help you see why I am so keen include a lot of those in this book!)

The very first time we listened to her healing-feelings was one early evening when she was three months old.

I loved breastfeeding her and usually fed her many, many times during the afternoon and evening. One evening, after many hours like this, her dad and I realised that she did have healing-feelings to express and decided that we would listen to those feelings instead of me continuing to feed her all evening. I'd become aware that she did have healing-feelings to express, that the breastfeeding and bouncing her while we were sitting on a fit-ball had been suppressing her feelings. I had seen signs of accumulated feelings – as I've already shared earlier in this book, she was starting to make less eye contact and was getting more tense.

That very first time we listened to her healing-feelings, her dad and I sat in comfortable chairs next to each other, listening to her feelings. We took turns in holding her on our lap, with her back lying along our thighs and with our legs bent at the knees (you can see a diagram of this at the back of the book) so that she could feel the support of being held and we could offer her eye contact and hold one of her hands. She cried for about 40 minutes. We didn't jiggle or rock her, and we were very still and present, offering our loving words and gentle touch.

I remember that I felt concerned that she might be hungry, even though she had fed many times that evening, including only just recently before we started listening to her.

However, at the end of that period of crying with us, she came out the other side of expressing the feelings – and WOW! Her dad and I both had the experience of her being more deeply present than we

had ever seen her. She simply lay there gazing into my eyes. She exuded a quality of presence which filled the room. We jokingly said that she was like a Buddha! We'd never experienced anything like it. Her dad knew at once that this had deeply benefitted her, and we went on to listen to her feelings almost every evening from then onwards for the next 3 years.

For me, I still had some concern left after the first time that perhaps she had been hungry after all, even though after the cry she was present, aware, happy and calm and showed no signs of being hungry at all!

I knew one person who had practiced Aware Parenting with her baby, so I phoned her and she listened to my thoughts and feelings. After getting to express myself, and observing our daughter again the next evening after listening to her healing-feelings, and seeing again how much more relaxed and calm she was and how much more eye contact she made, I felt a deep sense of reassurance. I clearly saw that the crying-in-arms *was* helping her feel more relaxed, relieved and present in her body and that all her needs were met while she was expressing her healing-feelings to us.

Remember that Aware Parenting spectrum I talked about? I was in a different place on that spectrum compared to when she was a newborn, and also compared to how I was with my son, four and a quarter years after that initial experience of listening to my daughter's healing-feelings.

As I mentioned, her dad and I went on to listen to her feelings every evening, usually for about 30 to 60 minutes. However, I didn't put much focus on aiming to differentiate between when she was hungry and when she had healing-feelings to express at other times of the day. It wasn't until later that I realised that I was still often feeding her when she clearly had healing-feelings to express.

If I did try to listen to her healing-feelings in the daytime, I would sometimes feel concerned that she might be hungry, and would stop her crying with feeding her, but then she would clearly show me she wasn't hungry and would come on and off the breast. Still, I thought that we were listening to the majority of her feelings.

It was only when she was 18 months old that I realised that I had given her a major breastfeeding control pattern because I still so often fed her when she actually had healing-feelings to express. How did I ascertain that information? One of the clear differences was that it became increasingly hard for her to cry with me, while she could cry as easily as ever with her dad. I felt really upset when I saw that, because I wanted her to be comfortable to express her feellngs wlth me.

Her dad and I could both see the huge effect that listening to her healing-feelings had, including how calm, relaxed and present she was, and how she slept all night while co-sleeping, as well as also seeing that she was still holding feelings inside of her. We continued to listen to her feelings before bed most nights until she was three years old as well as at times during the day. I think that many of those healing-feelings that she expressed in her second and third year were feelings from those early days that I had unwittingly suppressed.

Aware Parenting the second time around

When our son was born four and a half years after our daughter, I knew that I didn't want to give him a breastfeeding *control pattern* and that I wanted to differentiate between when he was hungry and when he had healing-feelings to express. I was also an Aware Parenting instructor by this point and realised that babies have even more healing-feelings than I had originally thought! So, I was in a very different place on the Aware Parenting spectrum by then.

It's natural that we move along the spectrum once we have both more cognitive understanding

of Aware Parenting, as well as more tangible reassurance and evidence from observation and experience about how deeply helpful listening to feelings is for babies.

I also started practicing Elimination Communication (EC) with our son from birth (I had only discovered it when my daughter was 8 months old and started it then with her). I loved practicing EC along with Aware Parenting. I share more about Elimination Communication later in the book.

Helping my son heal from birth trauma

I am so grateful that my son was born second rather than first, because after his very quick posterior birth, when he latched on for his first feed, he clamped on really tightly and I could tell he had a lot of tension in his jaw from his birth. If he had been my first baby, I would not have felt confident and comfortable to listen to his healing-feelings, but I was, and I trusted that through listening, he would release the tension he was holding in his body.

And that's exactly what happened. Within the first 24 hours after he was born, I listened to him crying in my arms three times, for about half an hour each time. And after each cry, his jaw was more relaxed when he fed. After the third cry in my arms, his jaw was much more relaxed and his latch was really comfortable and we went on to continue a lovely breastfeeding relationship for the next two years. I can only imagine what would have happened to our breastfeeding relationship if he had been my first baby, because I would not have been able to listen to those feelings right in those early days as a first-time mother new to Aware Parenting.

However, if you are new to Aware Parenting, and if your baby isn't clearly trying to tell you about their birth, you might want to wait for a week or two to establish your milk supply (if you are their mother and you are breastfeeding). Then, you might want to start listening to their feelings.

If you've had a baby before this one and have already breastfed and listened to healing-feelings, you might feel confident to listen to your baby's healing-feelings soon after their birth. If your baby has experienced a traumatic birth, and you are keen to start supporting them in healing straight away, I recommend getting the support of an Aware Parenting instructor.

Feyza, a doula and breastfeeding counsellor who supports infant mental health, had a similar experience to mine. Here, she shares her story:

"I experienced a traumatic birth for my third child, and I had a somewhat stressful pregnancy as well. Because I had learnt about Aware Parenting already, I wanted to apply my knowledge as soon as she was born. However, her being a newborn, I also wanted to make sure I responded to her cues for breastfeeding to make sure she was well fed, and to establish my milk supply. Over the first two days, she got fussy and seemed to want to breastfeed constantly and non-stop, and by day two of her life, her latch became painful. This situation was exhausting and difficult for me, so I decided to explore listening to her tears in my arms.

The result was nothing short of a miracle.

The day after I started listening to her crying, breastfeeding became comfortable, even though I was only listening for 10-20 minutes a day. She started making more eye contact, looking into our eyes with a lot of curiosity, enjoying our touch and holds, loosening her fists, and sleeping for very long stretches during the day and night. When she was 10 days old, our CranioSacral Therapist (CST) got to work on her. She was surprised at how little tension she felt in our baby's body given that she was born by C-section. When the CST felt her palate and tongue, she was very pleased about her mouth structure. At one point, she said something like, 'I've only seen a few babies who can extend their tongue below their lower lip'. She loved the way she latched on with a wide-open mouth.

When I asked her if more sessions would be necessary, she said she didn't think so; she said, 'I used to think every baby needed CranioSacral Therapy treatments, but now I see every child is different, no matter how they're born'. Based on my own observations and our CranioSacral Therapist's as well, it seems she is doing quite well. I definitely attribute this positive change to the fact that I've been listening to her feelings from soon after she was born."

Listening to healing-feelings is a powerful way for babies to heal physiologically as well as emotionally, as both Feyza's and my experiences showed.

Crying-in-arms isn't just about expressing feelings; babies are also releasing physical tension and innately know exactly how to heal from their birth experiences through particular movements such as arching their back or getting into particular positions and moving in unique ways.

Starting to listen to your baby's healing-feelings

If you want to listen to your baby's feelings, I recommend starting when you have two conditions in place:

1. You feel relatively emotionally calm and present yourself – and you are willing to listen to their healing-feelings;
2. You are as confident as you possibly can be that all of your baby's immediate needs are met.

I recommend listening soon after you have fed your baby so you can be confident that they won't be hungry again while you are listening to their healing-feelings. Some parents find that about 45 minutes after a feed can be a helpful time to start.

You could simply hold your baby in your arms[15] (if they are not mobile), or offer your loving presence (if they are), and avoid distracting them. See if you can be as calm and connected as you can be!

Talking to your baby is an important part of this process. That includes talking with them while you are listening, "I'm here. I'm listening. You're letting it all out".

Remember if at any time you feel concerned that your baby is hungry or has some other present moment need, you can do what you would normally do to meet your baby's perceived need, such as feeding them if you think they are hungry.

You might want to let them know, "I'm not sure whether you have feelings to tell me or you are hungry, so I'm going to feed you, because I'm guessing that you're hungry. If you do have more feelings, please let me know. And I will listen again when I'm sure you do have feelings to tell me".

---

15 There's a diagram at the back of the book showing my favourite crying-in-arms position.

I invite you to then observe them, in all the ways we've already talked about, to see whether your next actions bring about true relaxed presence, or dissociation, or whether your baby continues trying to cry.

Remember too, that from an Aware Parenting perspective, jiggling, rocking and dummies are not meeting real needs but are common ways to distract babies from their feelings.

Many parents ask whether stopping a baby from expressing their feelings before the baby themselves finishes crying is undoing all the listening they have already done.

I want to offer you reassurance that if you stop them before they have expressed a whole chunk of feelings, the crying-in-arms that they have done will still make a difference for your baby. They have had an experience of being heard and understood, and they've released some stress and tension from their bodies.

However, you may find that they try to finish expressing that chunk of feelings, possibly soon afterwards. For example, they might fall asleep but then wake up crying again soon after.

You may also find that the effects aren't as big as if you are able to support your baby to move through a whole cycle of crying and come to completion.

You will probably find that you want to gradually build up the amount of time that you listen to healing-feelings as you receive reassurance from observing them and as you have more emotional calm and presence in yourself to listen (particularly as you have your own feelings listened to).

If you *don't* get any reassurance that this is helping your baby, and you are observing all the things I suggested earlier, I invite you to pause in listening to healing-feelings, go back to your earlier responses to crying and to return to this book to understand more. If you still want to explore Aware Parenting, I recommend a consultation with an Aware Parenting instructor. You can find the main list at **www.awareparenting.com** and the list of instructors in Australia and New Zealand at **www.marionrose.net**.

What might you observe when your baby has feelings to express to you?

You might offer your baby your loving presence on your lap or in your arms. You might notice that they start to move into their feelings, squirming a bit, grunting, and then moving into a cry. You might notice that they stop if you sit them up or move positions or distract them in other ways, but if you are still again and offer them your warm presence and loving words, they may begin to cry again. If you keep offering this, the feelings will often intensify, as your baby goes into fully feeling and expressing accumulated feelings from past stressful or traumatic events.

Remember, this is how they release the physical tension mobilised to fight or flee.

They might already be crying, but you've realised from your observations that they are not crying from needs-feelings. For example, perhaps they cry every evening, or after you get home from a busy day. In this case, you might simply hold them in your arms and stay present with them.

If they are already mobile, I invite you to offer your loving arms and let them choose whether or not they want to be held. You can find out more about healing-crying once babies become mobile later on in this chapter. The more your baby feels your warmth, presence and eye contact, the more intense the crying is likely to be. This is because you are creating the *balance of attention* between emotional safety in the present while they revisit feelings from the past.

Suggestions for when you're starting crying-in-arms with a pre-crawling baby

Here are some practical invitations. I wonder if they resonate with you? These are what I did to support myself while being with healing-feelings. As always, I invite you to listen in to yourself and what resonates for you!

Please note: these positions are for non-mobile babies. Once they become mobile, they may still enjoy these positions, *or* the crying with loving support might be much more of an active process. I explain more about this later in the chapter.

You being supported: I invite you to set up a place where you experience being supported. I liked sitting on a soft armchair, with plenty of support for my back, and with my feet up so that my baby could lie along my thighs at a 45 degree angle. There's a diagram of this in the back of the book. Other parents like holding their baby in their arms. You might want to hold your baby in a position that is clearly different from any usual breastfeeding or bottlefeeding positions. Whenever possible, I made sure that I had already had a drink and some food and had been to the toilet so that I would be physically comfortable while I listened.

A comfortable position for your baby: Find a comfortable crying position for your baby. My favourite position was to have them lying on a cushion on my thighs, with their feet at my belly and their head at my knees, which were at a 45 degree angle. When they were bigger, they were in the same position but with their legs around my waist, like the froggy position of being in a baby carrier. As they got longer still, I had a longer pillow to support their head at my knees. I loved that position because I could hold them like that for long periods without getting a sore back or neck, I could always offer them eye contact, and they could feel the support of my body. It also meant that they had the combination of being supported and being able to move (remember the *balance of attention*, which is the combination of feeling our loving support and presence while revisiting past stressful or traumatic experiences).

Stillness and presence: I invite you to simply sit still, without jiggling or rocking or moving, and be as present as you can. You might want to connect in with your breathing, and consciously feel the support of the pillows behind you.

Inviting their feelings: You might want to say something to your baby, such as, "I'm here with you. I'm listening. Do you want to tell me anything?"

Holding one hand: When they were younger babies, I often used to hold one of their hands, putting my thumb inside their hand, and would let their other hand move around. I had the sense of that also being likely to support the *balance of attention* between feeling safe in the present and revisiting feelings from the past. *I wonder if that resonates for you too?* Again, not everyone does this, so I invite you to listen in to yourself and your baby and do what you feel called to do.

Continuing being deeply present and following their lead: I talk about the *crying dance* with older babies, but in a way it's like a dance right from the early days because we are observing our baby and being deeply responsive to them. I always think of this being like tango or salsa dancing, where we are just completely listening in and moving and following where the baby wants to move. Some babies might want to turn around over and over again when revisiting their birth. They might be crying and trying to turn, and we can just flow with that and support them to make these kinds of movements while they're crying-in-arms. It makes the whole experience rich and nuanced with this deep observation and presence that's required from us. We can keep aiming to stay connected, listening to them and following their lead. It can be the most wondrous experience to really be with the baby in that way and literally feeling the tension be released as we follow their lead.

What you can do when the crying intensifies: As you sit and offer them your loving presence, you may notice that your baby's crying intensifies. If they weren't crying at all to begin with, as you gaze at them and listen, you might notice that they start a low-level crying. The longer you listen for, the more the crying will probably intensify. This intense crying comes because your baby is feeling the safety of your loving arms and presence. Remember that you can always stop them from crying with whatever response you would usually have to their crying if you feel concerned or worried that they have an unmet need.

The longer you listen, the more likely they are to move into full intense crying. You might find it helpful to remember the fight/flight/freeze response and see if it makes sense to you that the sound they're expressing and the movements they're making with their arms and legs are releasing the energy that was mobilised to fight or flee.

It's when the crying gets most intense that your old beliefs and feelings are likely to show up. If you didn't ever get to cry in loving arms and complete the crying, coming out the other side into peace and calm, you might think that they are just getting worked up and will never come out the other side. If you feel scared, it may be that your own memories of being left alone to cry or other painful past experiences are coming up to be heard.

Them getting to feel and express those intense emotions through loud crying and movement is often what brings the biggest difference afterwards, particularly in terms of their relaxation and sleep.

What you can do if your own feelings bubble up: If you do experience your own feelings coming up, such as fear if you are thinking that they have a here and now need, you could do the things that you think might meet those needs and go back to observing your baby again. If you clearly see that actually they do have feelings to express, you might want to reach out to receive some empathy and get to share with a Listening Partner or Aware Parenting instructor so that you can see what is coming up for you and do your own next piece of healing. If they are feelings from your own infancy, you might want to imagine your own Inner Loving Mother[16] there with you, holding you, saying, "I'm here with you". This can help bring a literal sigh of relief, and more presence in your body. You might want to keep imagining being held and supported so that you can stay calm and present.

What you might say: During the crying, you might say things like, "I'm here. I'm listening. You're letting it all out. I love you. You're having a big cry," while communicating with your warmth and emotional and physical presence that you are right there with them. Again, I invite you to find words that are most a fit for you. You might want to imagine what you would have loved to have heard as a baby. If you sense that they are healing from a past experience such as their birth, you might feel called to say specific things, such as, "You made it!" "I'm sorry it was so hard," "I'm here to listen to all of your feelings". I also invite you to trust yourself in what you want to say to your baby. Each of us has such different ways of expressing ourselves! In my early days of listening to my daughter's feelings, I used to talk a lot more, and as time went on, I often said less. I also aimed to communicate empathy and mirroring with my facial expressions, and to give a sense that all is well, and I was feeling calm and confident that their crying was healthy and healing.

The end of the feelings: If we are willing to listen to crying-in-arms in the early months, babies may choose to cry often and for shorter periods compared to when they get a bit older and bigger. When I was listening to my son at this age, the cries reminded me of the surges during his birth. There was much less of a whole chunk of feelings being expressed and much more of little and often cries. However, if you want to just listen once a day or less often, you can still do that.

---

16 This is from The Marion Method.

Remember, Aware Parenting is all about finding ways of meeting the needs of both babies and parents.

As babies get older, in a crying session there might often be a crescendo of feelings, and then the feelings diminish. They might even stop crying or fall asleep if you do nothing else. However, if you stay present and keep telling your baby that you are still there and listening, they might have more feelings to share with you and there might be another crescendo and even another one or more. Once they have expressed a whole chunk of feelings, they often will come out the other side visibly clearer and more relaxed, with the kind of presence that I talked about seeing with my daughter.

Observe afterwards: Remember to observe your baby afterwards. Do you notice any differences? Perhaps you even noticed them becoming more and more relaxed as the cry went on? We can often feel a palpable sense of difference in their muscles as we continue to hold them while they are literally releasing tension and stress from their body.

Noticing how you feel afterwards: I invite you to connect in with how you feel. When you first start listening to feelings, you might feel tired or stressed afterwards.

You might find that you even need to cry during or after their healing-feelings session. If you feel called to cry while they are crying in your arms, you could let them know that you are there with them and are listening, and that you are also letting out your feelings. As long as you are still in your parent role, they can feel safe. If you have huge feelings bubbling up and you don't think you can be present with them in their feelings at the same time, this is a strong invitation for you to receive some emotional support from another adult.

As time goes on and you receive reassurance that your baby feels more relaxed and happy through crying-in-arms, and as you do your own inner healing, you may find that you feel *relieved* and *relaxed* after a crying-in-arms session.

Questions: If you have any questions afterwards, I invite you to take them to the Facebook group of any Aware Parenting courses that you're in (of mine or of other Aware Parenting instructors), or have a consultation with me, another Aware Parenting instructor, or Aletha Solter herself.

> Before a baby is mobile, it's important that they are either in our arms when they are crying, or that we are right next to them – for example, lying next to them on a bed, with physical contact.

That's for two reasons:

1. If we aren't right close with them, we cannot be sure that they aren't crying to indicate that they need closeness.
2. It's our closeness that helps their crying be healing – our baby needs us close to listen to the feelings and to give them that sense that they are safe, that they are not alone and that their feelings are being heard. Remember, it's the *balance of attention* – the combination of safety in the present plus revisiting the past – that brings the healing effects of crying-in-arms.

So, until they start becoming mobile, there are two key things to hold in mind:

1. Holding them or being right next to them (being sure that we have the *balance of attention*, so they feel safe in the present).
2. Being confident that they have healing-feelings to express and that they have no unmet needs in the here and now.

Once a baby becomes mobile – from crying-in-arms to the *crying dance*

From about nine months onwards (the exact time varying from baby to baby but usually related to when they start becoming mobile), the crying is less a 'crying-in-arms' process and more of what I call a *crying dance*.

Babies then generally want to move around more while they are crying. This can be really challenging to parents, to keep finding that balance between the safety and containment of our presence and their need to move as part of the expression and healing process as well as honouring their needs for agency and autonomy.

I call this the *crying dance* because I see it as like an attuned partner dance, such as tango or salsa. We can use all our observational skills and internal intuition to keep following our baby's lead. Perhaps they are on our lap and are rolling over and over – can we support them to keep doing that while they are crying? (This can be part of the process of healing from, or completing, their birth experience).

Did you ever play the 'colder, colder, warmer, warmer' game as a child? I see the *crying dance* as something similar. If your baby clearly has feelings to express but isn't expressing them, that's the invitation to find the exact *balance of attention* where they can feel their feelings and your warm loving presence, so they can cry and express and release those feelings.

If they are crawling away and you see they are distracting themselves from their feelings, you could crawl next to them, telling them that you're still there, and you're listening.

I think of us being an *'emotional shepherd dog'* here! When we stay close and stay present, we are inviting them to stay connected both with us and with their own feelings.

In comparison, if they start crying and distract themselves by moving away from the *balance of attention*, and then return to crying and then distract themselves over and over again, this process – for example if they are expressing feelings before bed – may take a really long time. Parents can often feel very frustrated if this happens. The more we can be that emotional shepherd dog, staying close to them and helping them stay connected with their body and their feelings through our emotional connection with them, the more quickly and easily they can let out a complete chunk of feelings, with big intense crying, and they can then feel relaxed enough to go to sleep.

Once they become mobile, the process of differentiating between needs-feelings (particularly agency and autonomy) and healing-feelings becomes a little more complex.

What can you do if you think that your baby has healing-feelings to express, and you come close to them and:

a. They crawl away and *stop* crying?

b. They crawl away and *continue* crying?

c. They stay close and *stop* crying?

To answer these questions, I invite you to consider three things:

1. Your understanding of the theory: especially the *balance of attention*.
2. Your interpretation: what you sense is going on.
3. Your observation: what you ascertain from observing your baby.

The balance of attention is what makes the crying healing.

I see the *balance of attention* as being a bit like a see-saw. On one side is the connection, closeness, empathy, presence, warmth, reassurance and love that we offer our baby.

On the other hand is whatever helps our baby connect with the feelings from unhealed past stress or trauma. That might be that they find something that reminds them of the past or they find a pretext to have a cry. It might be us offering a *Loving Limit*.[17]

So, when each of those situations occurs (a, b or c above), we can take into account the balance of attention, and ask ourselves where our baby is on that see-saw.

a. You think they have healing-feelings but they move away from you and stop crying.

If you think that they have healing-feelings to express, but when you are close with them, they crawl away and stop crying, the next thing you can do is observe them to discern whether they are moving away to meet a need or to distract themselves from their feelings.

Through observing them, you'll be able to see whether they are still agitated or not. If they:

- move from one thing to the next;
- avoid eye contact;
- express screechy or loud vocalisations;
- aren't concentrating; or
- start crying again soon,

they are probably telling you that they *did* actually have healing-feelings to express. They are showing you that this *wasn't* a need for

---

[17] A *Loving Limit* is when we say no to a behaviour that is being caused by unexpressed healing-feelings, and we say yes to the feelings that are underneath that behaviour. This is a term created by me based on an already-existing Aware Parenting practice.

agency or exploration; rather, they were trying to distract themselves from their feelings.

If, as they move away, they are:

- smiling;
- making eye contact;
- concentrating on things for long periods;
- relaxed; and
- making vocalisations with a calm tone,

then it is more likely that they *didn't* have healing-feelings to express and simply had needs such as agency or exploration.

So, you can observe them, and you can also listen in to your own sense of what is going on, from observing how they are before and afterwards.

If it becomes clear to you that they *did* need to cry, you might experiment with a few options to help them reconnect with their healing-feelings. You might:

- Come in close and stay close, (which might mean crawling along beside them) and offer them warmth, eye contact, and perhaps to talk to them and tell them that you are there and listening;
- Wait until their feelings bubble up again;
- Offer a *Loving Limit*, "I see that you want to go out of the bedroom, sweetheart, and I'm not willing for you to leave because I think you have some feelings to share. I'm here with you. I'm listening". Staying together in the bedroom with that *Loving Limit* might help them connect with those feelings again.

b. You think they have healing-feelings and they move away from you and continue crying.

In this case, I invite you to remember that *balance of attention.*

Once they are crawling, they can come close to you if they need to and don't necessarily need to be held to have the kind of connection needed for the crying to be healing.

But they *do* need to be able to feel the connection with you, the warmth, the love, the empathy and the emotional safety, which means, for a toddler, that you still need to be close to them. They need to be able to see you for the crying to be healing and for cuddles and closeness to be available if they need it.

If you've already been listening to their healing-feelings, it's also likely that they will have internalised your empathic listening which may affect how much they want or need to be held when expressing healing-feelings.

In this scenario, if they are still crying, you could keep playing with the *balance of attention.* You could:

- Stay where you are and tell them that you're listening and ask them whether they want you to come close;
- Reach out your arms and give them the choice of whether they want to come closer to you;
- Move a little closer and see what happens;

If the crying intensifies, it may be that you are getting closer to that balance of attention.

Again, it is only really through experimenting with this, listening in to yourself, talking to them, and observing their behaviour before, during and after, that you will understand what is really going on and what they truly need.

c. **They are crying, and when you come close, they stop.**

Again, the important thing is to observe their behaviour so you can discern whether they were needing closeness, and you've met that need, or they had healing-feelings to express and you have inadvertently distracted them from those feelings or they have dissociated.

1. If they are connecting with you in a present and connected way, then it is likely that their need was connection and you are meeting that need for connection.
2. But if you come close and they cling on to you in a way that seems quite dissociated and tense, or they avoid eye contact and get really busy, or they start twirling your hair or sucking on your top, or picking your skin or frantically asking for food or something else, then it is likely that they do actually have feelings to express and they're now dissociating – or trying to.

If we have frequently distracted our baby from their feelings, it becomes harder for them to express their feelings when we are physically close, because us holding them in particular positions might have become a *control pattern*. This makes the whole process more difficult.

There are a few things that we can do if that is the case.

As a preventative, at other times you could focus on getting clearer about distinguishing between hunger, the need for entertainment, and the need to express feelings. The more accurately you can tell the difference and respond to them aptly, the easier it will be for them to cry with you when you are physically close with them.

In the moment, you might want to play with that *balance of attention* see-saw.

What could you do that would meet their needs for connection and emotional safety, but would also helping them stay connected with their feelings from the past?

There are at least two main ways to do that if being close to your body leads to them dissociating. (This is common if breastfeeding has become a *control pattern*). I call them the *knees up hug* and the *bending down hug*.

The knees up hug

This is where you sit opposite them with your knees up and put your arms around them when they are asking to be held.

The bending down hug

This is where you are standing up and bend down to hug them, without picking them up when they are asking to be held.

In both of these, you are offering your warmth, closeness and love, but are unwilling for them to move into a position where they dissociate. Then you can continue to listen to their feelings.

> *The key is that you are sure that you are meeting their need for connection.*

If you are concerned, then perhaps you might like to explore your own feelings about this, such as expressing those feelings to your Listening Partner or an Aware Parenting instructor.

This happened for me and my daughter when she was a toddler. I was physically close with her all the time, and yet, often she would be agitated, would ask me to pick her up, and when I picked her up she would clearly dissociate even though she had healing-feelings to express. This was one of the effects of me regularly distracting her from her feelings with breastfeeding. I remember having a consultation with Aletha Solter when my daughter was 18 months old, and Aletha suggested that instead of picking her up when my daughter had healing-feelings to express, that I leant down and cuddled her, but without picking her up – what I'm now calling 'the bending down hug'.

At first, I found that impossible to do, because my own feelings of being left alone as a baby would come up, even if I was right there close with my daughter, offering her love and compassion and with my arms around her, but not picking her up. It was only as I worked more with listening to my own baby-self feelings that I could feel more comfortable with listening to her feelings while I was right there with her but without picking her up (when picking her up had become a control pattern).

Observing her behaviour afterwards, I soon discovered that if she clearly had healing-feelings to express, and she was asking to be picked up, and I picked her up, she would cuddle in and dissociate, and then she would continue to be agitated. Her body would be tense. She would avoid connection.

In comparison, at times I came right close, bent down to her, put my arms around her, and told her, "I see that you want me to pick you up, sweetheart, and I'm not willing to pick you up at the moment because I don't think that's most helpful for you right now, and I'm here and listening". If she then had a big cry with me, with my arms around her, afterwards she would smile more, make more eye contact, snuggle up in a connected way, and be more relaxed in her body. This is why this process is always about deep attunement with our baby by clearly observing their behaviour in all its nuances.

This is an example of a Loving Limit. *I said no to picking her up because that wasn't actually meeting her needs, but was helping her dissociate. I made sure I was right with her, offering her emotional presence and safety, so that the crying was healing. That is the 'yes' part of the* Loving Limit.

It really is only through experimenting like this – listening to yourself, observing your baby, finding the balance of attention, and observing them before, during and after healing-crying, that you come to understand them more and more, finding clarity about what is really going on for them in any moment, and gaining reassurance about how incredibly helpful healing-crying is.

What about *holding* a mobile baby?

If a baby is mobile, and clearly has healing-feelings to express, but will only cry in a parent's arms, yet also pushes against the parent's body with their arms and legs when crying, parents are understandably concerned and confused. The question is always: is the baby doing this because they need agency and autonomy, or are they doing this to heal from stress and trauma?

This is a very nuanced process and if you are experiencing this with your baby, I highly recommend having a consultation with Aletha Solter or an Aware Parenting instructor such as me.

Some babies in some circumstances might require this kind of support to heal from trauma – the pushing of their arms and legs can be them revisiting an experience from the past, such as a challenging or long birth or medical procedure. In revisiting this, they can get to feel powerful while also expressing all the feelings they felt back then, so that this time they get to heal from the experience.

However, *holding* a crying mobile baby is only something to do if:
- You are experienced with Aware Parenting;
- You're already practicing all the other aspects of Aware Parenting;
- You've tried *attachment play* and *Loving Limits* and they haven't brought healing;
- You are deeply calm and relaxed in your body;
- You're feeling connected with, and loving towards, your baby;
- You have a nuanced understanding of what's going on for your baby;
- Your *holding* is in tune with and responsive what your baby is doing, supporting them to move as part of the healing process.
- You only do it occasionally, not as a regular practice.
- They are hitting, throwing or biting and *Loving Limits* aren't enough to keep everyone safe.

If in doubt, stop and seek support from an Aware Parenting instructor. Holding a baby like this is an advanced practice and only to be used in some situations when these conditions are in place.

Some babies seem to need more *holding* to be able to heal from stress or trauma through pushing their arms and legs, for example if they were separated after birth or if they experienced birth trauma or a long or short birth.

But if we are finding that our baby only cries with *holding* (once they can crawl), it is often a sign that we need to learn to increase our repertoire – to learn more and become more familiar with *attachment play, Loving Limits* and the *crying dance*. I would recommend a consultation with Aletha Solter or an Aware Parenting instructor if so.

Self-Compassion Moment

How do you feel, after reading about *holding*? It's really normal to feel concerned, and to want to be sure that a baby's needs for agency and autonomy are honoured. I invite you to reach out to your Listening Partner or an Aware Parenting instructor if you want support with this.

Through a baby's eyes

"Bumpy, feelings, wriggly, me. Out of sorts, my body is awash with sensations. I wriggle and move. You're there, but I remember all the times I tried to share my feelings and didn't get to. I want to move away from you, because I feel all my feelings when I see your love. You come close. You stay close. Your eyes. You see me. I see you. You're here with me. But are you really? I try once more, moving away to the edge of the world, but you come close. You stay close. Ahhh, you are with me. Here with me. I'm safe. I let it out, the wail, the rage, the cry. You stay. You listen. I move, you move with me. You're here with me. I cry, I wail. You're here. You're here. Feelings flow through me. The rain flows through. The water moves and flows. Out and out and out. Ahh, it's gone, the water has gone. I'm sinking back into my body, I am here again now. I see you. I sink into you. Relaxed, relieved, we are here together".

A baby's words:

"Now I can crawl and I'm learning to walk, I'm learning so many new things. I can move. I can choose. I am so powerful. But also, there's so much I am not able to do yet. And I feel so frustrated. I really want to be able to walk, and it's so hard. I try and I try. It's evening and I'm tired, and I feel so full of feelings. But you've been so busy, and sometimes you used to stop me when I cried, so I don't know if you really do want to listen today. I start to cry, and I move away. Oh look! The tassels on the curtain are so interesting! This toy! I love this toy! Ooh look at this

blanket! I need it right now! I don't feel, I don't want to feel sometimes. Sometimes you used to stop me from feeling. Will you listen now? Oh, you are coming too! You ARE here with me! You look, I hear your love. You speak, you show me that you are going to listen. Ahh, I look in your eyes and I see how much you love me. YOU LOVE ME! The tears come, I cry, I cry. Oh Mummy! I feel so much! Walking is so hard! And you are so much bigger than me! I want to be able to do all the things you can do! And I feel so confused so often, and so powerless. Thank you for listening to me! I rage and I rage. I feel so frustrated. I move away. Do you really love me? Oh, you follow me. You do want to listen. You ARE listening. I will rage and I will rage. I rage and I cry. Oh you love me, you love me. I cry and I cry. Oh, the tears are less now. The feelings are less now. Oh I feel so much more relieved. Oh, the tears are done now. I cuddle in to you. I can feel my body. I feel the weight and I feel the depth. I can really see your eyes now, Mummy. I love you, Mummy. I feel so open and so loving. So relaxed and so relieved. Thank you for listening to me. I love you. I love you".

Big feelings are normal

Given the opportunity, ALL babies have big and intense feelings.

During a crying session, you might see the following while your baby releases accumulated feelings, stress and trauma:

- back arching (often releasing birth-related feelings);
- loud crying;
- their skin reddening with heat and sweating;
- kicking their legs;
- moving their arms; or
- crying for an hour or more.

And OF COURSE, it is ALWAYS important to make sure that your baby isn't in physical pain or discomfort.

The more familiar we are with the release crying that comes with healing-feelings, the more clearly we can differentiate that from a physical pain cry.

- **If a baby is in physical pain, the crying will generally be higher pitched.**
- **If the baby is expressing healing-feelings, it's more likely they will be able to dissociate by being fed or distracted.**
- **If your baby seems different, lethargic, or you are worried or concerned, then ALWAYS TRUST your intuition and seek urgent advice from a qualified health practitioner.**

Crying-in-arms often starts with a baby being a bit agitated, moving around in a wriggly way, and as we offer our loving presence, the crying will often intensify.

At its height, the crying can be very loud and our baby might be moving around a lot, perhaps sweating too, and that is often when we might feel worried or concerned.

And remember, if at any time you are concerned that something is amiss, then it is so important to listen to yourself. You can always talk to your baby, tell them you're concerned, and then do the usual things you do to stop them from crying.

If you can distract them from their feelings through distraction or rocking, that might give you some reassurance that they are relatively physically comfortable.

I invite you to take this process gradually for yourself. It's really only through observing your baby and seeing tangible signs that healing-crying is helping them, that you will feel more comfortable with listening to their big feelings.

What thoughts and feelings are showing up for you as you read this?

When you're not able to listen with full presence

What can you do if your baby is crying and you think all of their needs have been met, but you are unable to be fully present with their healing-crying? For example, if you are feeling exhausted, overwhelmed, sad or frustrated. If you're in that position, I'm sending you so much love and empathy.

Here is a list of suggestions from Aletha Solter[18] of specific things you can do:

These are in approximate order of most ideal to least ideal.

For all of these (except where noted), Aletha recommends some form of physical connection with the crying baby (such as holding them, having them in a sling or carrier on your front, lying down with the baby on your stomach, or in a carrier on your back for a toddler, etc.).

Aletha says; "Give the baby information. For example, you could say: *"I see that you're upset, sweetheart, but I'm not able to listen to your feelings right now, so I'm going to do some things to take care of myself. You are welcome to cry if you need to"*.

(For suggestion number 4, omit the second sentence.)

---

18 Personal communication

1. Find someone else to hold the baby. (The baby is free to continue crying with that person).
2. Release/express your own feelings. (The baby is free to continue crying with you).
   - *Cry while the baby is crying;*
   - *Call a friend or a Listening Partner to talk or cry with;*
   - *Draw or paint a picture depicting your emotions;*
   - *Write in a journal.*
3. Block the sound and use distraction/suppression/calming techniques with *yourself*. (The baby is free to continue crying with you).
   - *Wear ear plugs to partially block the sound;*
   - *Wear sound-masking earphones (the kind that cover the ears completely);*
   - *With earphones on, listen to music, white noise, or a meditation tape; or watch a video;*
   - *Do household tasks or pursue a hobby (cooking, cleaning, laundry, gardening, etc.);*
   - *Take a walk;*
   - *Go jogging with the baby in a stroller facing you (visual and auditory contact but no physical contact).*
4. As a last resort, use distraction/suppression/calming techniques with the baby.
   - *Rocking, bouncing;*
   - *Pacifier (dummy);*
   - *Breastfeeding, bottlefeeding, etc.*
5. As a VERY last resort, separate yourself from the baby (if you have tried all of the above, the baby is still crying, and you are feeling extremely overwhelmed or close to hurting your baby):

- *Put the baby down in a safe place (eg. cot), and leave the room. If possible, return from time to time to reassure the baby.*

For the first three suggestions, the baby is free to continue crying, which is why they are listed first.

For suggestion number 5, the baby is also free to continue crying, but leaving a baby to cry alone (number 5) is more harmful than lovingly trying to stop the crying while keeping the baby close (number 4), which is why it is listed last".

Aletha continues, "*Of course, none of these is ideal. They are short-term solutions when parents feel unable to listen to the crying. If you find that you are often not able to listen to your baby's feelings, that is a strong invitation for you to receive listening yourself for your own emotions. If you frequently feel an urge to harm your crying baby, I would strongly recommend that you find more support and also some form of therapy".*

Note that in Aletha's list, it's very important that our baby still has physical connection with us when they are crying to heal, so that even if we are not giving them our full emotional presence, they are feeling our physical presence.

Self-Compassion Moment
I wonder how you feel when you read this list and suggestions from Aletha?

I remember feeling all kinds of feelings when I first read it. I was much more comfortable to try to suppress my babies' healing-feelings (number 4 on the list) if I had my own feelings bubbling up. As I connected in more deeply with what was going on for me when reading the list, I realised that the idea of my baby crying while I was not giving them full attention helped me connect with lots of my old feelings from childhood when I was trying to express feelings to people and they weren't listening.

In summary, on those occasions that we are too stressed or too full up with our own feelings to be able to listen, we can still be physically present with our baby, trusting that if they feel enough emotional safety to continue to express their feelings, they will. Ideally, of course, if we find that we are too stressed to listen, we would reach out for more support on an ongoing basis, for example receiving listening from a Listening Partner or Aware Parenting instructor.

What do you really want for you and your baby with Aware Parenting?

What would you like to imagine for you and your baby? I wonder if any of these call to you?

Imagine, through observation, really getting to understand your baby – really knowing when they are hungry, when they are tired and when they are upset. Imagine having the honour of getting to listen to their biggest and deepest feelings, understanding that you are helping them heal from stress and trauma, so that they don't need to carry that stress and trauma throughout their lives.

Imagine seeing them relatively free of accumulated feelings, so that they smile more freely, their eyes look clearer, they make more eye contact, they feel more relaxed and comfortable in their body and they're able to sleep more peacefully and restfully and for longer periods.

Imagine them growing up with fewer *control patterns*, so that they're more present and more able to experience all the enjoyable things in life and have less need to turn to other ways to suppress or dissociate from feelings as an adult, like social media, eating, shopping, being busy, alcohol or drugs.

Imagine them knowing that when they feel a sensation of sadness in their body, they know that it's sadness, they can be present with those feelings, they can cry and express and release those feelings, all the while knowing that they are safe and that they will come out the other side feeling relieved and relaxed.

Imagine them knowing that when they feel a sensation of frustration or rage in their body, they know that it's frustration or rage, they can be present with those feelings, they can rage and express and release those feelings in healthy ways, with a deep body sense that they are safe and loved.

Imagine them knowing that they are unconditionally loved, however they feel, and that they don't need to hide or suppress certain feelings to be loved or accepted, either by you, or by other people in their lives as they grow up. Imagine them knowing that they are understood and they are heard, and them having a belief that their feelings will be welcomed by others. Imagine them being able to be with the feelings of others as they grow.

Finally, would you like to imagine how parenting would be if you were deeply compassionate with yourself, so that all the times you aren't able to meet their needs or listen to their feelings, you simply give yourself empathy, and are unwilling to judge yourself?

What would you love to imagine for you and your baby? And are you willing for that?

CHAPTER SIX

Differentiating between needs-feelings (especially hunger) and healing-feelings

Differentiating between hunger and healing-feelings

As I shared earlier in the book, one of the parts of Aware Parenting that many parents experience the most challenge with is differentiating hunger from healing-feelings. That makes so much sense, doesn't it, because we want to be absolutely sure that our baby isn't hungry whenever we're listening to their feelings.

This is where the triangle of research I mentioned earlier is particularly important, if you are wanting to clearly differentiate the two. That means getting really clear about the theory of Aware Parenting, listening in deeply to yourself, and observing your baby. In this ongoing process, you will gain more and more clarity about what's really going on for them.

You might decide *not* to differentiate between the two in general and to instead simply choose one time each day, perhaps the evening, when you are confident that your baby isn't hungry and you are willing to listen to one chunk of feelings. I see many parents taking this approach and this is what we tended to do with our daughter when she was a baby. This can make a huge difference to how a baby feels in their body, their level of relaxation and presence, and their sleep.

However, as I shared in the last chapter, doing this with my daughter meant that I often fed her when she needed to cry and as a result, she had a breastfeeding *control pattern*, and this affected her and also influenced our relationship. For example, it meant that it was, and still is, harder for her to express her feelings with me than with her dad.

If you *do* want to differentiate hunger from a need to express healing-feelings, I invite you to read this next section, where I share about my experience with my son when he was a baby. Wherever you are on the Aware Parenting spectrum, you might find the information you read helpful with whatever you choose to do.

My journey of differentiating hunger from healing-feelings with my son

Remember that spectrum of Aware Parenting? With my son, I aimed to listen to as close to 100% of his healing-feelings as I could, and to *always* differentiate between whether he was hungry and when he had healing-feelings to express. This was because I had found it really painful when I saw the effects of my daughter's breastfeeding *control pattern*, especially when I saw that it became much harder for her to cry with me, but she could still share her feelings with her dad. I wanted my son to have a really different experience and for him to be freely able to share his feelings with me. That was so important to me, and that's why I was so willing to put *a lot* of effort into distinguishing between hunger and healing-feelings.

I went back and re-read the chapter on food in Aletha Solter's *The Aware Baby*, over and over again. There, she offers guidelines for determining when your baby is hungry (p.84):

- *"Time since previous feeding (with certain exceptions). Intervals will increase with age.*
- *Careful attention to your baby's signals.*
- *Baby's behaviour after you offer breast or bottle".*

Once I really understood this, here's what I did.

As you read this, I invite you to listen in to whether this resonates with you, or even if there are parts that do and parts that don't.

I kept a diary (this was 2006, before phone apps were a thing!), and I noted down every time he fed, cried, or did a wee or a poo. I observed and listened to him closely; his different vocalisations, cries and movements.

From reading all of his hunger cues, I observed that as a newborn, he started off with a hunger gap of approximately two and a half hours between the beginning of one feed and the beginning of the next. I held that in mind, NOT to determine his feeding by the clock, *but as another piece of information to notice as part of my observation of what was really going on for him.*

My offering him the breast was ALWAYS determined by reading his hunger cues, NOT by the clock.

Feeding to a fixed schedule without observing a baby's cues is of course stressful and even traumatic for a baby, because it isn't attuned to them and doesn't meet their needs. Many of us adults experienced being fed on schedule as babies and understand how painful it is to experience being fed with no consideration for whether we were hungry or not.

I also didn't feed my son automatically at particular times, such as when he woke up, or to go to sleep, as I had often done with my daughter in the early months of her life, when I didn't know how to understand her cues for hunger and for needing to express healing-feelings.

Instead, I observed him and his cues and only fed him when I discerned from his behaviour that he was actually hungry.

I also had a piece of information that I didn't really understand with my daughter, even though it is in *The Aware Baby*, which is that rooting is a reflex action. Rooting doesn't indicate hunger. It's a reflex for obvious survival reasons.

With my daughter, I thought it was a sign of hunger, and fed her whenever she rooted.

If we are confident that our baby is not hungry through clearly observing and listening to their many nuanced behaviours and cues, we don't need to feed them simply because they are rooting, because we know that it is not an expression of hunger. Of course if they are showing other cues for hunger at the same time as rooting, then we can be confident that they are hungry and feed them.

I was able to correlate my observations of the cues of when he was hungry with the observations of when he was feeding. I knew that if he had actually been hungry before I fed him, he would:

- suck consistently,
- stay awake,
- stay on the breast, and
- be relatively calm in his body.

Whereas if he:

- sucked intermittently,
- fell asleep soon after getting on the breast, after not having fed much,
- came on and off the breast many times, and
- wriggled around a lot or was tense and agitated,

that told me that he was unlikely to be hungry.

If you are bottlefeeding, you might observe similar things. Whenever I talk about breastfeeding, please adjust what I say to fit with your experience.

I so appreciate Aletha Solter, who explains these points in *The Aware Baby*, which helped me so much. I highly recommend reading it if you haven't already read it.

I also knew from *The Aware Baby* that babies' stomachs get bigger as they get older and can hold more milk at each feed and thus go longer in between feeds. I therefore knew that if I was observing accurately, he would gradually start having a longer gap in between feeds before he became hungry again as he got older, as long as I was giving him a full feed each time (on both breasts) so that his stomach was full by the end of the feed.

If I observed that for several feeds in a row he was clearly displaying that he wasn't actually hungry (through my observation of those four things in the list above), I would conclude that I wasn't reading his hunger cues quite accurately, and that his stomach had got bigger and that he could now go longer in between each feed, and then I would add an extra ten minutes of my rough approximation of when he would get hungry.

Important note: I want to emphasise that I wasn't timing my feeding of him by looking at a clock. I was feeding him by observing him in great detail, and then seeing how that corresponded with an approximate amount of time.

Then I would observe him again. I'd wait until he was starting to seem a bit agitated in his movements and sounds and giving me

cues that he was hungry. If it was close to the approximate amount of time I was estimating in between feeds, I would feed him, and I would observe his behaviour while feeding.

If he clearly showed that he was indeed hungry, then I would stay with that time as an approximate marker. Over time, the gaps in between feeds became longer and longer, as his stomach became bigger and he took more milk at each feed, having a full feed each time.

If he was agitated in his movements and there were hours before he usually got hungry again, I had a big, long chunk of time where I could listen to his feelings, confident that they were healing feelings and that he wasn't actually hungry. Then I could offer him my loving presence and ask him if he had any feeling to express.

There isn't an inherent reason for bigger feeds and bigger gaps in between feeds.

In *The Aware Baby*, Aletha talks about how different spacings of feedings fit for different cultures and climates. If a mother lives in a hot climate where babies can easily become sick, dehydrated or malnourished, it makes sense to feed them little and often. In addition, being able to stop them from crying gives reassurance that they aren't sick. Whereas in a traditional culture in a snowy climate before the advent of modern nappies, it would have been advantageous to have longer and more spaced out feeds, to avoid less need of baring skin for feeding, weeing and pooing. In this case, giving a baby a full feed on both breasts and then waiting until they were hungry again before giving them another full feed would be most helpful.

However, longer gaps can be very helpful if you are practicing Aware Parenting and are aiming to differentiate hunger from healing-feelings and want to be confident when your baby is crying-in-arms feelings heard – present, aware, deeply interested in and engaged with life, relaxed and joyful.

My experiences with both of my children helped me know in a deeply embodied way that babies and children aren't what The Disconnected Domination Culture makes them out to be. At our core, when enough of our needs are met and enough of our healing-feelings are heard, we are deeply present, loving, aware beings. That is our true nature.

Seeing this in real life was a profound experience which has affected my core beliefs, the way I work with parents in their parenting and their reparenting, and in the way I perceive all humans.

Maru is an Aware Parenting instructor in the UK who had a similar experience to mine, also with her second child:

"I started differentiating between the need to feed for hunger and the need to cry when he was very little. Maybe about three or four weeks. And it took some practice, but he doesn't have the breastfeeding control pattern that my daughter did. I was actually amazed at the long periods of time he could go between feeds. He would generally feed just four or five times in 24 hours. That included night times and I noticed that he really didn't need to feed more than that. And often he would sleep for long periods, sometimes two, three hours in the beginning, and wake up and still not be hungry and sort of spend half an hour playing around happily. And it was only after half an hour that he needed to feed. So I really followed his lead on that. And I tried to be quite diligent, distinguishing one from the other.

He's slept completely differently to my daughter from very early on. He was doing almost a full night, like nine to five, when he would wake up and have a feed and then go back to sleep. His sleep is much deeper and it's been a lot easier to transfer him from one place to the other since he was very young. But even now, once he's asleep, he's properly asleep and he looks very peaceful and he's resting and he is relaxed.

It has been a completely different journey. Basically from the age of four or five months, he only had one feed at night and then he stopped around 12 months and began sleeping through the night. I can see the impact that feelings have on sleep because when he has accumulated feelings, he will wake up in the night and sometimes struggle and take about an hour or two to go back to sleep – so it's really obvious.

For example, we were travelling by plane and car once in Mexico when he was five months old. He was sleeping on the go wherever we were. It was quite a busy and overwhelming day even for the adults. I remember so clearly that night he was not sleeping as he usually did; he woke up at one in the morning, crying and crying for a good 45 minutes with us and then went back to sleep and woke up again at 3.30/4am. The following day he did more crying in our arms. Once that crying was done, he went back to sleeping again in his normal pattern; that's something that we've observed time and time again.

Also I noticed from the time we started listening to feelings that whenever we pick him up it's like his limbs are so relaxed, they hang off his torso, there's no tension. To this day we we can tell, for example, when he's not feeling well because his body feels different; he had a stomach bug when he was around six months and straight away I could feel his body felt different. This is something that I've commented on with my husband, how different this is to my daughter, with whom we started Aware Parenting later on.

The only way to describe it is like his limbs are supple and relaxed and there's no tension in his body".

This lack of tension is something my children's dad and I also noticed in our son and daughter. It was palpable. We could also see it later on in their posture too. If you've looked into therapies that discuss muscular armouring, you might be familiar with this. For example, my daughter's posture as a child and teen showed a complete relaxation, presence and openness in her upper torso which I notice is very rare in our culture.

If your baby's healing-feelings are being suppressed through breastfeeding

I want to let you know that almost every mother I've worked with has, with the most loving of intentions, given the first baby they practice Aware Parenting with a breastfeeding *control pattern*. Of course we are always going to veer on the side of thinking our baby is hungry rather than they have healing-feelings to express

> *Self-Compassion Moment*
> I invite you to drop any guilt sticks you might be picking up, and be deeply compassionate with yourself here if, like me, you unwittingly gave your baby a breastfeeding *control pattern*. You were doing what you were doing for the most loving of reasons.

So what can you do? You might want to aim to differentiate more between when they are communicating that they're hungry and when they're communicating that they have feelings to tell you. Maybe there are specific times that you know that they are not hungry. This might be at a particular time of the day, or after they've been feeding for a certain amount of time, or if they've already fed in the recent hour or two (depending on their age, of course!). Or perhaps you see that they are coming on and off the breast, are falling asleep or are agitated and you sense that they are not hungry.

Again, you could simply hold them in your arms or on your lap, and offer your loving presence, and listen.

Some mothers find that if their baby has a breastfeeding control pattern, it becomes hard for their baby to cry in their arms when they are in a similar position to the breastfeeding position.

If this is the case with your baby, you might want to offer a different position to them to listen to their feelings. And if you feel worried at any time that perhaps they are hungry after all, start to feed them and then observe whether or not they were hungry from how they feed. I also invite you to share your thoughts and feelings with an empathic listener such as a Listening Partner or Aware Parenting instructor because babies are acutely sensitive to, and are affected by, our emotional state. Babies will sometimes not express their feelings with us if we have a lot of our own feelings bubbling up that we are suppressing.

This process changes as a baby becomes older if breastfeeding has become a *control pattern*. Remember how we talked earlier on in the book about how babies will learn to interpret their sensations based on how we interpret them? Well, if we consistently feed them when they have healing-feelings to tell us, they will interpret the sensation of upset feelings to indicate hunger and will ask to be fed when they feel those feelings. That means, if we decide to listen to their feelings, they will often ask urgently to be fed, such as through pulling at our top.

This can be confusing for mothers. If you're in that position, I invite you to reach out for empathy and support from an Aware Parenting instructor, or Aletha Solter herself.

What I often say, and I wonder if this is helpful for you, is that *we were the one who originally gave them the control pattern*. Without picking up any guilt sticks, we can see that *they learnt to interpret and respond to their feelings in this way because of how we responded to them*. And any time that they do have feelings to tell us and we offer a *Loving Limit*, saying that we're not willing to feed them and we are willing to listen to their feelings, we are supporting them to come back to *interpreting their sensations accurately*. They will increasingly be able to tell the difference between the sensations of hunger and the sensations from feelings that want to be expressed. With the *Loving Limit*, you might say something like, "I see that you really want milk, sweetheart, and I'm not willing to give you any right now because I don't think you're hungry. I'm here, and I'm listening. I love you". At any time you are unsure, and think they might be hungry, you can tell them and give the breast (or bottle) again.

Loving Limits are when we say 'no' to behaviour being caused by feelings and 'yes' to the feelings underneath the behaviour.

In this case, we are saying no to the *control pattern* of feeding our baby, because *we understand that they aren't actually hungry*, and that the *deepest and truest* need they have in that moment is to express pent up feelings to us and heal from stress or trauma. In understanding them accurately, we help them feel much more comfortable in their body than if we were to simply suppress their feelings through feeding them.

Through a baby's eyes

"Feelings, feelings, oh milk makes them go away for a while, but this time you say no. I cry, tears come like rivers and the rain, they flow and flow and flow. Ahh, they are all coming out. Relief, different relief. I see you".

A baby's words

"Oh feelings are coming. I remember you stopped those feelings before with feeding me, and oh I do feel kind of relieved when you feed me, kind of like dreaming. Will you feed me this time? Oh, you are saying no! When you say no, all the feelings I've been holding in all day come tumbling out. I kind of want to not feel them, for you to feed me, so I will ask and ask for you to feed me, but I also feel this relief to finally tell you how I feel. Today I felt overwhelmed, and I felt frustrated, and I felt confused, and I felt scared. Thank you for listening to my feelings. Although they are kind of uncomfortable, I also really want to let them out. I feel free and open and spacious.

Ahhh, you are listening. You are here with me. You are listening. The feelings are going now. I feel calm. I snuggle up in your arms. Ahhhhhh...Thank you".

A breastfeeding *control pattern* can lead to a baby crying more easily with their other parent

When a baby has a breastfeeding *control pattern*, it can mean that they will cry whenever the mother leaves the room or tries to go out and leave the baby with their Dad or other parent. This can be really confusing and overwhelming for mums. I remember being in this position, and never taking time away from my daughter, because I thought her crying with her Dad when I left was because she needed me, despite the fact that her Dad was so involved with her and she was clearly securely attached to him. I have worked with many mothers over the years who have also experienced this.

Sonya was getting close to being burnt out:

"For a long time, I thought that my baby boy wasn't letting me do anything. My partner is really loving and attentive to him, but our son would cry any time I even left the room. I was desperate. His Dad was longing to do more of the caring, and I wasn't getting any time to even have a shower. Our little one didn't seem very happy either, despite everything I was doing for him, carrying him everywhere, co-sleeping and basically doing nothing else. After some sessions with Marion, I started to realise that it wasn't that he didn't feel safe with his Dad. It was because I was feeding him any time he had emotions to express, and that was why he cried whenever we were apart. It was a big deal. I had some super big cries myself as I recalled being left alone to cry and never wanting my sweet babe to feel what I had felt. Once we started listening to his feelings, things changed quickly and dramatically. His Dad and he gained this lovely bond, and the friction between my partner and I lifted. He felt powerful and valuable as a

Dad, now he could be with our son and even listen to his feelings before sleep (wow!). I went from being extremely sleep-deprived and never doing anything for myself to going back to doing things that I loved before becoming a mum – singing in a band and playing the piano. And our son blossomed. He smiled more, he was more relaxed, he was more interested in the world, and he slept! It really was like a miracle. If it hadn't been for Aware Parenting, I don't know what would have happened. We just couldn't have kept going as we were".

If your baby is dissociating from their healing-feelings in other ways

Dissociating through movement

You might choose to see what happens if instead of rocking them, jiggling them, putting them in a carrier and walking around, putting them in a pram and pushing them around, or putting them in the car to sleep, you simply hold them in your loving arms while you are still and present. You may notice that any initial feelings start to build and build, and your baby moves from an agitated state into crying.

You can always stop listening at any time if you get worried that they do have an unmet need, and you could start moving them again. You could also compassionately listen to whatever feelings and thoughts show up for you when you're not moving them, and express those feelings to a Listening Partner or Aware Parenting instructor, to help you then be able to more comfortably listen to your baby's feelings.

If they are mobile, you might want to offer a *Loving Limit* to their movement. For example, if they are really agitated and are moving from one room to the next, you might close the door to the room *you are both in*, and say, "I'm not willing for us to leave the room sweetheart, because I don't think that's most helpful for you, and I'm here and I'm listening". If they show that they want to leave the room with you, you might repeat that. "I really hear that you want to go into the other room, sweetheart, and I'm not willing for us to do that right now. And I'm here and I'm listening". They might then start expressing the healing-feelings that the movement was suppressing.

And again, if at any time you are concerned that they are expressing a need, such as for agency and autonomy, you could open the door and follow them and observe their behaviour.

If that was indeed a need, you will observe that they are calm and relaxed in their body and they will be willing to make eye contact.

If, however, they are agitated while they move around, they are probably telling you that they do indeed have healing-feelings to express to you, and that the *Loving Limit* of the door being closed was preventing the movement *control pattern* and helping them express the underlying feelings.

> As always, it's only through your experimentation and observation that you can really see what's going on.

For example, how are they after you've rocked or jiggled them when they were crying? And what about if you are still and listen to their crying instead? Do you notice any differences in their eye contact, muscle relaxation or sleep that give you reassurance that the movement had been distracting them from feeling and expressing healing-feelings?

Dissociating with a dummy

You might decide to not give them a dummy when you normally would, and instead, hold them in your arms or on your lap (depending on their age) and listen to as much of their healing-crying as you are comfortable to listen to. If they signal that they want the dummy, you can again offer the *Loving Limit*. "I hear that you really want the dummy, and I'm not willing for you to have it at the moment, sweetheart, because I don't think that's the most helpful thing for you right now, and I'm right here and I'm listening". If you feel concerned that they might have an unmet need, you can always give the dummy back again, "I see you still have feelings, sweetheart, but I'm going to give you the dummy back now. I would love to listen to your feelings again soon". You might also want to share your feelings with someone else, which will support you to be able to listen to a larger percentage of their feelings as time goes on.

India, a parenting mentor in training to become an Aware Parenting instructor, and who uses Aware Parenting with children in her childcare setting, shares her experience with a dummy, sleep and Aware Parenting:

"I came across Aware Parenting when my baby was six months old. We had a soother/dummy/pacifier and it was clipped to her clothes. I was so anxious about it being there in case she cried. She was waking up every half an hour at night from four months of age and I was losing my mind. I read The Aware Baby *book and I hated it. I wanted to scream at this woman who was telling me to let my baby cry. I wanted to throw the book across the room! I can't remember what it was I read in it that resonated but thankfully something did. I experimented little by little with listening to my daughter cry in my arms until I felt comfortable and not afraid anymore – then I let her go for it and she cried in my arms for two hours. That night she slept for five hours straight for the first time ever. I was so joyous and in tears when I woke up and realised I had had more than one hour of sleep!!!*

My baby did exactly what Aletha described in the book. After her big cry she went into this happy, contented, tranquil state just staring at me and smiling and so happy. Then she drifted off to sleep so peacefully. When I reassessed her hunger cues as it describes in The Aware Baby *I realised that I'd been feeding her every time she niggled and she only fed for five minutes here and there on and off constantly. After realising her new cue I found she fed deeply! All the listening I did in between helped her become less hyperactive and sleep better for naps.*

Since then I've been hooked and every drop of information and support from the books and the community is sheer heaven. I LOVE exploring the workings of raw humanity and coming back into connection with our natural stress release processes. It has brought me so much healing after four decades of being lost in trauma. I finally feel free, peaceful, balanced and most importantly, normal. There is nothing wrong with me or my baby. We were just in pain. And I now know how we can release that pain. So joyous! I'm so in love with Aware Parenting, I share it everywhere I go. I love to spread the information and support I have gained from it to as many families as possible. What a transformative, insightful and wise approach Aletha Solter has created. I'm so grateful for her work and to all who enrich it".

Dissociating with thumb or finger sucking

Because this is something they are doing themselves, it's different to the *control patterns* where we are doing things to them, such as feeding them or giving them a dummy.

This means that we *don't* recommend ever taking a baby's thumb or fingers out of their mouth.

Instead, we can indicate to them that we welcome their feelings.

Before even working with a thumb-sucking *control pattern*, I like to invite parents to see it as a symptom, and to start by looking at the cause.

Here are the questions I generally ask:

- When did the thumb-sucking start? What was going on in the family at that time? Was there any increased stress?
- Did it start on any particular occasion? eg. when in the car or when you were on your phone? Is there anything you can change to offer more presence at those times?

- How are you feeling as the parent/s? (If our baby senses that we are frequently agitated, stressed, overwhelmed or dissociated, it is common for them to move into mild dissociation when they have healing-feelings to express.) [I invite you to put down any guilt sticks and see this as an invitation for more emotional support for you!] Helping ourselves become more emotionally present is one of the most important things if our baby is sucking their thumb, including through expressing any thoughts or feelings we have about their thumb-sucking to an empathic listener!
- Are you inadvertently frequently distracting your baby from their feelings, eg. by feeding them, rocking them, or offering toys when they have healing-feelings to express? Are you willing to offer loving presence instead of distracting them at those times?

Once you've understood and attended to the cause, there is a process that I have found helpful in supporting babies to reconnect with their healing-feelings when they are sucking their thumb:

1. Checking in with whether I really do have the emotional presence to listen to their feelings.
2. Connecting with the baby through touch – such as gently touching their hand.
3. Offering playfulness – such as 'blowing a raspberry' on their hand or making funny faces or sucking my thumb and popping it out of my mouth with a big loud 'pop' sound.
4. If they take their thumb or fingers out of their mouth to laugh in response to my playfulness, I might hold their hand gently. When supporting babies in this way, I put my thumb inside their fist at this part of the process and imagine love from my heart going into my hand, connecting with their hand, and going to their heart.
5. If they start crying while I'm holding their hand, *and they are not trying to desperately put it in their mouth*, I will keep holding it. This is a form of *Loving Limit* – I'm saying a no to them putting

their thumb or fingers in their mouth while saying yes to the feelings that were lying underneath the thumb or finger sucking. However, I'm also holding in mind the *balance of attention*, making sure that they are feeling enough emotional safety and presence for the expression of feelings to be healing. If they are *desperately* trying to get their thumb, fingers or hand back in their mouth, it tells us that *there isn't the balance of attention and they are not experiencing enough emotional safety to freely express the feelings*, in which case, I would let go of their hand so they can put it back in their mouth. If they are simply pulling or pushing a little bit against our hand, we can assume that there is the *balance of attention* and that they are experiencing the crying as healing.

Feyza, a doula and breastfeeding counsellor supporting infant mental health, who you've already heard from in this book, shares her experience of helping her baby when she started sucking her hand. You can see so clearly how much she was taking into account all of her observations of her daughter to make sense of what was going on:

"At one point, I was trying to better understand how to support my newborn when she had feelings built up, but she resorted to sucking her hand. It would be clear to me that she was not happy when she started crying, but then frantically put her hand in her mouth and started sucking it. She did this many times during a crying session. It got tiring for me to be there and present for her during this time because she seemed like she wanted to dissociate. When she sucked her hand, she would stop making eye contact and tense her body up before bursting into tears again.

I knew she was not hungry because I always made sure I fed her to the max before listening, and she even got spit ups after our long feeding. When she removed her hand from her mouth, she started crying again which suggested to me that the sucking was not comforting her. Lastly, when she showed this behaviour, I did try breastfeeding her to see if she was still hungry, but she did the same thing by sucking, then popping off to cry, then sucking again, etc. I also did not think there was any allergy because she only cried during the evening. During the day she breastfed and went back to sleep or became calm. If it were an allergy I thought that it would affect her all the time.

It was clear to me that she had feelings bubbling up, but she had a hard time crying in my arms. After consulting with Aware Parenting instructors in the free Facebook group, I gained some clarity as to why she may be sucking her hand. They suggested that she may be feeling my own emotional tension, and asked me whether I have a loving listener. That resonated with me. I am trying to let go of any feelings of shame that come up, but rather, to continue to stay present with her and show compassion for her even when she wants to dissociate, just as I'd want it to be done for me".

I had a similar experience with my son, which I'd love to share with you.

At four months old, he started sucking on his hand. Unlike with my daughter, I had been doing the majority of the listening to his feelings myself, because his Dad was by then working a lot. And I also listened to a much higher percentage of his healing-feelings than we did with my daughter, which meant that I listened to a lot of crying, especially because of his quick birth. When he started sucking on his hand when he was four months old, I connected in with myself and realised that I was getting burnt out from all the hours of listening to feelings I had been doing. We'd stayed in the bedroom for those four months, me focusing 100% on being with him and my daughter. When I realised the burnout, I chose to have a week where I was still listening to his feelings, but not as many of them, and I also started to go out a bit together, to meet my needs more. While we were out, he was more distracted from his feelings. After that week, I felt recharged and present again, and I went back to being more present with him. He stopped sucking on his hand, and never did it again.

Our babies live in the sea of our feelings and pick up on our emotional state. If we have feelings at the surface that we're suppressing or dissociating from, they will feel that, and may wait until we are more present again before expressing their feelings to us.

> *Self-Compassion Moment*
>
> How are you feeling, having read this? If your baby sucks their thumb, or even if you sucked your thumb as a baby or child, this information might help you connect with painful feelings. I invite you to put down any self-judgement sticks if your baby is or has sucked their thumb! If you did suck your thumb and your baby does too, you might find it particularly helpful to share your feelings, particularly if you experienced being told to stop or being judged or shamed for doing it. I'm sending you so much love and compassion if you do explore thumb sucking.

When working with parents, I will generally see thumb or finger sucking as a symptom, an indication of what is going on or what has happened in the past.

Sometimes that can be our own feelings we're suppressing, in other cases it might be, for example, when a baby is going in the car seat twice a day because their parent is taking an older child back and forth to school and they aren't getting to express their healing-feelings then. At other times it can be because a parent is unknowingly distracting their baby from healing-feelings. This symptom of thumb or finger sucking invites us to be an emotional detective, to work out what is really going on.

I will generally ask the parent when the baby's thumb or finger sucking started, and what else was going on in the family or for the parent/s at the time. They often have an 'aha' moment, as they make sense of why their baby wasn't feeling the emotional presence to express their feelings back then. Often it turns out that a parent was feeling more stressed than usual, or more distracted, perhaps using their phone more to dissociate from their feelings themselves. Again, this is why self-compassion is so important!

Attending to the cause of the thumb sucking, whatever that is, is far more likely to be helpful than just trying to stop a baby from sucking their thumb. That exploration might invite us to receive support, or do something that we love that lights us up, share our feelings with someone, or whatever will help us return to feeling more relaxed and present.

Map of indications that your baby probably has healing-feelings to express

Here are some clear ways you can tell that it's likely that your baby has healing-feelings to express:

- They're avoiding eye contact;
- When you are lovingly present and still with them, they start to cry;
- You are rocking or jiggling them and they start crying when you stop doing that;
- You are rocking or jiggling them for longer and longer as they get older;
- They had a dummy in their mouth and then drop it and start crying;
- They are sucking their thumb or fingers with a glazed look in their eyes;
- They are feeding on and off all evening;
- They move around a lot when they're feeding;
- They are feeding more and more frequently as they get older;
- They're taking longer and longer to get to sleep;

- They're waking up more and more frequently as they get older:
- They move around a lot in their sleep;
- They frequently wake up crying.

> *Self-Compassion Moment*
> How are you feeling, having read this chapter?
> Did you experience any 'aha' moments?
> Would you like to do anything differently as a result?
> Did you feel any uncomfortable feelings?
> If so, do you feel called to do some journaling, or reach out to a friend, Listening Partner or Aware Parenting instructor?

It's so understandable and natural to feel big feelings when reading about this information. I want to remind you that most of us grew up in a culture and family where needs-feelings and healing-feelings weren't differentiated, and healing-feelings weren't listened to. Changing core beliefs and putting into place new practices in a culture that doesn't support us to parent in ways that are most optimal for babies is bound to be hard. I'm sending you so much love and compassion on your journey of reading this book!

CHAPTER SEVEN

The relationship between sleep, needs and feelings

You might wonder what accumulated feelings from stress or trauma have to do with sleep, yet I invite you to reflect on your own experiences as we start answering that question.

Have you had times when you were worried about something or feeling really stressed and you found it hard to go to sleep, you woke up in the night and couldn't go back to sleep, or you woke up early, unable to go back to sleep although you were really tired?

Babies are very similar in that their sleep is deeply affected by how they feel – both in terms of needs-feelings and healing-feelings. Their sensations and emotions profoundly influence how relaxed they are and thus also the quality and quantity of sleep they have.

We can put ourselves in our baby's shoes to see this more clearly, and I invite you to do that now.

Imagine being a baby, with very few concepts about the world. If you're newborn, you don't have any sense of time, so being alone seems like forever. You don't have the understanding of what sleep is, nor the knowledge that if you are left alone, someone will return. Everything is new and so much is overwhelming.

From this perspective, let's look at the three things babies, children and adults need for peaceful sleep. I created this map as a shorthand way of understanding sleep from an Aware Parenting perspective.

The three things babies, children and adults need for peaceful sleep

1. To feel tired *(sleepy)*;
2. To feel connected *(closeness creating a sense of safety)*;
3. To feel relaxed *(by releasing any healing-feelings present)*.

1. To feel tired (ie. sleepy)

This may seem obvious, but if we're trying to get our baby to sleep and they are not tired, it will be difficult for them to go to sleep. Sleepiness/tiredness is a needs-feeling, signalling a need for sleep. We can often see this if a baby has red eyes, rubs their eyes or is wanting to cuddle up and be close.

The next piece of information I'm going to share about tiredness is one of the major differences between Aware Parenting and other parenting approaches.

> If a baby is tired and is 'fussing' or crying, the tiredness is not the direct cause of the crying, nor is tiredness painful for them.

If this is the case, *why* do some babies cry *when* they are tired?

I'd love to explain! When babies are tired, their natural healing and relaxation responses come into play – to cry in loving arms, expressing and releasing healing-feelings. This is an inbuilt part of their stress-release process and is designed to bring about homeostasis – a state of relaxation – so that they can sleep peacefully and restoratively.

This understanding fits beautifully within a somatic perspective. Relaxation is required for restful sleep, so of course our bodies have a system to release stress and tension and provide deep relaxation and thus the most restorative sleep. Our bodies are so wise! I will be sharing more about this relaxation process in point three of the map.

The more a baby gets to express healing-feelings and release tension before they go to sleep, the more relaxed they feel in their bodies. As you've read earlier in the book, this relaxation is a truer, deeper, more long-lasting form of relaxation than the calm that occurs when we distract a baby from the feelings that bubble up when they are tired. When we distract a baby from their feelings so that they are calm enough to go to sleep, they are in a mild form of dissociation rather than a true state of relaxation. The quality of calm is not as deep and they are likely to wake up again when they move into a lighter phase of sleep, when healing-feelings bubble up again to be expressed.

In comparison, if we cooperate with their natural healing and relaxation response, this deeper form of relaxation means that it's easier for them to go to sleep and stay asleep until either they have had enough sleep, or they become hungry, whichever comes first. We'll talk more about this in the section on relaxation.

The same confusion we talked about earlier in the book can arise here – where we've been taught to interpret healing-feelings as being needs-feelings.

If we think that the baby is crying because the tiredness is causing the crying, of course we will want to help our baby to go to sleep as soon as possible, to meet the need we think is there and remove the apparent reason for the crying. But if we see that these feelings aren't needs-feelings at all, but are healing-feelings, we interpret things in a very different light.

> The feelings are not *caused* by the tiredness but *facilitated* by it, so they can be expressed and released to *support restful sleep.*

When we understand this, our aim is to cooperate with our baby's innate desire to express these feelings so that they can feel really relaxed, which means that they will be able to sleep much more peacefully and restfully and for as long as they need.

I'd love to tell you about my experience with sleep and healing-feelings.

Once I understood the power of crying-in-arms, I focused on prioritising listening to my daughter's healing-feelings before sleep. Connection and feelings were my focus. I didn't focus on sleep, I didn't worry about her sleep or how many hours she was sleeping. Instead, I put my attention on meeting as many of her needs and listening to as many of her feelings as I could. (And as you will have read in earlier chapters, I wasn't listening to as high a percentage of her healing-feelings as I thought I was). After experimenting with this for a while, particularly when she was nine months old, I found that sleep came easily as a result and continued to be easy throughout her childhood, and my son's too. They slept long hours and slept in, often until 8 or 8.30am. The idea that babies and children need to wake several times in the night for the first few years really doesn't need to be the case with Aware Parenting.

Caroline shares her experience of the transformation in sleep she experienced when she started practicing Aware Parenting:

"I was in a desperate place – a walking zombie – as my son woke every hour by the time he was six months. I didn't want to let him cry alone but neither dummy nor boob nor anything else I tried was helping. A friend recommended the Aware Parenting Babies Course *with Marion and Helena [Mooney, another Aware Parenting instructor]. And I learned that sleep issues are just a symptom of accumulated feelings.*

I started the course because of sleep and continued it because it changed the way I saw my baby's emotions. I connected more with him, I enjoyed him more, I connected more with myself and my partner and yes, better sleep followed pretty quickly".

This is a completely different way of looking at a baby's behaviour in relation to sleep, both before naps, and particularly in the evening. Rather than 'witching hour' or the invitation for long periods of rocking, singing, feeding, or giving a dummy, we are invited to simply be present with our baby, hold them in our loving arms and listen to their healing-feelings. Again, we will talk more about this in point three.

2. To feel connected

I have used the phrase 'feeling connected' for brevity, but connection is actually a need. Babies have a core need for connection and closeness and it's vital that that need is met for them to be able to have a relaxed sleep. Let's think about why this is, while holding in mind our evolutionary past as hunter-gatherers. Since babies cannot fight or flee, they need us to carry them away from danger or protect them from it. So (particularly before a baby can crawl), they need to be held or need to feel us right next to them to know that they are safe enough to go to sleep.

After they begin crawling, when babies have some capacity to flee from danger, they can't crawl as fast as an adult can run, and have very little capacity to fight, so they are still highly dependent on us to stay safe, so it's natural that they still require connection to feel safe enough to sleep. If they do sleep away from us, it's important that they are able to get to us, rather than being in a cot or in a room with a door closed. If you think about it, fleeing is their major way to escape from danger, and if they are in a cot, they cannot do that. This is why, if our babies are away from us and cannot get to us (either because they are not yet crawling, or because they are mobile but are in a cot), attending to them *as soon as they call out* is very important.

Self-Compassion Moment

I invite you to put down any guilt sticks if you have put your baby in a cot in a different room. However old they are now, if you want to offer them more closeness before sleep and/or during sleep, you can offer them reparative experiences.

Some parents start co-sleeping with their older baby who has been in a cot since birth, once they learn about Aware Parenting.

I also want to remind you that the practice of babies sleeping alone, including in cots, in separate rooms, is also a recent one and was spread around the world through industrialisation, colonisation and The Disconnected Domination Culture. In most Indigenous and traditional cultures, babies and small children sleep in the same place as their parents, often with the rest of the family or community.

If your baby is in a cot in a separate room, I invite you to listen in to see how you have been affected by The DDC to make that choice. You have probably seen movies with babies in a cot in a nursery, read books, seen adverts, as well as seeing friends and relatives do this. Most of all, you may have experienced this yourself. Cultural conditioning is powerful.

And, as you read this book, I invite you to *listen in to yourself and your own views and values*. If your baby is in a cot in a separate room, is that what you want? In this book, I am inviting you to tune in to yourself and listen to your baby, free from the confines of Disconnected Domination Culture conditioning.

If you've co-slept with your baby and have been judged by others for doing so, I want to remind you that you've come up against those people's cultural conditioning. From a Marion Method perspective, The Disconnected Domination Culture wants to keep babies and parents separate, because disconnection is necessary for domination to occur. The DDC keeps those beliefs in place through shaming and judgement of those who don't do that. I invite you to be unwilling to be hurt by those judgements, and to keep on listening to yourself and to what most deeply resonates for you in your parenting.

I also want to remind you that Aware Parenting is a form of attachment-style parenting, which understands that closeness is one of the core needs of babies and children and supports you to do that in whatever way that you can, while also acknowledging and honouring the importance of getting your own needs met, particularly in The DDC where families do not receive the support they need and so attachment-style parenting is going to be way more difficult than if we lived in a community of 20 or 30 or 100 people.

I have worked with many parents who wanted to stop co-sleeping because their baby was wriggling and moving around a lot during sleep. When they understood that this wriggling was caused by accumulated healing-feelings, and listened to more of those feelings, their baby became more relaxed at night and they continued co-sleeping.

Similarly, other parents were going to stop co-sleeping because they thought that was the next step when their toddler was waking several times a night and breastfeeding. Here's one mother's experience with this.

Sammy did my *Sound Sleep and Secure Attachment with Aware Parenting Course 1.0* several years ago. One day, she wrote to the Course Facebook group about moving her son into his own bed.

"We are planning to night wean in a few weeks ... Leo currently sleeps beside me and he is now 16 months old (feeding multiple times per night ... I think because boobie is right there) and it's been an amazing journey being right by his side. I now feel he is ready for a bit more independence and some of his own sacred space for sleeping and I feel night weaning will make this easier ... Has anyone done night weaning and moving bubba into their own bed? I would love any pearls of wisdom please if you have any to share ..."

In response to Sammy, I suggested that his waking might be more to do with feelings, and that instead of stopping breastfeeding at night and putting him in his own room, she might want to focus on listening to more feelings instead.

A few days later, she responded, telling us she'd put that into practice, and wasn't going to be 'night weaning' or putting him in his own room after all!

"I took Leo into his room for nap time; he is good at distracting himself from his feelings so I did the crying dance. *He cried, he laughed, he pushed me and I turned it into a power reversal game which he thought was hilarious and then when he kept distracting himself with the pillow case or the nearby curtain or jumping on the bed, I used lots of* Loving Limits *and that helped him to release. I did feel a deep sense of connection to him this whole time. He eventually relaxed and fell asleep at 1.15pm. His previous feeds were at 3.30am and 10.30am. This is much less than normal. Plus he enjoyed a delicious breaky yesterday of hempseed pancakes – he couldn't get enough and normally he isn't really interested in food.*

He slept from for an hour and a half and on waking we had lunch together where he ate a good amount of food. Then we played and connected all afternoon. He had boobie at 3.45pm and again before his bath at 5.30pm – this was his last boobie before bed. Then he did high-octane play with his Dad and I disappeared for 20 minutes for a micro-me moment. Leo's Dad lay beside him after story time in the bed and he went to sleep easily and relaxed with not much of a release at 6.45pm. He slept soundly with a few tiny peeps that didn't need much for him to go back to sleep – really just a loving presence and he was asleep within 20 seconds. He slept deeply until 12.30am. Amazing! That was almost six hours of deep, sound, rejuvenating sleep in-a-row! (Normally Leo would have had boobie about three times in that period and about four wake ups.)

I am very excited about this development. Here is what we have learnt:

- *Releasing with crying in the day is easier than in the night.*
- *At this age (16 months) Leo was eating at most eight teaspoons of food and I now think it was because he was always full of milk.*
- *I was using boobie to 'shut him up' (inadvertently).*
- *Attachment play including power reversal games and 'Present Time[19]' are invaluable tools to support connection and healing for the WHOLE family.*
- *My cup needs to be full; get as many macro-me and micro-me moments as possible.*
- *Delete the Facebook app from my phone – Facebook never EVER fills my cup (except for The Aware Parenting page ☺).*
- *Express my own feelings regularly (I was pretty good at that – ask my hubby!).*
- *Loving Limits are amazing (I realise I was 'avoiding conflict' and letting Leo do 'everything' and trying to be a carefree mum but now I see that Loving Limits create so much connection and trust. Even if it doesn't feel like it in the moment!)*

In the short time we have been doing Aware Parenting, we all feel more connected as a family and there is so much more balance and more happiness. Leo is more and more happy to have independent play now too! So I doubt we will have to 'night wean' at all, let's keep going on this path of release and deep connection in the day and all will be more balanced.

So much thanks to you, Marion for this amazing work you do. This path hasn't been easy ... There have been no examples in my past that I can call on in my family or others where this sort of parenting was implemented. My husband reminds me 'when Leo was a newborn it was YOUR mum that taught us about jiggling/rocking/boob to quiet

---

19 A term I created to describe offering our full presence to our baby.

our baby'. This was done in love (of course). The thought was if the baby cries you aren't meeting their needs! We are so beyond that and thank goodness! We are very grateful! Thank you Marion for connecting me to the mama I sooooo wanted to be! P.S. I love your 'Sound Sleep' course!

P.P.S. I am actually so proud of myself for my commitment and patience these past few days – being a mum is definitely the most challenging permanent position I have ever had, and now I feel like my deepest desires about being the mum I want to be are coming to fruition!!!! YIPPPEEEE! I am also so proud of my amazing hubby for his unwavering commitment to Aware Parenting. I am so glad he joined me on this sleep course. It was a push – he kept saying, 'How about you do the course and tell me what you learn!' and I said, 'No, we are parents together, so we do this together'. I am so glad he listened ... it REALLY helps to be on the same page."

Self-Compassion Moment

I wonder how you feel when you read this, and what you think?

Sammy's experience is one I have heard many times. Parents thinking that their baby or toddler will sleep more if they are moved to a separate bed, but then when they have more support themselves, and offer more connection, play and listening to their baby's feelings, they find that they can have ongoing closeness and restful sleep.

I know we're talking about sleep, but I want to respond to what Sammy said about her toddler and milk and food. I have also seen this many times over the years. When we are breastfeeding a toddler a lot, they are less likely get the chance to feel even a slight sense of hunger, so they often have very little interest in food. I sometimes think it's like us, if we were continuously drinking smoothies, we might never want to eat a meal. And of course, I support you in trusting your toddler's timing in relation to food. However, for many parents who are concerned that their toddler has no interest in food, understanding this can make a big difference.

I've also heard many parents sharing that they think that their toddlers wake up a lot at night if they are breastfed and co-sleeping because they can 'smell the milk'. Some parents then do things that they really don't want to do – such as giving up co-sleeping or breastfeeding or both.

However, it really is possible to keep breastfeeding and co-sleeping and get plenty of restful sleep, when we're listening to enough healing-feelings.

I also want to remind you that co-sleeping can be much harder in a culture that doesn't support it, where cots are seen as the 'normal' thing to do, where there's lots of advertising and media input on the necessity of cots, and where there's still a lot of judgement and fear in relation to co-sleeping.

You may find lots of thoughts and feelings coming up for you when you think about co-sleeping. Perhaps the thought that your baby will become a child who always wants to sleep in your bed. Perhaps you fear that you will be judged by your friends or family. Perhaps fears come up from your own childhood – if you were in a cot and left alone to cry, those feelings might show up if you think about co-sleeping with your baby. If you do notice feelings showing up, I invite you to reach out to a Listening Partner or Aware Parenting instructor, including me, or Aletha Solter herself, for a consultation.

If you do choose to co-sleep, of course I encourage you to do that in a way that is safe and to read up on all that is needed to be known about co-sleeping safely. I recommend James McKenna's work on safe co-sleeping.

I also invite you to think of a baby's needs for closeness and how you can meet them as being on a spectrum, with the most physical, visual, auditory and emotional closeness on one side, and the least on the other. Here's how we could look at that spectrum:

The way they are *most* likely to experience their closeness needs being met is if they are being held by you when they go to sleep (or lying right next to you) and if they are close when they are sleeping, so they can touch you if they need to.

However, for many reasons, you might not want to do that. If this is the case, you might want to put them in a bassinet close to where you are once they are asleep, and then wait until you go to bed to have them in the bed with you. You might do that until they first wake up.

Along that spectrum, you might choose to have your baby:

- next to you (with two mattresses on the floor);
- on a sidecar cot right next to your bed;
- in a bassinet or cot right next to your bed;
- in a bassinet or a cot in your room, so that they can see you from where they are or can hear you;
- in a cot in another room.

In terms of the closeness spectrum, the more they can feel your touch, the more their connection needs are met. If they can't touch you, then at least being able to see you or hear you will meet their needs more than not being able to sense or connect with you at all.

Being in a cot as a toddler can not only create feelings of loneliness, it can also lead to feelings of powerlessness. Once a baby is mobile, being in a cot means that they cannot get to us if they need to be close, even if we aim to respond promptly. If you don't want to co-sleep, once they can crawl, you might want to have them sleep on a mattress on the floor in your room (and have your room toddler-proof) so they can get to you if they need closeness. If you really want to have them in another room, once they can crawl, perhaps you might have them on a mattress on the floor in a room that is safe for them, where they can get to you if they need to be close to you.

> *Self-Compassion Moment*
>
> I wonder how you feel when you read this?
>
> Would you like to change anything about your baby's sleeping arrangements?
>
> I invite you to remember that you get to choose what you do!
>
> And that you can experiment and find a way that fits for everyone in your family.
>
> I invite you to listen in to yourself and what resonates with you, and what would work for everyone in your family. For example, if you have cats or dogs or other animals roaming in your home, that's something else to hold in mind in terms of safety.

Let's go back to our original list of three things. We've been talking about point two for all this time!

So, babies need to feel tired *and* connected to be able to sleep restfully. But that's not all.

What if they are clearly tired and you are holding them, but they are not going to sleep? What's going on here?

This is where parents may think that their baby is 'fighting sleep'.

However, from an Aware Parenting perspective, it simply means that they are not feeling *relaxed* enough to go to sleep. We'll talk more about that in point 3. Before I do that, I'd love to turn to another question.

What happens if a baby is tired and is put into a cot alone and *does* go to sleep? How do they go to sleep, if babies need closeness to be able to sleep peacefully?

To understand what's going on here, we need to return to the topic of dissociation.

> *Self-Compassion Moment*
> If you have put your baby in a cot and left them, I invite you to be deeply compassionate with yourself and drop any guilt sticks. It's never too late to do things differently, to repair past experiences and to listen to their feelings so they can heal.

Babies can mildly dissociate from loneliness, fear or other feelings that they might feel when their need for connection isn't met before sleep. They might suck their thumb or on a dummy, or they might clutch on to a soft toy or blanket, or they might get into a very particular position, or they might tense their muscles or simply just dissociate. That way, they don't feel those needs-feelings, and they don't feel any healing-feelings that might be bubbling up, and the dissociation helps them feel calm enough to sleep. They might wake again, even several times, and will generally do the same thing again to again feel calm enough to go back to sleep again.

3. To feel relaxed

If a baby is tired and we are doing all kinds of things to help them feel relaxed – jiggling, walking, feeding, singing – and they are taking a long time to go to sleep, in Aware Parenting we don't see them as 'fighting sleep'. In fact, what is happening from an Aware Parenting perspective is that we are probably fighting their natural healing and relaxation processes. They need us to cooperate with those processes for them to work.

In The Disconnected Domination Culture we are taught to not trust babies and their innate knowing, so we think we need to do things to them to help them feel relaxed, rather than trusting that they know how to feel relaxed and are trying to do that through crying in our arms or the *crying dance* and it is us who are working against that.

It's a really different way of looking at sleep, isn't it?

> *Self-Compassion Moment*
>
> I want to remind you of two things. The first is to put down any guilt sticks that you might be picking up. The second is to remember the spectrum of Aware Parenting. If you love feeding your baby to sleep and really want to keep doing that, I so support you in that. There are no have-to's here.
>
> My intention instead is to offer you this information to see if it resonates with you. If it does, then I invite you to listen in to whether you would like to change anything about how you are with your baby and their sleep. You get to choose, always, what you do in your parenting!

Babies feel deeply relaxed through expressing healing-feelings from experiences that day or from the past, including from their birth. The kind of relaxation they can feel after crying-in-arms has a very different quality to the kind of apparent calmness that comes from us doing things to sidestep those feelings.

If you've ever tried really hard to tiptoe away from a sleeping baby, only to find that they wake up with the slightest noise or movement, or tried to transfer a sleeping baby from one place to another, being as quiet as you can, you'll know what I mean about that apparent calmness.

There's a big difference between relaxation and dissociation.

As adults, we know that from our own felt experience too. Relaxation is an *embodied presence* and an enjoyable experience. Dissociation might also feel kind of *pleasant*, but we don't feel *present* in our body.

So, a baby who is sucking on their thumb, fingers or a dummy and staring into space might fall asleep that way but isn't relaxed enough to sleep soundly or for very long – because they are mildly dissociating, and that dissociation tends to wear off once they stop sucking. In comparison, if a baby has expressed a chunk of healing-feelings before bed in our loving arms, and they fall asleep and we wait for about 10 minutes until they fall into a deeper sleep, they will generally be sound asleep. We can move around and make noise and they are unlikely to wake up. We can move them from one place to another without them waking up. This is a deeper level of relaxation and sleep.

I have so often heard from parents who tell me what a difference this makes to their parenting, for example, if they want to leave their baby to sleep and get something done, or if their baby is asleep in one place and they want to move them somewhere else. The depth of sleep is quite different when a baby feels that true and deep quality of relaxation.

Have you ever experienced being restless in your sleep, tossing and turning, worrying about something, and woken up not feeling very refreshed by your sleep? This can help us understand what our baby might be experiencing.

Sarah Louise shares her journey of understanding sleep and Aware Parenting, just a week after she restarted listening to her baby's healing-feelings:

"I have a five month old baby boy. I first came to know about Aware Parenting when he was a few weeks old and I heard about the concept of 'crying in loving arms'. This made a lot of sense to us that this was the natural way for a baby to process and release stress and in the moments when nothing seemed to be settling him and his basic

needs were met we would stop our crazed (honestly, crazed!) attempts to calm him and just looked at him lovingly while I held him and he cried. He would cry deeply before relaxing into me and calming completely. I was sold, I ordered The Aware Baby *by Aletha Solter and queued some podcasts to listen to and learn more. He was a calm and beautiful baby to be around who slept well, waking generally twice a night for a feed and settling easily back to sleep.*

As is often the case, the book sat unread for the next few months. I essentially forgot about this concept of crying-in-arms as my baby was bright, happy and alert. We were on cloud nine with our baby.

From three months he began waking more often and during the day seemed unsettled or upset easily. He was very active and curious and we put it down to him being a busy boy with lots of big feelings. He had the happiest energy a lot of the time and a beautiful personality but was becoming increasingly sensitive.

From four months his sleep went completely downhill – I was not one to count wakings or focus on this so I accepted it as biologically normal for his age and continued on as he was still happy most of the time and was developing perfectly.

By five months old his sensitivity was increasing and I was at a loss. He started waking 10-15 minutes into naps and two hourly or more at night. I noticed lots of agitation and that he was arching his back in frustration regularly. He was frustrated while breastfeeding and would unlatch and cry repeatedly.

Not sleeping was one thing – but he was now seeming more unhappy. I couldn't shake the feeling I was doing something wrong. We would work so hard to help him sleep and even harder to keep him happy during the day. I was highly responsive to his needs as I understood them, I breast fed and co-slept when he needed, contact napped[20] and

---

20 Please note that this isn't a term used in Aware Parenting.

baby wore regularly. I pumped extra to top up his feeds in case he was hungry. We got out in the fresh air every day and both me and his Dad poured lots of love and energy into our play and interactions with him. I would attribute his fussiness to teething or a developmental leap but I knew deep down it was something more.

For a week I repeatedly said to my partner, "I am doing something wrong. I am missing something." Like any supportive person he reassured me I was doing a great job and our baby was healthy and happy a lot of the time, but I couldn't shake the feeling that I was missing something and my boy needed more. I was filled with self doubt and becoming anxious and frustrated.

A week into his fifth month, I listened to Marion's Q & A episode about sleep on The Aware Parenting Podcast. *It was such an aha moment. I couldn't believe I hadn't considered that every time he cried and I would rock, distract, pat, feed or use a dummy that I was stopping him from expressing his feelings. I thought I was being attuned to his needs. This was building up in his body as accumulated stress which was showing in his behaviour and temperament.*

That night I tried crying in loving arms. He cried deeply and arched his back repeatedly for about ten minutes and then relaxed and softened and began a quiet babble as he looked in my eyes. He gradually drifted off to sleep, his arms fell above his head in total relaxation and he did little smiles as he drifted off. I was reminded of his behaviour as a newborn. That night he only woke twice to feed. I couldn't believe it.

Over the coming days I read and absorbed as much as I could about this approach and applied what I learned. What is incredible is that it is not a technique, it is a whole new way of understanding babies and their innate knowing and capacity. It has brought a whole new layer of joy to being his mum.

I have felt so deeply connected to him and know I am doing what is right for us now. He has become so easy going and joyful and when he is not, there is almost always a clear reason. For the first time since he was about six weeks old, he will drift off happily to sleep in the pram or in my arms when we are out and about. He is relaxed in his body and not easily fazed by minor things like someone talking loudly near him or the dog barking occasionally.

He falls asleep without any 'aids' like white noise or the dummy and does 4-5 hour stretches, waking to feed.

He is CUDDLY and more affectionate than he ever was before. He generally breastfeeds calmly until he is full. Nap schedules and even wake windows are gone as we go by his cues and it is falling into a lovely, still relatively predictable pattern. If needed I am generally able to move him from my bed to his cot, car to cot or pram to car without disrupting a nap.

I can't believe that it was only just over a week ago that I nearly cried when I realised I had left the dummy at home and sat in my car with white noise blaring through the speakers to help him finish a short nap in the car as moving him would not be an option. Just that short time ago, I needed the dummy or white noise through Bluetooth in the car to help him go to sleep in the car and would never have dared interrupt a nap.

Now I can trust that he will sleep when he needs and if he is deeply asleep a bit of noise around him or anything like that doesn't disrupt him.

Things have changed completely – literally overnight. It's incredible, the change that has happened in a short time. I have tingles thinking about it and feel soooo grateful to have found this and be able to relax into motherhood and learn from my baby. For added context, we had a traumatic birth and a car accident (no injury, just scary) at four weeks old. There was definitely some catch up crying and accumulated stress.

The real moment of bliss for me was having a day time nap in the sunroom together, sunshine glaring through on us and my lovely boy snuggled into me. The dog even jumped up on the bed and it didn't disrupt him. When he woke up he looked so relaxed and looked in my eyes and smiled with loving eyes as if to say – yes mama, this is what I needed all along!

Sleep is really just the added bonus to this way of fully connecting with and understanding my son."

Waking soon after crying-in-arms

What is going on if you *do* listen to your baby express their feelings in your loving arms before they go to sleep, and they fall asleep and you wait for a while and then put them down, and they wake up straight away?

I remember when I first experienced this a few times with my daughter and I felt frustrated. However, after a while I worked out that she did that when I hadn't supported her to express a *complete* chunk of feelings.

What do I mean by a complete chunk? I'll give you an example.

Remember we talked about how babies will often reach a crescendo of intense crying, and then the volume and intensity will decrease? If we are newer to Aware Parenting and perhaps more uncomfortable with feelings, or perhaps we have less emotional presence to listen that day or are just wanting to get something else done, or we just think that they've expressed all the feelings that they need to, we may see them moving out of the cry and looking sleepy and think that they have finished.

But often, babies can go through another or several more crying cycles, ramping up again to more intensity, and quieting down again. Sometimes they need reassurance from us that we are still listening and are willing to listen to more of those cycles. We might ask them, "I'm still listening. Do you have any more to tell me?" We might also change their position and offer more eye contact. That might help with the *balance of attention* for them to express more feelings.

Once I realised this and understood what was going on for my daughter, I then listened to more crying cycles and stayed with the process so she could express a complete chunk of her feelings. I then found that if I did want to get up and do something while she was napping or sleeping, I could wait about 10 minutes or so and place her somewhere safe and she would continue sleeping.

The same can be the case if a baby often wakes up after one sleep cycle – which can generally be about 45 minutes. When they move into lighter sleep, the healing-feelings near the surface call to be expressed and they wake up again. This can happen if we haven't listened to any feelings, or even sometimes if we've listened to some feelings but not a whole chunk of feelings. Those feelings are still there, ready to be expressed.

Sometimes (but rarely, because babies have so many healing-feelings to express!) babies will have expressed all the feelings they needed to already that day, in which case we just need to hold them in our arms when they are tired and they can fall asleep without us 'doing' anything to them.

In fact, you might have experienced that when your baby was a newborn, particularly if they didn't experience much birth stress or trauma. Before they have accumulated many feelings, they generally feel relaxed in their bodies and thus only need the tiredness and connection elements to go to sleep because they are already deeply relaxed.

I wonder if you've noticed that shift over time, from your baby being more relaxed and not needing much to go to sleep, but as they get older you need to do more and more and it taking longer and longer for them to go to sleep?

Jess, an experienced early childhood teacher, shares about how different her experience was between her first baby and her second baby's sleep, before and after Aware Parenting. She shares:

"I found The Aware Parenting Podcast *with my second daughter and started to practice Aware Parenting when she was around six months old. I noticed a huge difference in her sleep at around nine months old when I listened to her feelings. She would have a big cry/release with me before she fell asleep for the night. If I rushed her emotional release by trying to distract her because it was going for a long time or if I breastfeed her to sleep and cut the releasing short she would just wake multiple times through the night and continue her release then. In contrast, I noticed how when she had finished expressing her feelings with me listening she would relax and sleep so deeply."*

Sommer, a student doula, also shares about how sleep changed dramatically once she learnt about Aware Parenting:

"I noticed a big difference in my baby and our family after crying-in-arms. He lived on me from day one and didn't like sleeping anywhere else, which was fine during the day but trickier at night where he would sleep in small bursts. Then his day sleeps started shortening and shortening until he really wasn't getting the number of hours a small babe needs. One day, after he'd been awake for about 10hrs at maybe three or four months, I called Lael [Stone co-host with me of The Aware Parenting Podcast *for episodes 1-123]. She explained about crying-in-arms.*

After hanging up the phone I rapid-fire explained it to my bemused husband, over the screams of our baby. We all sat on the couch, I held our baby and my husband held me. I softly repeated calming phrases which became quite meditative and soothing for all of us. After 20 minutes or so Nico (my son) fell asleep for six hrs. After that night I stopped with the rocking and bouncing and singing and shushing. I let him cry in my arms while I spoke softly to him. It was so much more relaxing for everyone and helped Nico off to sleep immediately after."

What happens during the day affects what happens at night

How we respond to our baby's needs and feelings – particularly in relation to feeding and crying – affects what happens at night, in the following ways:

1. **Feeding.** If a baby is also getting to express plenty of healing-feelings, I have found that there is a relationship between the gaps between feeds during the day and how long a baby tends to sleep at night. Many babies will sleep for the amount of time in between feeds in the day plus approximately an extra two hours. My hypothesis is that they are using less energy during the night than in the daytime, hence they don't get hungry again for that longer period. So, if you want to help your baby sleep for longer, another thing you can do is gradually increase the length of time between feeds in the daytime, giving them time to increase and adjust how much milk they are taking in, and of course making sure you always feed them when they are hungry. That way, they will also go for longer during the night, unless they have lots of feelings to tell you. Added to what I already shared in the chapter on hunger, this is another reason why longer gaps between feeds can be helpful. And as always, I invite you to listen to yourself, observe your baby, experiment, and see what is most a fit for your family.

2. **Crying.** During the night, there is more quiet and stillness, which generally means less distraction from feeling healing-feelings. Whatever feelings we have distracted our baby from in the daytime will often come up to be heard in the evening and

then during the night. The more feelings that are not being heard in the day, the harder it will be for them to go to sleep and the more likely it will be that they wake up in the night. Again, this waking isn't a sign that something is wrong (unless at times the baby is unwell or is in pain). In fact, it is a sign that their body is working beautifully – trying to express healing-feelings that need to be released. You may like to consider this reframe: something isn't wrong, in fact it is a sign of the release process working the way it is meant to.

But you may say, "I *am* listening to their feelings during the day!" And I honour *everything* you are doing. I know that you are doing so much. And I know that this requires so much of us, to listen!

So, why do some babies and children still wake up even if we are listening to their feelings?

Well, it can often be because we really *underestimate* quite how much babies and children feel. It can be hard for us to really imagine how many feelings they have, how deeply they feel things and how incredibly affected they are by what happens to them.

So, what tends to happen, especially practicing Aware Parenting as the first generation and first time around, is that we listen to some of their feelings, but not as many as need to be heard in order for them to feel deeply relaxed enough to sleep.

Chiara, an Aware Parenting instructor in Australia, shares about how she came to Aware Parenting after her baby was waking very frequently, and the mammoth change she saw in his sleep and many other things once she started listening to his healing-feelings. She also describes how much he needed to cry.

"I'm a mother of a 19-year-old girl and a 17-year-old boy. My 19-year-old daughter was a really dreadful sleeper and would wake through the night every hour practically from day one after birth. She would also quite often be awake at about two or three in the morning for a couple of hours. I was a single parent – I still am a single parent, so I didn't have, and I don't have family here to support me so I just put up with it and led a life of complete sleep deprivation. Luckily I had a friend who was going through the same things, so we would call each other up all the time and keep sleep diaries and I just knew that I didn't want to do any form of sleep training, no matter all the euphemisms they used.

Then when she was nearly three, I gave birth to my son, who was an even worse sleeper, and he would wake every 45 minutes. And the thing with him is when he was four months old he was really fat – he was really big. People kept telling me in the attachment parenting world, "No you can't overfeed a breastfed baby, you can't," and I had been going through some really stressful stuff with family court and some awful stuff with my daughter's sister on her father's side – she was dying of a brain tumour aged one and a half – so it was really high stress times. And here I had this beautiful fat really healthy amazing looking child, very bright in every way – but he was waking all the time and feeding a lot through the night. I just put up with it as I didn't know any alternative and I certainly wasn't going to let him cry it out or do any of the things that anyone in the mainstream was suggesting, so I just sort of gritted my teeth and went through it.

But the trouble with him is that – my daughter didn't do this – he was refluxing terribly, and so after many feeds was throwing it up (and there was a joke, because he's called Omri so we would call him Omri Vomri) and it was really inconvenient! Not only that, I felt really sorry for him because it must be awful to vomit after every feed. I could smell it was quite acidic and that would irritate him but I just did not know what to do. I tried – I spent a fortune going to naturopaths, I tried all sorts of remedies. I thought it was zinc deficiency, I thought it was something that was wrong with me. I was told the second child often has this because their digestive system is compromised, and I don't know... blah blah blah. Until that amazing fateful day when I was looking through Kindred Magazine *that someone had given me and I saw a tiny little advert of Marion Rose's and it said, "Do you need help with sleep?" and I literally remember this advert jumping out at me and for some reason I called Marion straight away and we had our first consultation and my life changed forever after that. Marion reaffirmed what I really deep down knew – I just couldn't bring myself to allow my child to cry, because I was so programmed to think that a crying child is in pain and in trouble and we need to do everything in our power to soothe those feelings and so I would jiggle and bounce and distract and feed and feed and feed.*

I remember the first time I allowed him to cry in my arms and I timed it – it was seven minutes, and it was probably the longest seven minutes of my life. And after only seven minutes he actually stopped. I remember this so clearly, he stopped crying and his skin looked different and his eyes were sparkling and he actually made this profound eye contact with me – he looked to me like – you know when they say that they look right into your soul? He looked right into my soul and he let out this almighty, all body, giant sigh. It's funny, I'm not a Buddhist at all, but the closest thing I can describe is that he was a little fat Buddha; he was so serene and Buddha-like after that, and I noticed it throughout the day. He was so different and less agitated in his body. His little fists let go and he slept really well.

Literally from that moment on I knew that I'd found the Holy Grail. It was really hard for me to continue to listen to him crying. It was something I really had to re-learn and I'm so grateful for the support Marion gave me and my friend Joss at the time, who I called up straight away (and Breeda and Karen as well). And so we also have supported each other through this. I knew there was no going back after that moment. I started to also notice he just was sleeping so much better every night. Eventually after a couple of months he was doing sometimes three hour cries and they would hit a crescendo and then they would die out again and then he'd start again. Sometimes I did stop him from crying because it was the middle of the night and I was worried about neighbours hearing it or worried about my daughter waking up. But it was nothing short of miraculous and I remember that so well.

I'm literally every day grateful for finding that advert and finding this modality and I'm still learning about it 17 years later. I have incredible teenagers as a result who are really centred and really know themselves, and emotionally so intelligent, and I know it's because of finding that advert when he was four months old."

Listening before sleep or listening during the night?

If a baby wakes up during the night and they are clearly waking up to express healing-feelings, many parents ask whether they 'should' listen then and there, rather than distract the baby. What I want to remind you is that there are no 'shoulds' and that you get to choose. Sometimes babies do seem to need to express feelings at a certain time of night – such as if there was a particularly traumatic part of their birth that happened at two in the morning and they wake every night at two to express the feelings that they experienced then.

However, often it's simply that they are waking because they didn't get to express enough feelings during the day, or particularly in the evening, and so they are waking up to express them when they move into lighter sleep and aren't being distracted from their feelings. In this case, we might choose to listen in the middle of the night, or we might see this as an invitation to focus on listening to more feelings before sleep, particularly focusing on supporting the big cries and not stopping them before they've expressed the whole chunk of feelings. Most people tend to prefer listening in the evening rather than the middle of the night!

The bigger the percentage of feelings we listen to during the day and evening and the more they get to complete whole crying cycles, expressing their feelings fully, the less they will wake up at night to express the feelings then.

Helping your baby to sleep for longer stretches at night

From an Aware Parenting perspective, there are at least five things that might be waking your baby up in the night.

1. They are hungry;
2. They are feeling physically uncomfortable;
3. They are feeling lonely or scared and need closeness;
4. They are stirring to wee, since babies cannot wee when they are asleep[21];
5. They are being woken up by feelings that are bubbling up to be expressed.

If we are wanting them to sleep longer stretches, we can go through this list.

1. If they are hungry, we can feed them.
2. We can make sure they are physically comfortable, eg. that they are not in physical pain, they are not ill, they don't have a rash, they aren't too hot or too cold, and that they have nightwear and bed linen in natural fibres rather than polyester, checking out for food intolerances, gut issues, and the effects of EMF, dirty electricity or blue light, etc.
3. We can co-sleep or have them close to us when sleeping;
4. If they stir to wee and don't have many feelings, they can stir to

---

21 This is from an Elimination Communication perspective.

wee and just go back to sleep again with closeness (I practiced Elimination Communication with my son from birth, and when he stirred at night, I would put his little bucket underneath him or take him to the bathroom for a wee and he would fall back asleep again. When I had listened to fewer feelings that evening, he would wake to wee and then the feelings would prevent him falling asleep again so I would listen to feelings then.)

5. The more feelings you are able to listen to, and the more concentrated, free-flowing and intense those feelings are, and the more your baby gets to complete a whole crying cycle, the more relaxed your baby will be and the more they will be able to sleep until they are either hungry or have had enough sleep, whichever comes first.

If babies have accumulated feelings, they will often start to wake at shorter and shorter intervals as the night goes on.

If you are wanting to help your baby sleep for longer, you can either simply listen to more feelings during the day or evening, and/or you might decide to gradually increase the length of time between night-time feeds.

For example, you might decide that if they wake up after four hours, you will feed them, but if they wake up sooner than that, you will listen to their feelings.

Eileen decided that she would gradually increase the gaps in between feeding during the night and would listen to her daughter's feelings then. She shares her journey:

"My partner and I started navigating Aware Parenting together when our daughter was 12 months old. We were drawn to Aware Parenting as we still weren't getting more than two hours sleep at a time. I had been 'advised' by sleep counsellors, family members, other mothers

and almost anyone I mentioned my situation to that things would improve if we moved my daughter to her own room, weaned her and of course 'left her to cry'. Every part of my being told me that none of these were suitable solutions.

But without anyone for guidance and support on an alternative solution I had come to accept that I would be chronically sleep deprived until such a time that she was old enough to suddenly sleep better. But my belief that she would somehow grow out of these endless night wakings was gradually burst by conversations with other mothers who were still waking multiple times with their 2, 3 or 4 year olds. That's when I realised I couldn't bear this way of existing for that long. I was already an emotional mess. I kept becoming unwell and had even been to hospital three times with my physical ailments. My state of chronic exhaustion was taking a toll on my family as well.

So my heart called out for some guidance, some other way of maintaining closeness with my daughter while also allowing better sleep for all of us. I had already become curious about what could be causing my daughter to wake much more often than other babies of a similar age. When my daughter was 9 months old, I talked with a group of women; we were all deeply dedicated to developing secure attachment through practices like co-sleeping, breastfeeding and staying close with our babies. I was surprised and confused that by doing these things we weren't in fact seeing peaceful, well-rested babies.

So when I bumped into one of the midwives from our pre-birth course I was deeply curious when she mentioned a friend who had gone through similar challenges but was seeing great improvement since listening to a particular podcast. Most interesting for me was to hear that her friend was still breastfeeding and co-sleeping but also managed to improve their baby's quality of sleep! Eureka! I thought! An alternative that I could finally get on board with, at least I hoped I could.

After listening to a couple of episodes of The Aware Parenting

Podcast, I sill knew very little of all that Aware Parenting entails. And admittedly, I had skipped ahead to an episode on sleep. But I already felt that what I had heard had struck a chord. I started with the nights, as they were the biggest issue for me. And the first step we took was talking about what would change. I knew that expecting my daughter to go from waking and breastfeeding every two hours to sleeping all night was unrealistic, and I still wasn't confident that she could go that long without milk. So we set our first goal of aiming for her to sleep until midnight without breastfeeding.

One of the first big lessons I gained from Aware Parenting was simply communicating this goal with her. I had already told her little things like, "We are going to the shops today," or, "Let's put your nappy on," but it had never occurred to me to share long term plans with her. But here I was, telling her that, "In a few nights' time, we are going to start sleeping until midnight." Most importantly, I shared the full picture with her, explaining what would happen when she did wake up before midnight and what would happen after midnight. Through this process, I felt I was setting expectations for her as well as myself.

But even with all this groundwork, I struggled listening to her feelings as she cried when she woke and I didn't breastfeed her. Often I would eventually offer the breast, doing what I needed to still get through the night. In retrospect, I took these early steps quite gently, not wanting to do anything radically different. I was too depleted to risk making things even worse.

But after the first few weeks, I was already amazed to see tiny signs of progress. My daughter would often stir and wake to cry, but she was often less distressed about me not breastfeeding her at these times. She was only having small releases and then returning to sleep, which wasn't ideal in some ways, but we were getting better nights overall, which gave me the tiny bit of energy I needed to try more.

Bit by bit we were able to reduce her breastfeeding overnight, and within a couple of months she was sleeping fairly well from bedtime through to four or five in the morning. By this stage I had listened to a few more podcast episodes and was just starting to see the bigger picture of how Aware Parenting is more than just a way of improving sleep. So I finally found the strength to really listen to her big cries in the full light of day. These days were the hardest for me, and I realised the importance of sharing my emotions with someone else, to allow me to be most present and available to listen to my baby.

Looking back over these past seven months, I still can't believe how far we have come in our journey together. Not only is sleep less stressful and less fractured, but our bond and trust has become so intensified. I now see Aware Parenting is a pivotal step in completely transforming the way I think about my role as a parent and how to better meet the full range of physical and emotional needs of my daughter. Every day, I still have moments of self-doubt and second-guessing whether I am doing things 'right'. But when I can play with my daughter and see her pure delight, or listen to her tears and watch her peacefully drift into sleep, I simply know in my heart that there was never any doubt we were meant to discover this whole new paradigm together."

Aimee shares the huge difference she experienced between the sleep of her first baby and her second, once she learnt about Aware Parenting:

"I have a four month old baby and a three year old. With my three year old toddler, my partner and I were up day and night holding her through every nap, crying and screaming. From 5-8pm every night she would scream non-stop and I would put her in the baby carrier, bouncing her on the ball, doing everything I could, singing. I remember rattling and singing so loud that she would go to sleep. It was exhausting. It was so overwhelming. I had postpartum anxiety and postpartum depression.

A few days after the birth of my second child, I picked up The Aware Baby, *after a friend introduced it to me, and I read it. I started holding my baby while she cried. I made sure she had been fed and she had a clean nappy and she was healthy and she cried and she would just go to sleep. And now she is my miracle baby. She slept for 11 hours last night! And I still do it. I've had so much inner rewiring going on when I hold her. Because in the beginning, I told myself helpful things while I held her skin to skin the whole time.*

I've just had to file through all the old parenting programmes that say I need to fix something. My mom was here and she was really upset seeing my daughter cry in my arms, and I said, "Mom, she's fed. If I offer her my breast, she won't take it. She's very clear about what she wants. I'm not going to breastfeed her if she doesn't want to feed." I have had doubts, but the moment I see her fall asleep in my arms and sleep so peacefully and then she's wide awake and she's so happy, I feel so confident and happy.

And this is how we are designed to feel. We are designed to feel happy. With my first child, we spent five or six hours trying to put the baby to sleep and I don't do that any more. If I have any advice for new moms, it's, "Don't try to put your baby to sleep. Your baby will fall asleep when they are ready." I went through old parenting paradigms that said that a particular cry or rooting means hunger. When mom friends come around I say, "Just because she's getting fussy does not mean she's hungry. It means that she needs to cry and it's going to be okay. She's just fed."

When I hold her, I know that I've done everything that I could and I know she's safe being held in loving and present arms. I've been super present, gazing in her eyes. I've done SO much inner child healing for myself. Letting my baby have her grief and express it – most of the time when I've let her know that it's safe to cry, I've cried and released as well. That has been a beautiful part of this experience."

If we want to listen to feelings before sleep, this requires us to have enough emotional presence in ourselves.

If we are wanting to listen to feelings in the evening, this often invites us to change practical things around so that we have enough spaciousness to listen. That might mean if we have a partner, asking them to do things so that we can have a ten minute break to go and do some yoga or stretching or dancing around the kitchen, or taking turns listening to our baby crying with our loving support. If you are exhausted and are just desperate for your baby to sleep, they are likely to pick up on that, and will find it harder to feel the emotional safety and presence they need to let out their feelings.

It's often harder for babies to express feelings if they've been recently fed, or if we keep distracting them from their feelings through reading books, singing, or through a busy routine. They need a sense of presence to be able to feel connected with their feelings and to express and release them. You might want to play around with how you do things, for example feeding them earlier, skipping reading books, or changing around the order in which you do things. Remember that you get to experiment with things, observe what happens, and go back to the drawing board!

So often, in working with parents, I find that it is through them playing around with how they do things before bed, and focusing on closeness, *attachment play* and listening to crying and raging, that profound changes happen with sleep.

Kim, a Registered Nurse and Aware Parenting instructor in training who works with mums and babies in a mother and baby unit shares a story about sleep from her circle group, with their permission:

"The mum walked into the room in a fluster and apologising for having to bring her baby as her baby sitter fell through. She said she was worried about him crying and interrupting the group. We welcomed them both and welcomed all the feelings in the room. As we got started in the session her little babe started getting upset and his cries got louder; the mum became flustered and said, "Kim I have no clue what

to do now – should I put him in the pram and walk outside?" I asked her if she felt comfortable in the group to stay holding her bubba while she (and the group) listened to his feelings. She was willing and so I talked her through it.

Her little babe started to back arch and kick and she looked at me and said, "Do you think he is saying he needs space?" I invited her to stay with him, and just see what happens. I told her that he may kick harder and back arch and be more restless – which he did right on cue. I then said, "When he finishes releasing all of his emotions he will probably fall asleep in your arms." She looked at me like I was crazy! And I went on to talk about melty baby moments and how when our little babies release all of their feelings they are so relaxed you can put them down and you will not have to commando roll away trying your hardest not to make a peep. We were all laughing and sharing our experiences of doing this. That's when the mum looked down and almost burst into tears. Her baby had fallen asleep in her arms! She said he hadn't fallen asleep in her arms since he was a newborn. He was a melty baby!"

Attachment play before sleep

As babies get older, *attachment play* has an increasing role in babies expressing healing-feelings, including before sleep. Offering our loving presence and particular forms of play (as described in the chapter on *attachment play*) helps babies feel both connected and relaxed, since laughter and play both create release and relaxation. It's also very common that after some concentrated *attachment play*, bigger feelings will bubble to the surface and a baby might then have a cry – either through them finding a pretext to access their feelings (I call this the 'emotional coat hanger') or because we offer them a *Loving Limit* (where we say no to the behaviour and yes to the feelings causing the behaviour) – such as if they start biting or pinching.

Different sleep perceptions and concepts compared to other parenting paradigms

'Overtired'

In Aware Parenting, we don't hold the concept of a baby being 'overtired'. Rather, if they are tired and they're not sleeping, it either means that they don't have enough connection to feel relaxed enough to go to sleep, or that they have accumulated feelings that are preventing them from feeling relaxed enough to sleep, or both. (Remember the three things we need for sleep: to feel tired, connected and relaxed!)

'Sleep windows'

Nor do we hold the concept of sleep windows, for the same reason. Babies can sleep when they feel tired, connected and relaxed. There aren't other complex calculations to take into account.

'Sleep regressions'

In Aware Parenting, we don't think that there are events called sleep regressions. When babies are waking up a lot, this can often be because uncomfortable feelings have accumulated. Those are often at similar ages to other babies because they are when infants are going through new developmental phases where they feel more frustrated and so have more feelings to tell us, and if we're not listening to those feelings, the accumulated tension will make it harder for them to go to sleep and stay asleep. Hence the more frequent night waking.

Nixie shares her experience of moving away from concepts such as 'sleep regressions':

"Thank you for your podcast, it has helped me to turn away from the sleep apps, wake windows and all the other things they tell you babies need to sleep. Every time I logged onto Instagram I was overloaded

with sleep training advice and it was just so painful for me to do. It never felt right to let my baby cry alone. I think I lasted five minutes the very first time I tried. Finally I found The Aware Parenting Podcast *and I could now relax. My baby can come anywhere with me while I work and he will get the sleep he needs when he can.*

I have been listening to my nine month old cry in my arms for about two months now. The difference between the first time I tried listening and now is phenomenal. The first time I held my baby before bed he cried, thrashed his body around and hit his head. It took all my strength to hold him and watch this happen. After 45 minutes his body fully relaxed and he fell asleep. I cannot explain the feeling this gave me, it was absolutely beautiful. The next time I did this he cried for about 20 minutes. Then 10 minutes, now he usually fusses for about 2 minutes. One day he even babbled in my arms and laughed and fell asleep.

Now when I go out if my baby is tired I can hold him and he will fall asleep in my arms anywhere. Then if I choose to, I can place him down somewhere. I was at a BBQ the other night, people talking and music going and he was tired, he had some crying to do, so I walked away and sat down with him and he fell asleep in my arms. My friends were shocked. I have learnt so much more about my baby. We were connected before but this has connected us more. This is just a small example of how letting a baby cry in your arms gives you the ability to go out and do the things you need to do and not race home to a dark room, with white noise on. With a little trust and patience, the baby will sleep anywhere."

'Settling'

We're not settling a baby. If they wake up and we go to them, we're either meeting their need for closeness that they were signalling, so they go to sleep again, or they wake up to express feelings, and we can listen to those feelings so that they feel relaxed enough to sleep.

'Winding down to sleep'

Hannah shares her experience of doing my *Sound Sleep and Secure Attachment with Aware Parenting Course*, offering one of the most fun and powerful descriptions of this old belief about 'winding down to sleep':

"Four years on from doing the course I'm still so appreciative of it and everything we learnt. I was just reflecting last night as my two year old fell asleep how grateful I am for this approach and understanding. She worked through the hurts of the day – the balloons popping at the party, Daddy picking her up and carrying her across the kitchen rather than Mummy, etc., crying about them one by one, telling me while I listened lovingly and then she said, 'Sleepy now,' and happily fell asleep (and slept all night!).

Initially the course was a life saver with a five month old waking up more than seven times a night. Within a few months we were all getting more sleep but more than that it has totally changed our parenting approach. Aware Parenting has been such a blessing. It's a radical thing that could change the world! But it's also a really practical tool for being happier as a family and feeling more connected every day. I'm still so grateful for the lessons I learnt on this course and through your work Marion and we have so much fun at bedtime.

> When there's squealing laughter and silly games as we put on PJs and brush teeth, I'm so glad that I don't share the cultural belief that we have to get children to 'wind down' at bedtime! That would be like trying to squeeze an octopus into a Tupperware box ... fighting their nature!

But with rough and tumble, and laughter and tears if they need them, bedtimes are much more relaxing for all of us. Sometimes I forget and find myself moving towards old patterns and then I have to give myself a little refresher...I especially turn to The Aware Parenting Podcast *which re-ignites my understanding and connecting and for which I'm so grateful too! Basically thank you wonder woman for all that you do. It still holds true that Aware Parenting has been the most tremendous gift for our family life."*

Toddlers who move all around the bed

There is often a perception in *Classical Attachment Parenting* that all toddlers will move all over the co-sleeping bed, kick off covers, and wriggle around. There are many classic memes that show older babies or toddlers doing just that. This is seen as just how toddlers are. However, from an Aware Parenting perspective, this would be seen as a likely sign of accumulated feelings. Toddlers who regularly get to express healing-feelings tend to sleep restfully, without moving around a lot. They also don't need parents to be in one particular position. Often this means that parents also have much more restful sleep, not only because of the longer patches of sleep, but also because there's less movement and agitation.

Sarah, an Aware Parenting instructor in Australia, shares her journey with Aware Parenting and sleep, and all the observations she made:

"From birth, my daughter had big crying sessions where no amount of feeding, rocking, dummy or carrier walks would soothe. I felt anxious and worried that I was missing something, and I didn't know how to help her. I knew that there was nothing physically causing her to cry. I noticed things in my daughter that made me curious about what was really going on. Sometimes, when I offered her a dummy she would suck vigorously, and have agitated, stiff body movements. Sometimes when we would breastfeed, she would clench her fists and feel stiff

in her body, or she would be fussy, and sometimes come on and off the breast. I felt powerless as I didn't know how to help her in these moments, yet I was determined to understand what I was missing.

In those early days, even before I came to Aware Parenting, after trying all the things, I would just hold her as she cried, and I noticed how calm she was after the crying stopped.

Before I found Aware Parenting I had experimented with many different approaches with helping my daughter to become more soft and calm in her body, so she would fall asleep easier and stay asleep. Each week that passed she was waking more frequently and daytime naps were short. By six months, she would wake up 45 minutes after falling asleep for the night, where I would breastfeed her and place her back into bed. She continued to wake up every two to three hours all through the night, and I chose breastfeeding to help her to fall back asleep. I was exhausted and sleep deprived.

I learnt about Aware Parenting and we started practicing crying-in-arms before bed when she was six months old. We started to see small improvements in her sleep and in the relaxation in her body. However, I really had no idea what I was doing. 'What does crying-in-arms look like? What is meant to happen?' I wondered. I had so many thoughts running through my mind as I sat with her on the bed, surrounded by pillows as I held her on my knees to maintain eye contact.

Despite the uncertainty, what I did notice was how she was after crying in my arms. Seeing how she was afterwards was the reassurance I needed that what we were doing was helping her. At first it was small changes: she was more content to play and engage for longer periods, and she had less agitation in her body while feeding. After about one week of listening to her feelings her sleep improved and she was now waking only once a night.

Four weeks later, we went on a camping trip. I was so nervous and concerned about what the other campers might think with a crying baby, so for the three nights that we were there I breastfed her to sleep. For the first two nights she slept with one wake up, although I noticed her wanting to get closer to me through the night (we were co-sleeping). On the third night she woke up three times.

When we came back home, I really observed the difference in her after only three nights of breastfeeding to sleep. I was so surprised at how quickly using a control pattern to help her sleep could affect her sleep. I was ready and willing to restart the crying-in-arms again and to listen to all the feelings that she didn't get to express for the previous three days. However, it didn't come as easily as before. For the next few weeks, I was exploring the crying in arms approach before sleep. Listening to feelings was a big learning curve, as I had never had my feelings heard by an empathic listener. What I discovered was that supporting my baby as she cried really came down to how available I was in the moment. In those early days, I placed so much pressure on myself for the crying to come that I was no longer offering her a safe space to express when she was ready. Rather, I was placing an expectation on her that she needed to cry before bed. The next part of my journey was so much about my own compassionate connection with myself, which naturally flowed into offering her the kind of presence she needed to be able to express her feelings."

Aware Parenting is simple in philosophy yet deeply nuanced in practice. As Sarah shared above, if we tell ourselves that we 'should' listen to our baby's feelings, or that we 'have to,' if we coerce ourselves, judge ourselves or pick up the guilt sticks, all these deeply affect the quality of our presence.

This is why our own inner work and reparenting are so vital. This is why I developed The Marion Method – to support parents to stop 'shoulding' themselves and coercing themselves, and instead listening in to their emotional presence and willingness to listen to their baby or child, as well as developing a compassionate inner dialogue.

Our babies live in the sea of our presence, and all that inner coercion and judgement actually gets in the way of offering the kind of relaxed presence that they need to be free to express their feelings to us.

Family co-sleeping and waking

Another common scenario I have seen many times with families is where one parent is sleeping in one bed with the baby, and the other parent is sleeping in another room with the older sibling, because the baby is waking the older child and the parents. If you are doing this and you are finding that it is meeting the needs of everyone in the family, I so support you in doing this. However, this sleeping arrangement can place a huge strain on the parents, who may often have years sleeping apart.

Over the years, I've worked with many couples for whom things have changed when starting to implement Aware Parenting. When the baby gets to express more feelings during the day, and particularly before sleep, they sleep more and more restfully, move around less, and wake up less. This means that everyone else is woken up less. In addition, if the older child's feelings get heard too during the day, they also sleep more soundly and are less likely to be woken up if and when the baby wakes.

When I was pregnant with my son, my then-husband and I put a single bed next to our queen bed, and then all four of us slept together in the bed, making sure of course that our baby son and four year old daughter were sleeping safely. Our son didn't ever wake up our daughter – she had expressed a lot of feelings and slept peacefully. There was so much lovely family closeness that we all really enjoyed.

An invitation to reframe sleep

Would you like to avoid focusing on or even counting how many hours sleep you and your baby get?

Would you like to remember that if you keep on focusing on connection and crying-in-arms, sleep will come as a result?

If your baby has fallen asleep and you move away and they wake up again, would you like to choose to see that as an opportunity for them to cry more and express more of their healing-feelings to you?

Would you like to see sleep as a natural result of sleepiness, connection, and relaxation?

Would you like to trust that every time you focus on connection and expression, your baby is moving more and more towards having more restful sleep?

Are you willing to deeply honour your own body's needs for rest, and find ways to rest, even small moments?

Would you like to choose to be grateful that sleep was an issue for your baby, so that you could see that they had more feelings that needed to be heard, while being deeply compassionate with any feelings of exhaustion, frustration, powerlessness or outrage you feel in response to what has happened in relation to your baby's sleep?

Would you like to talk about your feelings in response to what has happened with sleep with a compassionate listener, where you experience being heard, understood and supported?

Are you willing to deeply trust that your needs and your baby's needs can both get met, including for sleep, and that the key is always connection? Connection with yourself first, and then connection with your baby and a willingness to listen to their healing-feelings.

Are you willing to experience the time before sleep as a beautiful opportunity for the deepest and most profound invitation for intimacy and connection, and deep knowing of your baby?

Would you like to see how you are feeling at the end of the day as a signal, telling you what might need shifting in your relationship to yourself?

Are you willing to believe that it really is possible to have restful sleep as a parent?

Are you willing to believe that it really is possible for your baby to have restful sleep?

As we move towards the end of this sleep chapter, I'd love to share something Kari told me. I wonder if it inspires you to talk to your baby about what's going on!

"Actually I am also ignited with curiosity after the last Zoom call in the Sound Sleep and Secure Attachment Course *and yesterday evening I said to to my baby son something like, "I want to see if it's possible to wait with your feed at four am until the morning, so check in with your belly if you need to eat some more now," and he ate a little more for later supper. And at four, I said, "Hey love, I am right here and I wonder if you want to share something with me," and he had a quite small cry with me and went back to sleep for two more hours. I want to keep exploring, perhaps it was only this night, but it felt right to communicate with him like this. Let's see! It also makes me think how much he actually understands, it's a humbling and sweet reminder that they understand a lot even though they don't speak yet with words (in our case). Also in the day I feel I chose my words and my way of communicating with more awareness after this reminder."*

Through a baby's eyes

"Eyes getting heavy, getting woozy. Feelings bubble up from within. You hold me. So easy to cry. Tears come and come and flow and fade. You listen. You're here with me. Tightness leaves, softness comes. Ahh, eyes closing. Relaxed, falling asleep in your arms."

A baby's words

"I'm getting tired and I can't hold the feelings in any more. I want to let them all out. I've been holding them in all day and it takes so much for me to do that. Oh, you're taking me into the bedroom, and we're on the bed. I'm so glad that I can let them all out. I cry with you and I rage, and I get all hot and sweaty. I move around. You are here with me. I want all the feelings to come out. I have so much to tell you, Daddy. I want you to know all about what I've been through. You're listening. You see me. I cry and I rage some more, and I feel my body relaxing. Oh I feel so relieved, Daddy. I start to drift off to sleep in your arms. You talk to me, and I feel more feelings. I cry more. You really are listening. I'm so glad that I'm heard. Ahh, so relaxed now, so sleepy. Night night, Daddy."

CHAPTER EIGHT

Why listening to babies' feelings can be so hard and how we can help it be easier

I'm sending you so much love and compassion. I think it's the most normal and natural thing in the world to find it hard to listen to your baby expressing their feelings through crying-in-arms when all their needs are met. There are many reasons for this, which I will start off by listing and then will share about in more detail.

1. We live in a culture that has demonised feelings and the body for centuries and we grew up in that soup of consciousness.
2. We grew up in The Disconnected Domination Culture, which is designed to disconnect babies from their families.
3. The majority of us are not given this information about babies and their feelings and have never seen a baby crying in the loving arms of someone who was able to listen, having met all of the baby's immediate needs, and who felt relaxed, calm and confident that all was well and that the baby was doing exactly what they needed to return to relaxed presence.
4. Our human heritage is to live in large communities, with many different adults taking care of a baby's needs and supporting one another. In contrast, in The DDC, most parents don't receive enough emotional support, which is so important if we are to be

able to listen to our baby's needs and feelings.
5. Understanding needs and feelings isn't taught to us as children.
6. Most of us have never had the experience of being held in loving arms and listened to while we expressed all our feelings, once all of our immediate needs were met.
7. Most of us don't have communities of other parents practicing Aware Parenting around us, where we would be discussing, listening, observing, and having a sense of belonging as we all practice it together.
8. Many of us were left alone to cry, and the fear, terror, loneliness and overwhelm that we felt then can bubble up in the here and now when we hear or see a baby cry, even in loving arms when all their needs are met.
9. Many of us will have been distracted from our feelings when we needed to cry as babies, and so those similar themes of distracting ourselves are likely to show up when we see or hear a baby cry-in-arms.
10. Many of us will have learnt to dissociate when we felt feelings that we needed to express, so we will tend to dissociate when we see or hear a baby crying-in-arms.

When you read this, do you feel more compassionate towards yourself when you think about crying-in-arms?

It is SO understandable that we can find this hard; that you might feel scared, overwhelmed, outraged, confused or many other feelings, even when reading this information, let alone actually practicing crying-in-arms. It is SO natural for us to dissociate when we think about it or practice it.

SO, what *can* we do, given these things?

The three key areas we can focus on

1. Our thoughts;
2. Our needs;
3. Our feelings.

1. Our thoughts

This includes getting as much information as you can about Aware Parenting with a baby so that you can keep listening in to whether it still resonates with you, and also to counter all the conditioning you've received about babies, having grown up in The Disconnected Domination Culture.

If you haven't already read it, I highly recommend reading Aletha Solter's book *The Aware Baby*. You might want to listen to the various Aware Parenting podcasts too, including *The Aware Parenting Podcast*. (I invite you to type 'Aware Parenting' into your podcast search to find them!) Perhaps you want to read other Aware Parenting books, including Aletha Solter's, my other books, and *Raising Resilient and Compassionate Children*, the book that I co-authored with Lael Stone.

While you are resonating with and exploring Aware Parenting, I recommend *not* reading about other paradigms. I have found that parents can easily feel confused if one day they're reading about how to help their baby 'self-soothe' or about 'sleep regressions' and 'sleep windows' and the next day they're reading about Aware Parenting and *control patterns* and how accumulated feelings affect sleep.

Continuing to dive in deep in learning about Aware Parenting is not just so that you understand the theory, but it's also so you can deeply understand the practices. The more you understand how they work, the easier you are likely to find them to practice.

Another way of working with your thoughts is to continue to observe your baby in the ways I invite in this book. It is through your experimentation and observation that you will receive information that will support your theoretical understanding of Aware Parenting.

One more part of our thoughts work is more related to The Marion Method (first mentioned in Chapter 1) and to the thoughts you think about yourself – those emotional sticks. I invite you to put down those sticks if you notice yourself judging yourself, comparing yourself, or thinking that you 'should' be doing this 'perfectly'. (Concepts created by The Disconnected Domination Culture). All of these sticks will make practicing Aware Parenting harder, and conversely, the less you hit yourself with those sticks, the easier parenting will be.

I'm here to invite all humans to put down the guilt and shame sticks forever. This is key to The Marion Method work – freeing ourselves from Disconnected Domination Culture conditioning. The more we are unwilling to pick up those sticks, the freer we are to learn about what babies and children need, feel and experience, because we're unwilling to guilt or shame ourselves when we see the ways we haven't understood our baby or child, and the ways in which we've done things that weren't helpful for them or haven't done things that would have been beneficial for them.

Parenting is an ongoing invitation for learning more and becoming more. If we are willing to learn and grow, and we are also willing to hit ourselves with those emotional sticks, we are going to feel guilty or ashamed a lot of the time.

I invite all parents to get to a place where they can absolutely see things that they have done to their baby that weren't helpful and can also see things that they didn't do that their baby needed, *without feeling guilty or ashamed*.

We might mourn, yes. We might feel sad as we reflect back. Sadness and mourning invite healing. Guilt and shame are simply cultural forms of self-punishment. When we can see clearly, without guilt and shame, we can also be curious about the ways we can create repair and recovery from those past experiences for our babies.

So, as you read about all the ways we have been taught to respond to babies, from distracting them from their feelings with jiggling, dummies and feeding, to not really seeing them as feeling beings, I offer an invitation to you. I invite you every step of the way to let go of any guilt and shame, perhaps with the phrase, "I'm not willing to judge myself." I invite you to become compassionately curious instead. From there, you will be able to take action from lovingness and willingness (another core part of The Marion Method), rather than from guilt, shame and self-coercion.

2. Our needs

Just as the extent to which your baby's needs are met has a profound effect on how they feel, so the same is the case for you. Your needs for safety, for reassurance, for empathy, for support, for community and for sleep are likely to be particularly important when practicing Aware Parenting, and probably so many more.

Emotional safety

Why do I include safety? For most of us, being with our baby's feelings will help us connect with our own feelings as a baby, and many of us would have been left alone to cry, which would not have met our needs for emotional safety and would have been traumatic for us.

Those feelings of fear are likely to show up when we are with our baby crying in our arms. Helping our own inner baby self know that she is safe in the here and now, that she is not alone and that what our baby is experiencing now is different to what we experienced back then, is very important. Emotional safety can also be met by having someone there with us while we listen to our baby's feelings, whether that's our partner or friend, or a Listening Partner or Aware Parenting instructor in person or on a platform like Zoom.

Reassurance

Our needs for reassurance (that this is helpful for our baby) are most likely to be met when we see, through our own eyes, that our baby is happier, more relaxed, more present and more connected when we listen to more of their feelings. This is one of the most important things we can experience to help us also reassure the younger parts of us that our baby is safe and we are safe in the here and now.

The only real way you can receive reassurance that your baby is helped and not harmed by listening to their feelings is by observing them. Your baby is the only one who can give you that information.

Empathy

If we were living in healthy communities, our needs for empathy and support would be met plentifully. But in the culture that most of us live in, which demonises feelings, many of us grew up not having our feelings heard as babies, nor as children, teens or adults. If you do have friends and family who can listen to your feelings with loving compassion, I'm so happy to hear that. If you don't, I invite you to reach out to The Aware Parenting community for a Listening Partner so that you can receive (and give) frequent listening, empathy and understanding for all that you're going through on your parenting journey. That really is vital in the Aware Parenting journey.

3. Our feelings

As I've mentioned many times, it's very understandable that your own unexpressed feelings will bubble up when you listen to your baby's feelings. If you were left alone while you cried, it's normal that those feelings will bubble up too. So, you might feel deeply sad, outraged, scared, confused, overwhelmed, terrified, powerless, or many other feelings. Just as babies do, your own innate healing processes are in operation here – you are experiencing something in your present (your baby crying in your loving arms) that reminds you of your past (you crying as a baby) and the feelings that didn't get to be felt, expressed and heard then will come up to be felt, expressed and heard now.

However, just like for a baby, you need to feel a balance of attention between a sense of emotional presence and safety in the present alongside revisiting those feelings from the past in order that feeling and expressing those feelings is healing for you.

That's why getting support from others is vitally important. Over time, we do internalise the loving presence of others so that we can increasingly be present and safe with those big feelings ourselves, just as babies and children do over time, so that they become adults who can stay present in their bodies with their painful feelings. However, most of us didn't receive that listening and presence as babies and children so we haven't internalised that yet.

If we have lots of big feelings sitting at the surface, it will be almost impossible for us to listen to our baby's feelings. And if we have a lot of big feelings bubbling, our baby will feel it and may not feel enough of the balance of attention to express their feelings with us.

Attending lovingly to our own feelings and emotional healing is an essential part of Aware Parenting.

Self-Compassion Moment

How do you feel when you read this?

Are there any changes you'd like to make in relation to your thoughts, your needs or your feelings?

Are you willing to make those changes?

CHAPTER NINE

Attachment play with babies

Alongside crying and raging with loving support, *attachment play* is another way that babies naturally use to heal from stress and trauma and release tension, this time though particular forms of play and laughter. Because this is innate, it also means that many parents naturally do this. Play is one of our inbuilt healing processes that often stays intact, even in The Disconnected Domination Culture. However, understanding what *attachment play* is and how it works can help us practice it in more conscious and effective ways, and can also encourage us to refrain from certain kinds of play that are harmful, e.g. tickling. If you want to dive deep into understanding *attachment play*, which is a central part of Aware Parenting, I invite you to read *Attachment Play* by Aletha Solter.

I also want to remind you of the importance of the balance of attention. Just as crying-in-arms requires the balance of attention to be healing, so does play. That means that the play needs to help children connect with past experiences and feelings while they also feel emotionally safe in the present.

Chiara, an Aware Parenting instructor you've already met in this book, specialises in *attachment play*, She says:

"In the age bracket of 0 to 12 months the main benefit of being playful *is bonding with your baby. Play with infants isn't raucous and doesn't involve lots of toys and needn't as they grow older either. In fact, I would like to remind you that the best toy in the entire world for an infant is you. You can see their little faces light up when you play with them, look at them, spend time with them and connect with them."*

There are nine types of *attachment play*, which you can read more about in Aletha Solter's book of the same name.

For now, we will just talk about three types – contingency play, separation games and the baby version of non-directive child-centred play.

Contingency play

These are games we play where what we do is contingent on, or caused by, our baby's behaviour. So many mirroring games do this – our baby puts their tongue out and we copy them, they smile and we smile, they move their hand and we mirror that with our hand, they touch our nose and we make a squeaking sound. Contingency is a vital way that babies come to have a sense of agency, power and trust that they are seen and heard. They have a bodily sense that their actions lead to specific things happening. As parents, we are wired to mirror our babies in this way, and it has powerful effects on how they feel.

> *Self-Compassion Moment*
>
> Do you notice yourself playing this kind of play with your baby?
>
> If so, how do you feel when you do?
>
> What do you notice in your baby?
>
> If you don't do any contingency play, would you like to?

Separation games

Peek-a-boo is one of the most common games we play with babies, but did you know that this kind of play has powerful effects? Babies are learning all about what is called 'object permanence' in the psychology world – the knowing that people and objects are still there even when they can't be seen or heard. When we put our hands in between our baby's face and ours for a short while and then take our hands away, we will often see them smile or laugh.

The laughter indicates that they are releasing a bit of fear. They are feeling relief when they feel when they experience that we really are still there, even though they couldn't see us for a little while. Just like with healing through crying, healing through laughter requires that we hold in mind the *balance of attention*. If we hide from our baby for too long, they will start to cry. This isn't healing. The separation is too long for them.

Chiara shares again:

"With babies, I find that the best ideas are to get the classics and then to build on those and be slightly more creative. For example, with peek-a-boo, we usually do it with hands or behind something, but you could involve fabric. And then while you are also doing that, maybe also reach out and touch their hand as well. So you are incorporating touch and they know you are definitely there because they can feel you. I like making it a little bit more three dimensional when you're playing those simple games."

Rebecca talks about her experience of the power of *attachment play*:

"Before reading about and starting to implement Aware Parenting, my baby had only slept five hours at a time once or twice and four hours at a time a handful of times. Most nights, her first wake up would be after two or three hours, and then would be every hour or two for the rest of the night.

Since Aware Parenting, yay! We are making huge progress. Yesterday, she had a couple of good cries and we really did a lot of play too. In the evening, lots of attachment play. And today, after her sleep, she was in the best mood pretty much all day. She wasn't clingy at all like she can tend to be, but I still made sure to give her a lot of attention and focused play.

I have always spent a lot of time with her, but I'm seeing now that the type of focus I give her really matters. When I really focus on her and make the effort to make her laugh as much as I can, she actually goes off and plays by herself! And bedtime now is an enjoyable and special time instead of me feeling resentful about how long she takes to feed to sleep.

You've changed my perspective about bedtime, so instead of thinking that I need to calm her down and getting frustrated that it's not working, I'm following her lead and really loving the bedtime chit chat that's happening.

It's so sweet to get this glimpse into what she's thinking about while we're snuggling and giggling in the dark.

One of the best parts is that it takes her less time to fall asleep now than it did with her feeding to sleep every night."

Self-Compassion Moment

I wonder if you see any of the games that you play with your baby in a different light now? I invite you to consider that these games support your baby to heal and to release feelings, as well as being connecting and fun for both of you.

Why tickling isn't recommended

Although babies may laugh when they are tickled, tickling can easily be overstimulating for a baby's nervous system.

They might still laugh, but they are probably also feeling overwhelmed and powerless. Instead of tickling, a few seconds of blowing raspberries, or moving towards your baby with a delighted face, can provide fun, connection and release, without being overwhelming for them.

Offering a baby your loving presence (non-directive child-centred play)

In Aware Parenting with children, we talk about non-directive child-centred play, where we offer a child our undivided attention and follow their lead. From a young age we can offer this same kind of presence to our baby. Babies thrive on this and need it as much as we can possibly give it. This is a part of the attachment-style parenting we talked about before.

Have you ever noticed a baby searching out for eye contact, searching for presence? They are longing to be met in deep connection. Holding your baby on your lap, being present with them, mirroring their expressions, and following their lead, is a powerful form of connection.

Most babies will not want or need toys in the first several months, since you are the toy they really want to play with.

The other wonderful thing about this quality of presence is that if they have feelings to tell you, they will be free to share those feelings when you are still and present with them.

Offering them this quality of presence as much as you can will be a profound gift for both of you.

Cazza shared the following about sleep, connection and *attachment play*:

"I would like to share our progress: last week, my almost 11 month old baby slept through the night for the first time ever! He slept from 9pm to 6am, then woke for a feed and actually fell back asleep until 9am! He repeated that the next day and since then has, with the exception of one night, only been waking once, between 5:20 and 6. I didn't think I would ever see this day, certainly not when we started the Sound Sleep and Secure Attachment with Aware Parenting 1.0 Course *at the beginning of this year.*

Just four weeks ago he was waking four+ times at night, often as much as three times before we went to bed. We had already been doing crying-in-arms successfully from September last year when I started the Aware Parenting Babies Course *and I felt that that had made a huge difference to my baby's sleep, especially during the day with his two day-sleeps being regular and for two to three sleep cycles each. However, some piece of the puzzle was missing and I had this massive a-ha moment when Marion was talking about connection in the first week of the course. Instead of focusing on crying-in-arms before bed, this is now just one part of the routine.*

We added attachment play and although my 11 month old won't always have the hearty laugh that is so releasing, he is definitely enjoying this play, grinning from ear to ear. He is initiating the play, for example throwing himself down and peeking over his shoulder to see if I come to pick him up and kiss him all over. We are doing hide and seek, catch me and peek-a-boo as well. Marion, I can definitely see why you call it high-octane connection! When he starts to slow down, I put him on my knees or in my arms for crying but even then he often prefers to play and for example puts his foot in my face and giggles when I make funny muffled noises that there is something on my face.

I was worried a bit that he was just using the playing to distract himself but he is always maintaining beautiful deep eye contact and seems very present, not distracted. Both my husband and I are feeling very connected to him.

I also appreciate and prioritise my mini- and maxi-me moments much more, seeing how much more energy I have at the end of the day as compared to my husband who works outside the home. This has been an important change with this course as well, taking time for me when bub is sleeping – first, before doing the washing, the dishes or whatever else is on the long to-do list. I am listening to my baby's feelings more during the day now and he seems more willing to share them with me during that time too. I found a good time is when he wakes up after naps.

This shift went hand in hand with the other changes, so it could be because I am spending more time on me during his naps and my batteries are charged and he feels that, or because he himself has shifted because we have this deep connection time in the evening now. Whatever the reason, it works for us!

I also noticed how one evening last week, he was whiny but didn't want to release with me, even though he had a deep and intense cry with me during the day. He kept moving towards his dad so I passed him on and the floodgates opened. The crying and 'babbles' sounded exactly like the ones he had earlier in the day with me. I had the feeling that he wanted to share the same story he told me with his dad as well.

Afterwards he fell into a peaceful and beautiful sleep. I am so forever grateful to you for introducing us so beautifully into this exciting journey that is Aware Parenting."

> ### Self-Compassion Moment
> How do you feel when you read this? Does it inspire you to do anything differently with your baby?

Kata shares about the first time she consciously chose to put into practice *attachment play* with her son:

"He was around nine months old when he started so-called 'testing' behaviours, such as pulling down his socks and throwing them on the ground, watching my reaction. This happened again in a tram station while we were waiting for the tram and he sat in the stroller. I tried to put it back on (it was winter), and got a little agitated as he did not let me put the sock back on, and when I did, he pulled it right off again!

As I was participating in Marion's Attachment Play Course *right then, which was my first course with her, I thankfully remembered to play! I tried the game to playfully put the sock on my nose, and on his nose, and the top of my head, and on his hand instead, and to act shocked when he threw it down, and he giggled so beautifully! I was like, wow, this feels sooo good! What a delight, instead of the suffering and agitation!*

When I saw the tram arriving, I put the sock back on his foot without any issues, and that was it!"

Through a baby's eyes

"Your eyes, you, coming closer, smiles, ahhh, you're here, you're gone, you're here again! Joy! Sprinkles in my heart! I smile, you smile, we are we. We are one. We are here together. I light up when I see you see me. Love. Smiles, Laughter. Joy. More, more. I love this."

A baby's words

"I love it when you come and do that smiley play with me. My heart lights up when I feel that joy and laughter bubbling out of you. I catch it and we ride the wave of laughter together. We are here together and this is my favourite thing in my world, when we dance the laughing dance of play and joy together. Dancing, singing, laughing. I love this. This is what I love. This is an eternity of love for me. My whole body relaxes as we laugh and laugh together. I love this."

CHAPTER TEN

Aware Parenting and Elimination Communication

Many of the elements of Aware Parenting are practices that were in existence before industrialisation, and that still exist in many Indigenous cultures today – practices such as having babies close when sleeping and carrying them in the daytime. For millennia, parents understood their babies' elimination cues in ways that are rare nowadays. However, just as co-sleeping and baby carrying have been reclaimed, so has what is now called 'Elimination Communication' or EC. In this chapter, I will talk about how Aware Parenting and EC can work together.

I also want to clarify that the majority of parents who practice Aware Parenting use nappies with their babies, and don't practice Elimination Communication.

However, some parents who practice Aware Parenting do also practice Elimination Communication (EC). EC is the process whereby parents read a baby's elimination cues and also use their intuition to support a baby in weeing and pooing in a receptacle rather than in a nappy. With Elimination Communication there is also a spectrum of practice, just like with Aware Parenting. On the one side of the spectrum, parents might *never* put nappies on their baby, and might aim to catch *all* eliminating, or on the other end of the spectrum, they might *always* put nappies on their baby and *occasionally* catch poos.

Aware Parenting and Elimination Communication can fit well together, because with EC we are learning to understand and perceive more cues and feelings. We also get to observe more clearly the relationship between digestion and the effects of stress and trauma on the body, and the difference that crying to heal from stress and trauma makes physically on our baby. Crying, dissociation, weeing and pooing can be very interrelated.

Certain behaviours indicate that babies are about to wee or poo, and we can learn to notice these cues. In addition, some babies will express discomfort if in a wet nappy.

I practiced Elimination Communication with my son from birth, and in the early weeks, I found that he would often signal quite clearly, either with movement, agitation, or a bit of crying, that he needed to wee or poo. As soon as he had eliminated, the crying stopped. I loved the additional information to understand him even more! Those signals were really clear, yet I hadn't noticed those with my daughter because I didn't start Elimination Communication with her until I found out about it when she was eight months old.

From my experience, I would say that babies might cry a bit before they eliminate, particularly in the early days, but it wouldn't be the kind of huge crying that we see when they are expressing feelings from stressful or traumatic events.

I also found that understanding more about my son's elimination needs and cues helped during the night. I discovered that he wouldn't wee in his sleep, so if he needed to wee during the night, he would move and squirm and become wakeful, I would offer him the little potty, and he would go back to sleep again if he had already expressed a lot of feelings that day. I didn't feed him or do anything apart from lying back down together. If he had feelings to express because he had expressed less in the day, or had experienced more stimulation, he would wake to wee and then he would have a cry in my arms and would then go back to sleep.

So, if we are practicing Elimination Communication and Aware Parenting, we might respond differently at night compared to if we are doing EC with another style of parenting, or Aware Parenting without EC. If parents are practicing Elimination Communication but not Aware Parenting, their baby might stir to wee, but when they stir, feelings might start to emerge then too, and they might not be able to go to sleep again after weeing, so they might then always be fed back to sleep.

With Elimination Communication and Aware Parenting, once they've woken up, we might choose to feed our baby back to sleep, or we might just be with our baby as they drift off to sleep again, if they have no or few feelings to express, or we might listen to some crying if they have feelings bubbling up.

If we are practicing Aware Parenting but not EC, we might *not* realise that that is why our baby is stirring (to wee) and thus might take different actions.

Another thing that I found incredibly interesting was the interconnectedness between weeing, pooing, and feelings. I knew theoretically that there is a correlation between digestion and feelings, but seeing it in action was amazing to me. For example, whenever my babies had more accumulated feelings, such as if they'd done less crying-in-arms when we had had a busy few days, or I'd been going through something and hadn't had as much emotional presence to listen to their feelings, then that would affect their weeing and pooing.

In EC circles, they talk about 'strikes,' and 'resistance'.

However, from an Aware Parenting perspective, I saw this in a different light. I found that if they had more accumulated feelings than usual, then in order to wee or poo, they might also need to let out some feelings too. So at times, they signalled a need to wee, I took them to a receptacle to wee, and then they had a cry with me before they were able to let the wee out.

The way I see it, tensing muscles to hold in feelings often results in tightening muscles that hold in wee and poo. When a baby is holding on to feelings, they will often hold on to wee and poo too. The more relaxed their muscles are, the more they are connected to their natural signals and ability to wee and poo. It's hard for them to feel what is going on in their bodies when they are holding in lots of feelings, or dissociating from them. So, I found that EC gave me lots of other clues and more information about what was going on for my children when they were little.

Another thing I found fascinating was clearly seeing my intuition in action. Often I would be thinking about something elimination-related, such as putting things that had been wee-ed on in the washing machine, and a few moments later, my son would wee! It helped me see how much we would be deeply connected with that intuition had we all stayed connected with EC, as in some Indigenous cultures. We would not need to reconnect with it again. I also found it similar to experiences I had when my babies were crying in my arms and I would find myself remembering something about their birth experience. I trusted that the intuition and interconnectedness was similar there, and that I was tuning in to what they were revisiting and healing from.

If you're practicing Elimination Communication and Aware Parenting together, my biggest invitation is to be compassionate with yourself.

Learning to offer something that we didn't experience and don't see being practiced around us is inevitably going to be hard at times. I recommend focusing on every time you *are* aware of when your baby is going to wee or poo, or you have that intuitive sense and act on it, and catch it, rather than counting the number of 'misses'. I invite you to celebrate all that you are doing, rather than what you are not doing! I loved practicing Aware Parenting and Elimination Communication together. As for missing signals – I did miss quite a few and definitely needed to do more washing because of that. I bought organic protectors that I placed on the bed, on the sofa and in their car seats which made a huge difference! And I was quite harsh on myself, because I hadn't yet learnt how to put down those emotional sticks, which is why I am inviting you to put those sticks down!

Maru Rojas is an Aware Parenting instructor and EC and Potty Learning Consultant. She shares about her journey of combining the two:

"I discovered Elimination Communication (EC) when my daughter was eight weeks old. It took me two weeks to gather the courage to take off her nappy and hold her over the sink. To my surprise, she started eliminating consistently within two days of offering the potty. Over time, I became more skilled at reading her cues, similar to how I learned to recognise when she was tired. Unfortunately, I wasn't introduced to Aware Parenting until she turned six months old, so my focus was primarily on meeting her needs, and preventing crying.

With the birth of my son three years later, I felt much more confident with EC (and Aware Parenting!). This allowed us to distinguish between his discomfort or fussiness due to needing to empty his bladder or bowels and his agitation caused by accumulated stress or emotions. EC seamlessly fit into our caregiving routine, and my son preferred the feeling of cleanliness, resulting in very few poop misses from five months onward.

What I truly appreciate about EC and Aware Parenting is that it reaffirms that we can trust in our babies' innate wisdom. Regardless of how regularly we practice EC, simply recognising that babies have body awareness is a significant shift in perspective. By maintaining this awareness, we save them from having to relearn it a few years later.

There are lots of benefits to practicing EC, including using fewer nappies, reducing the occurrence of nappy rash, and gaining a deeper understanding of your baby's fussiness. Usually, EC facilitates an easier and earlier transition to using the toilet. However, the most significant benefit of EC is the heightened connection and bond between you and your baby.

As the name suggests, EC is all about communication and responsiveness. It doesn't require completely forgoing diapers or spending entire days catching every wee or stressing about misses. It's about meeting everyone's needs, and that will look different for each family. I've supported parents who never used nappies and parents who used disposables full-time but were adept at reading their baby's cues and using sign language to maintain their awareness of elimination, without necessarily offering the potty. There are countless ways to practice EC, as diverse as the families who embrace it. I will say that the most daunting part is simply getting started. If you're curious, I encourage you to take off the nappy for a bit, hold your baby, and observe what happens.

EC is simply a shift in perspective from the nappy being a toilet to a nappy being a back-up. I would love for EC to be a normal part of the caregiving routine one day (whether using nappies or not), so the responsibility of taking baby to the potty could be shared amongst the community."

Please note that Aletha Solter[22] says this about Elimination Communication; "Several people who practice Aware Parenting, including some Aware Parenting instructors, have used this approach and have found it successful. I consider the approach to be fully compatible with Aware Parenting. However, I am not convinced that the use of nappies is a source of stress for infants (as some proponents of EC claim)."

If you aren't practicing Elimination Communication, but you'd like to, one way to start is to start noticing cues and timings. Pooing cues are often easy to catch, and you are probably seeing those already! You might also notice some patterns, for example, maybe your baby always eliminates as soon as they wake up. If so, you might want to take their nappy off and offer them a place to wee and see how that is for both of you. Noticing and responding to timing and cues like this can support you to be even more attuned to your baby!

---

22 Personal communication.

Through a baby's eyes

"Tension building. Tighter and tighter. Fullness, fullness,..... Ahh, relief. So many sensations, so much is new. I feel it all."

A baby's words

"This is all so new to me. When I was inside your tummy, I didn't have these sensations of fullness and emptiness. Now, there is filling. I feel pressure, sensation, tension. It starts off mild, and gets stronger. When I wee, aahhh, I let it out, aahh, I feel relief."

CHAPTER ELEVEN

Frequently Asked Questions

I invite you to read all of the Questions and Answers, because I share things here that aren't in the rest of the book. In addition, answers to questions that you don't have may well give you information and clarity about issues that *are* relevant for you. And if your situation is similar but a bit different, please adjust the response to take that into account.

These are generalised responses. I cannot really know what is going on with a family without a consultation, with a pre-consultation questionnaire beforehand. If you are ever unsure, please reach out for a consultation with Aletha or an Aware Parenting instructor, or for longer-term work with me.

General information and preparation

How can I know if my baby is benefitting from crying-in-arms?

I know that the idea that babies have feelings to express through crying in our loving arms can be an enormous paradigm shift! The Disconnected Domination Culture has demonised the body and feelings for a long time, and yet, there is a cultural shift towards understanding that our bodies and feelings have deep wisdom, including the innate mechanisms babies have to heal from mini-traumas and larger traumas including birth trauma and early separation. When all of our baby's needs are met, and we are present, we can hold them in our loving arms, offer our eye contact and warm voice and (without jiggling or rocking or trying to distract them in any way) simply listen to their feelings. "I'm here with you. I'm listening. I welcome all of your feelings."

The wonderful thing is that we can try this out for ourselves if it resonates with us, and we can clearly observe our baby, to see if listening to their feelings makes a difference. If we receive reassurance when, after crying in our loving arms, they gaze into our eyes with a more relaxed presence than we've ever seen, if we feel in their bodies that their muscles are deeply relaxed, if they smile and there's a quality of peace about them that spreads through the room, if they make more eye contact in a relaxed way, if they then feed more calmly and connectedly, concentrate for longer periods, smile more, have more relaxed muscles, sleep more peacefully and for longer, and melt into our hugs more than ever, this gives us direct evidence that they really did release tension, express feelings, and heal from stress or trauma. In my own parenting and in working with thousands of parents, I have seen this time and time again. When we know what to look for, babies tell us how relaxed they really are, and we can then differentiate between true relaxation and dissociation. On the front of the book is a picture of my son when he was a baby, where this quality of presence, spaciousness, clarity and relaxation shines through.

I'm pregnant. What can I do to prepare for practicing Aware Parenting?

With Aware Parenting, the main areas of focus with young babies are:

1. Promoting secure attachment;
2. Preventing stress and trauma, including *in utero*;
3. Listening to your baby's healing-feelings and helping them

release the stress that all babies experience, however sensitive and aware we are as parents, as well as any trauma they might have experienced.

Here are a few ideas for how you might attend to each of these:

I invite you to aim for a calm pregnancy, with lots of connection with your baby. Research indicates that babies whose mothers were anxious or depressed a lot during pregnancy cried more than those whose mothers who weren't anxious and depressed (which makes sense from an Aware Parenting perspective, doesn't it?). There are a few books I recommend to increase connection, such as *Prenatal Parenting* by Frederick Wirth; *Nurturing the Unborn Child* by Thomas Verny and Pamela Weintraub, and *Tomorrow's Baby* by the same authors. I suggest doing whatever you are drawn to do to have a calm and empowering birthing experience. Birth trauma is very stressful for babies, and babies whose mothers have a more difficult birthing experience also cry more and wake up more at night. From an Aware Parenting perspective, they will have more feelings to tell us. Personally, I found *The Gentle Birth Method* by Dr. Gowri Motha, and *The Calm Birth Method* by Peter Jackson really helpful.

A main stress for babies is unmet needs. One of a baby's primary needs is closeness and gentle, present touch. Consider always keeping your baby close to you or your partner in the early weeks and months. I invite you to look into co-sleeping. Research by people such as James McKenna shows that babies and children who co-sleep experience favourable long-term effects. You can also find all about safe co-sleeping from his work. I recommend accessing *The Aware Baby* by Aletha Solter, and reading and re-reading it, with a particular focus on the chapter on sleep. I also recommend re-reading the chapter on sleep in this book. If you feel uncomfortable with the idea of co-sleeping, I invite you to explore this more – first of all giving empathy to the feelings, and then listening in to where the discomfort comes from. What are your thoughts? What are your concerns? What feelings bubble up for you when you think of co-sleeping? This is an opportunity for you to be compassionate with yourself, tend to younger parts, free yourself from cultural conditioning, and make true choices based on your research and what you most resonate with.

I'd suggest avoiding buying a pram while you are pregnant, and instead research baby carriers. Hold in mind that you will have your own unique preferences and body type for which carriers are most comfortable and easy for you. Parents often find they need to change carriers after their baby is about six months old, although with certain carriers, like wraps, they can be used from birth to beyond toddlerhood. Carrying a baby means that you can give your baby the closeness they need, while also meeting your needs for ease. Choosing the most suitable carrier is important so that your body is comfortable too! Carriers can be a really helpful way to meet everyone's needs if you have an older child or children too. They also minimise over-stimulation for babies when you are out and about.

One of the biggest stresses for newborn babies is indeed over-stimulation. Overwhelm for a baby means everything that they don't understand, which is a lot for a baby. The more you can protect a baby from this, the less stress will build up in their body, and the less crying-in-arms they will need to do to release the stress. I'd recommend a babymoon, where you stay at home, preferably in your bedroom, for a period of time that feels apt for you. I suggest avoiding loud noises, bright lights, and aim for plenty of skin-to-skin contact and presence in the way you hold and touch your baby. Avoid letting lots of other people hold your baby in the early days, and later on, ask the baby if they are willing to be held by anyone new, and wait for a signal from them to indicate a 'yes'.

The more you give your baby a chance to make a gradual transition from the dimmed lights, muffled sounds, and complete skin touch of being in the womb to the outside world, the less stressful their early weeks will be. As they get older, slowly increase stimulation, such as with outings – and remember that, even going out in a car to a shop is a stressful experience for a newborn baby. Keeping them close to your body in a carrier facing you will minimise the stress, and yet they will still have healing-feelings to release when you get home. As much as possible, avoid loud and crowded places, travel, and moving house for the first six months.

The next thing to consider is your relationship with crying. How are you with your feelings? What are the habitual ways that you avoid feelings? Consider starting practices like a Listening Partnership, counselling, therapy, or working with an Aware Parenting instructor to bring more awareness and presence to your feelings, and your beliefs about feelings. These practices will also help you to become more comfortable with feeling and expressing your own feelings, especially from your experiences of stress and trauma in infancy and childhood. I invite you to read and re-read the chapter on crying in *The Aware Baby* and to re-read this book. I invite you to watch parents with babies and notice how you feel when you see a crying baby, and what your habitual response is. Perhaps you'd like to connect with someone who is practicing Aware Parenting with their baby and ask them if they are willing for you to be with them while they listen to their baby's feelings – and see what comes up for you. Would you like to ask them questions about their experience with their baby's feelings? The more you can get clear and work through old feelings and beliefs, the more present you will be able to be with your baby's healing-feelings, and the more you will be able to see what is going on for your baby, rather than see them through the filter of your own unexpressed feelings.

I'd also suggest you explore your relationship with food, and whether you eat when you are upset. I invite you to enquire into whether you eat when you are hungry and whether you stop eating when you are satiated and receive listening support as you explore this. One of the main differentiations first-time parents practicing Aware Parenting find difficult is between their baby's hunger and their healing-feelings.

The clearer you are on the difference between when you feel hunger, and when you feel upset, the more easily you will be able to see the difference in your baby. I'd recommend reading and re-reading the chapters in this book and the chapters on crying and feeding in *The Aware Baby* – particularly getting clear about the ways to distinguish between hunger and a need to release healing-feelings.

Finally, I invite you to deepen your connection with your own needs. It is so tempting for parents, particularly mothers, to ignore their own needs. The more you keep connected with yourself and your needs, and put in place ways for you to get your needs met once your baby is born, the more you will have a full cup, and will have so much to offer your baby. For example, consider starting a regular empathy swap with your Aware Parenting friend, so that you know that someone is there to simply listen and be present with you as you share what parenting is like for you. Find a local Aware Parenting group and consider going to meetings before your baby is born, or perhaps you'd like to start one of your own!

You have a unique opportunity to be as fully prepared as you can be for Aware Parenting, for understanding your baby's needs and cues, and to respond accurately and empathically. And remember that the rest of it is a learning in process experience – you will learn and grow as your baby does! Have fun!

What kind of inner work will help me with Aware Parenting?

Any kind of counselling or therapy that helps you to be more connected and compassionate with your own needs and feelings and that supports you to revisit your own childhood hurts and traumas to be healed will help you with Aware Parenting, particularly those that support crying, raging and laughter. I developed The Inner Loving Presences work, The Inner Loving Presence Process and The Willingness work to support parents in their reparenting process. These are all part of The Marion Method.

How will I be able to listen to my baby's feelings when I also have another child?

Listening to the healing-feelings of a baby and a child can be challenging, and I invite you to be compassionate with yourself as you remember that we are designed to live in community, not in nuclear families. I invite you to reach out for as much practical and emotional support as you can and also set up your home environment to bring about more ease to meeting needs and listening to healing-feelings. What I did was set up an environment so that I could listen to my baby son's crying while also being with my four-year-old daughter. For the first four months we were in our bedroom – I set up two big comfy chairs, one for her and one for me. I had big bottles of water and lots of snacks, and lots of activities for her to do – activity books, weaving, craft, etc. I could listen to my son crying at various times throughout the day while also being right there with my daughter, responding to her needs, chatting, etc. It was such a beautiful time. This is just the way that I did it, and each family is in a unique situation. I wonder if you might like to change something about the environment so you can listen to cries while also attending to your older child? I notice that parents sometimes try to leave their older child while listening to their baby's feelings before sleep and that this can be challenging for the older child. Finding ways to stay close to your older child/ren while caring for your baby can really help meet their needs, especially if you can find ways to include the older child/ren. Some parents are concerned that if the baby and child are both crying at the same time, that one parent's presence is not enough, but I invite you to trust that if your baby is in your arms, and your older child is close, perhaps even with physical contact, that your presence is enough for the crying to be healing for both of them.

Closeness and presence

Is swaddling helpful?

When babies first come out of the womb, we can help their transition into the world and support them to be less overwhelmed by the big change by making things as similar now to what they experienced in the womb, and then to gradually make small changes. For example, having muted sounds and light and lots of physical closeness. Swaddling a baby in the early days *can* be part of that. Swaddling can help some babies have a sense of containment and can help prevent the startle reflex in the very early days. However, the needs for containment and preventing the startle reflex can also be met in other ways. For example, having your baby in a sling or carrier helps them feel that similar sense and also has the added benefit of closeness and our heartbeat sounds, which are vital needs for babies in the early days.

However, before long, most babies *do* need to have a sense of autonomy and choice in relation to their bodies. Being able to move their legs and arms is an important developmental capacity. Sometimes parents swaddle their baby longer than is helpful for their baby. Swaddling can become a way that a baby's feelings become suppressed, especially if it's paired with things like rocking. You may notice the typical signs of dissociation – tense muscles and a staring look. So, as always, please observe your baby and stop swaddling them when they show you that this is no longer meeting their needs.

Self-Compassion Moment

If you've swaddled your baby for longer than this, I want to remind you to be compassionate with yourself, and also to remember that it is never too late to listen to feelings from the past.

If you are still swaddling and are unsure about whether it is helpful for your baby, one thing you might do is, when you would usually swaddle, to hold your baby in your arms or on your lap, facing you, and simply be present with them. As you hold them, you will be meeting their needs for closeness and physical safety and containment. If they start moving around and crying, it is very possible that the swaddling was preventing them from expressing feelings that they were trying to express. *I invite you to always listen to yourself, observe your baby, explain to them what you are doing, and only do what resonates with you.*

Do I have to carry my baby in a carrier to practice Aware Parenting?

Aware Parenting is a form of attachment-style parenting, which means it values the attachment needs of babies and children. One of the ways we can meet those attachment needs is to keep our baby close as much as possible, and a sling or carrier can help with that.

Self-Compassion Moment

Before we continue, I invite you to drop any guilt sticks if you haven't used a carrier, or if you put your baby in a pram or stroller from a young age.

We can offer reparative experiences for closeness at any age and we can listen to feelings of overwhelm from earlier times at any age.

I find it vital to repeatedly remind ourselves that we are designed to live in communities where babies would be carried by many adults as well as by children, so one person doing a lot of the carrying is a very different experience and can be exhausting and hard. We are not meant to be doing this in isolation. Aware Parenting is also all about valuing both a baby's needs and the parents' needs, within the culture and society we live in.

Having said that, slings, wraps and carriers don't only promote secure attachment for our baby and bonding with our baby. They also help reduce a baby's experience of overstimulation and overwhelm, particularly if the baby can choose to snuggle in and stop the stimulation visually. I don't generally recommend front-facing carriers because some of them don't support the baby to be in the 'froggy' position that's most helpful for their hips (The froggy position is when their legs are out wide like a frog rather than dangling down), and also because the baby is more likely to feel overwhelmed.

I particularly recommend the use of slings, wraps and carriers if a baby has experienced separation after birth, as it helps them feel more connected, helps promote secure attachment, and helps repair the earlier separation. Remember too, that babies can also express feelings of overwhelm after being out in busy environments, through crying in our loving arms when all their needs are met. In addition, overwhelm can also happen even if a baby was carried and babies will commonly have feelings to express after an outing, particularly in the early months.

When I put my baby in the baby carrier, she starts to cry. I think she doesn't like it.

I have spoken to many parents over the years who have experienced this, and who have stopped using the carrier or sling for several weeks or months. I want to remind you that with Aware Parenting, we are always asking ourselves, "Is this an immediate need they are expressing, or are they trying to express feelings here?" We can do this with the carrier example. The first action, of course, is to check that they are comfortable. Some carriers can put undue pressure on a baby's hips, which can be uncomfortable. It appears that having a baby with their legs wide is more helpful for her hip development than carriers where a baby's legs dangle down. If her legs are dangling down, it may be that she is telling you that she is uncomfortable. In any carrier, it's important to check that there aren't any clips that are rubbing her skin or anything that is too tight, or that she isn't too hot or too squashed.

However, being uncomfortable isn't the only reason that babies may cry in the carrier. Remember, in Aware Parenting, when the present situation reminds a baby of a past situation that they haven't expressed the feelings about, those feelings come out to be expressed and heard now. If there's the *balance of attention* between being safe in the present alongside being reminded of unhealed stress or trauma from the past, babies will naturally try to heal through crying in our arms. So, if your baby cries when you put her in the sling or carrier, and she wasn't crying before, it could be that the containment is helping her remember feelings from when she was in the womb or was being born. I've found that babies who had a challenging time *in utero* or during birth are more likely to cry when they are put in the carrier.

What can you do if you think this is the case? You could check in with yourself and see how you feel when you imagine listening to your baby's healing-feelings about the birth. You could keep her in the carrier, and without rocking or walking or jiggling, you could give her your full attention, tell her you are listening, and listen to her crying, for as long as you are sure that she is crying to tell you about those earlier experiences.

You could sit down and take her out of the carrier, or simply loosen the carrier so you can put your arms around her, and hold her close, and tell her that you'd like to listen to her. You could refrain from jiggling, rocking and distraction, and simply listen to her feelings. It may be that she is still connected to those healing-feelings from having been in the carrier and can still tell them to you now.

As always, it is important to listen to yourself, and observe your baby. If at any time, while listening to her crying, you start feeling worried or scared or unsure or panicky, then I invite you to listen to yourself. If after checking in with yourself you still feel those feelings, then explain this to your baby and then do whatever you might usually do to stop the crying, e.g. to feed her if you think that she might be hungry. Ideally you might, at some point that day or in the next few days, share those feelings with your Listening Partner, or your life partner, or do some journaling, or speak to your counsellor, or listen to the feelings yourself, and see what was coming up for you. Listening to your feelings and what comes up for you is such an important part of Aware Parenting. *The more you can feel and express your feelings in ways that are emotionally safe for you, the more you will be able to listen to your baby's feelings.*

Is it okay for my baby to fall asleep in the carrier or will it create a *control pattern* for movement?

Again, I want to remind you there is no 'okay' or 'not okay' with Aware Parenting, because there isn't judgement about what you do or don't do. However, if you carry your baby in a carrier and they often sleep in there, it *can* be the case that it makes it harder for them to express their feelings, and it *is* possible that movement could become a bit of a *control pattern*. Again, you could do your own experiment to see. What happens if you sit down with your baby on your lap and offer them your loving presence at a time where you might normally have them in the carrier and be doing things? What do you notice? Do they tend to move into a cry before falling asleep?

In my own experience, I found that if I was carrying my babies around in carriers, I wasn't offering the same quality of emotional presence for them to express feelings. If I carried them in a carrier all day, they wouldn't cry much – and this wasn't because of meeting more needs – because I was comparing this with holding them in my arms, offering them my loving presence, not doing anything else, offering eye contact, and letting them know I was available to listen to their feelings. To me, there was a clear difference between the kind of presence I was offering in those two scenarios. Both lovely, but different.

If you are carrying your baby around in the carrier a lot for a few days, you might want to choose to have the next day to offer more presence to your baby to offer them opportunities to catch up on expressing healing-feelings that they didn't get to express in the previous few days.

If I sit still with my baby, he will start to grunt and then start to cry.

If I get up and walk and talk, he stops crying. Are we creating a control pattern by standing up and are we delaying crying? Is it preferable to stop standing up and just be with him as he gets to a point where he expresses his feelings?

I love your question and I invite you to experiment – and then notice the difference between when you move him and when you are still and listen to his feelings. How is he afterwards? How much eye contact does he make? How much tension is there in his muscles? How does he sleep that night? Over time he will tell you whether moving him or staying still and listening to his feelings is most helpful for him! From an Aware Parenting perspective, it's likely that your still and calm presence is an invitation for him to tell you about his healing-feelings, and when you stand up and move, that is subtly distracting him from those feelings. Does that resonate with you?

My partner scoops up the baby and he isn't present at all in his body with her. What can I do?

Many of us are quite dissociated a lot of the time and few of us have received really present touch from someone who is not dissociated or in hyperarousal but who can feel the sensations and feelings in their body and thus can really sense in to what another person is experiencing on that physical level. For us to offer present touch and holding to our baby, we need to have experienced that ourselves. I wonder if you might like to have connection time with your partner and see if he is willing to experience the difference between when you touch him on the shoulder when you are present in your body and when you touch him on the shoulder from a place of lack of presence? This can be a way to help people to start being able to notice the difference in themselves and thus be able to be more present with a baby. Having bodywork with a practitioner who is deeply present in their body can also be a way to help adults gently move towards more presence in their body.

My baby has a soft toy bunny to go to sleep with.

I've read about transitional objects or comfort objects. Isn't that a healthy thing for them to have, to get used to being away from us? He cries when I wash it and put it on the line.

I'd love to answer your question by telling you about my experience! When I was a baby, I was given a toy bunny, and as I grew, I carried it everywhere and slept with it always. There's the family story of when my Mum washed it and I cried and cried while it was drying on the line. I even took it with me when I went to University and still cuddled up with it at night! It was there, doing my psychology degree, that I learnt about transitional objects, a term coined by Donald Winnicott. It was seen as a soft object such as a blanket or soft toy that was held on to as part of a normal process from "absolute dependence on the mother and is a vehicle towards objectivity and autonomy". Later on, when I was doing my PhD at The Winnicott Research Unit, Cambridge University, I learnt more about this philosophy of transitional objects. However, when I came across Aware Parenting, I then saw the idea of 'transitional objects' in a different light, as objects babies and children use to suppress or dissociate from feelings, which made complete sense to me. My bunny helped me in that I had it with me when I was alone as a baby and a child, and it helped suppress the feelings of loneliness and fear. However, I would have much preferred to have co-slept with my parents and had my healing-feelings heard so that I didn't need my bunny!

Self-Compassion Moment

As always, if your see your child doing this, I invite you to put down any guilt or self-judgement sticks. This isn't an invitation for judging ourselves as parents – it's an invitation to understand children and have clarity and compassion about how they suppress and dissociate when they need to.

We can also help children express more of the feelings that clutching on to the bunny or blanket is holding in, all the while aiming for deep compassion for ourselves. Like with other *control patterns*, we can offer *attachment play* and *Loving Limits*, listening to their feelings, but giving the bunny back when we don't have presence in ourselves to listen to any more feelings.

> **My breastfed baby cries whenever her Dad holds her. Does she need me or is she expressing feelings to him?**

Your experience and question is a very common one. From a *Classical Attachment Parenting*[23] perspective, you might think that your baby doesn't want to be with her Dad (or other parent), and only wants to be with you. This can mean that mothers end up doing all the bedtimes, and most of the caregiving, and not having much time to meet her own needs.

From an Aware Parenting perspective, we can see that something else might be going on. I want to remind you that the research on attachment shows that babies can have secure attachments with multiple caregivers, and that it is helpful for a baby's development to have more than one attachment figure. Again, in Indigenous cultures, that is generally how things would have been – babies and children securely attached to multiple family and community members. Historically, when we lived in large communities, that would have always been the case. *And* of course your baby's connection with you is special. If you are their biological mother, growing in your womb does bring a very special connection and understanding. If you breast-feed, that is a special connection too. *And* secure attachment is also more than those two experiences. It is about the quality of our presence and attentiveness to our baby, which can happen with people who didn't carry the baby in the womb nor who breast-fed them.

---

23 This term refers to the original attachment parenting paradigm, which was first described by William and Martha Sears. The Aware Parenting version of attachment parenting has several key differences from this original version. (This term was created by Marion Rose and has been adopted by Aletha Solter.)

Dads can be bonded with their babies, and babies can be securely attached with Dad or other parent, as long as they are having regular times to connect with each other and the parent is present, attentive and attuned. Given this information, what might be going on when our baby cries with their Dad or other parent? Well, remember that babies have two reasons for crying – to communicate their immediate needs, and to heal through expressing and releasing healing-feelings through crying-in-arms.

As mothers, we might generally tend to assume that our baby is hungry rather than needs to express feelings – because of course we want to make sure they are never crying from hunger, as well as because we are first-generation folk practicing Aware Parenting and are learning to read our baby's cues for when they have healing-feelings to express. So, we will probably often feed our baby when they need to cry in our loving arms. What happens then is that particular positions with us become *control patterns* where our baby dissociates. Then, they might find it harder to cry with us when they need to. We might notice that when we are holding them, they tend to dissociate – which we can observe from their tension and avoidance of eye contact. They might cling to us even if their Dad or other parent or attachment figure is around. When they are with the other parent, they will be freer to express their uncomfortable feelings. In other words, not all clinging is an attachment behaviour. This is very common and something I have witnessed in thousands of families.

Obviously, this will be a different scenario if a baby is bottle fed and both parents are bottlefeeding the baby. If one of the parents is more likely to feed the baby when the baby has healing-feelings to express, the baby may then be less likely to cry with that parent (or carer).

> *Self-Compassion Moment*
>
> Does this resonate with you?
>
> If so, I invite you to be compassionate with yourself. It's so natural and normal to veer on the side of feeding our babies to make sure that they never experience being not responded to accurately when they are hungry.

And our babies can relearn to express their uncomfortable feelings with us. *And* we can nourish the relationship between our baby and their Dad or other parent by giving them opportunities to care for the baby and listen to the baby's feelings.

Over the years, I've seen many parents who, once given this information, have transformed things in their family.

Dad (or the other parent) gets to have more bonding time with his baby. The baby gets to be more securely attached with their Dad. Dad can do things like help the baby sleep and can gain confidence in his own capacity to care for the baby. Mum can get more time to care for her own needs. Babies can get to release more feelings, which means that they sleep more calmly and for longer, and are generally happier, which of course is more enjoyable for all the family. Babies internalise core beliefs that men welcome their feelings as well as women.

And, this situation can help bring up big feelings for everyone. For mothers, it often brings up fears of whether Dad is present enough. Seeing our partner listening to our baby crying in his arms can help us connect with times when we were left alone to cry as a baby. It can help us revisit feelings in relation to our own Dad not listening to our feelings or times when our Dad got angry when we cried as babies or children. We might be concerned that our baby is crying to express a need rather than immersed in healing-crying. For dads, it can bring up their own unheard feelings from when they were babies and little boys, including if his Mum didn't come when he called. They can also think that their baby is rejecting him and that their baby doesn't want to be with him.

So what can you do? Having empathy time with each other, where you each talk about your feelings and listen to each other with empathy and compassion, can really help. You can talk about your fears and what this reminds you of and what feelings are bubbling up in you. You can also experiment with the actual process itself. Remember that there are no 'should's' or 'have-to's' in Aware Parenting. You might not be confident that all your baby's needs are met with her Dad. Your own feelings or your partner's feelings of being left alone to cry might feel so big that you aren't able to have your baby cry in the loving arms of her Dad. There are no 'have-to's'.

But if you want to, you could play with this. For example, if you are going out to do something for yourself, and your baby's Dad (or other parent) is at home with your baby, he could listen to her feelings. He might say things like, "Mummy isn't here, sweetheart, and I'm here with you and I'm listening. Mummy will be back soon. You love being with Mummy, don't you? I'm here and I'm listening." You could both observe afterwards how your baby is. Is she more relaxed? Does she sleep more peacefully? Does she make more eye contact? Does she seem more peaceful when she is feeding? Does her Dad feel more connected with her? Does she seem more connected with him? Again, it is only through observing your baby that you will gain the reassurance that she is crying because she feels freer to cry in his arms, rather than because she wants to be with you. As always, this is about listening to yourself, going slowly, and observing your baby.

If you are unsure whether your baby crying with their Dad (or other parent) is needs-crying (wanting to be with you) or healing-crying and you don't want to experiment in the above way, you could research it in a different way. You could make sure that your baby is having plenty of connected presence with their Dad and you could increase the amount and intensity of healing-crying your baby is doing with you. If your baby tends to stop crying and dissociates when you hold them, you could hold them in a position different to your breastfeeding position/s. If they are a bit older, you could sit on the floor with them when they're crying, and put your knees up so you can still put your arms around them and hold them, but not in the position where they dissociate. For toddlers, you could bend down and put your arms around them but also not get in that same position. If after doing some healing-crying with you like that, where you are confident that you have the *balance of attention* and they are doing healing-crying, you could then observe what happens when your baby is with their Dad (or other parent) after they have done more healing-crying with you. If they cry less, or don't ask for you, it would confirm that the crying earlier on was indeed healing-crying. You might then feel confident to leave your baby with their Dad after that.

I would also recommend lots of *attachment play* with both you and your baby's Dad (or other parent) – particularly following your baby and offering separation games like peek-a-boo, as well as contingency and power-reversal games. You might find then that your baby's feelings bubble up with you and then come out in crying or raging.

My five month old baby never cries with me. Does that have something to do with breastfeeding and what can I do to help her express her feelings?

I invite you to read the answer to the previous question to make sense of this. It's of course natural that we would always want to make sure our baby is never hungry, and because of this, many of us as mothers will be breastfeeding our babies when they actually have healing-feelings to tell us. This means that the positions that we breastfeed our babies in can become *control patterns*, where the baby mildly dissociates. If you want to support your daughter to cry with you, you might try holding her in positions that are different to the ways that you breast-feed her in. Another option is, if you have a partner, to ask your partner to hold your daughter when she needs to cry.

Crying-in-arms

Sometimes I get worried when my baby daughter is crying in my arms. What can I do?

There are several reasons why you might be feeling worried:

1. You are accurately picking up that your baby has an immediate need that hasn't been met, including a sensation of physical discomfort;
2. You have a need to understand more about Aware Parenting and how it works;
3. You're needing reassurance that this is helpful for her, and you haven't yet observed enough differences after crying-in-arms to give you that reassurance;
4. Your own feelings are being stirred up from when you were a baby or child and cried or were left alone to cry or were distracted from crying.

I invite you to listen to yourself to discover which one of these it is.

If you are picking up on a need that needs meeting, the most important thing is to find out what that need is and meet it for her. You could feed her if you think she might be hungry, and observe her while feeding. If she comes on and off a lot, is agitated and moving around, or falls asleep quickly, it's likely that she wasn't hungry. If you are concerned that she might have digestive issues, allergies, a tongue tie or other physiological issues, please follow those up with a trusted healthcare practitioner. It's so important for you to listen to yourself.

If you need more theoretical understanding of Aware Parenting, then the most helpful thing would be to read and re-read this book and also read and re-read *The Aware Baby*, and take in other information about Aware Parenting, such as through listening to *The Aware Parenting Podcast*.

If you need more reassurance that crying-in-arms is helpful for your baby, then I invite you to observe her very closely. I also recommend having a journal for noting down what you see. I suggest observing things like her eye contact, how much she melts in to your body, how relaxed or tense her muscles seem, whether she clenches her fists and toes, how long it takes her to go to sleep, how much she moves around when she is asleep, how she is when she wakes up, how much she is happy to observe and explore her world, how much she smiles, how calm or agitated her vocalisations are, and so on. Noticing differences in any of these between when you listen to crying-in-arms compared to when you do things to stop the crying will give you the reassurance that the crying-in-arms is helping her feel calmer, more relaxed, and more connected (with you and herself). You may also want to observe the difference between when she has a shorter and less intense cry and when she has a longer and more intense cry and between when you stop the crying short or support a whole crying cycle.

If your own feelings are coming up, then I recommend finding someone to listen to them. That might be a friend or partner, that might be your Listening Partner, it might be a counsellor or therapist, or it might be consultations with Aletha Solter herself or with me or another Aware Parenting instructor. The more you get to express those feelings and be heard with love and compassion, the more comfortable you will feel with listening to your baby's big and long feelings.

What can I do to feel more comfortable with crying-in-arms?

Here are some suggestions and invitations:

1. Learn more about the theory of crying-in-arms and why it is so helpful, and what a difference it makes for babies (and parents). The more we understand, the more of a cognitive foundation we have for our practice.
2. Read or hear more about other people's experiences with Aware Parenting, such as through re-reading the stories shared in this book. This will probably help you feel more comfortable.

3. Observe what a difference it makes to your baby when you listen to them crying in your arms. This really is the most tangible way to get reassurance. When you clearly see, over and over again, that they feel more relaxed, relieved, connected, at peace, aware, calm, present, and so on, when they get to regularly cry-in-arms compared with if you distract them from their feelings, the more comfortable you will be to listen to your baby's healing-feelings.

4. Express your feelings, thoughts and memories to someone else to be lovingly heard, particularly in relation to being left to cry, crying when you were hungry, and other painful feelings in relation to your feelings as a baby or child. This might be with your partner if you have one, a dear friend, a counsellor or therapist, your Listening Partner, in our free Facebook group or by an Aware Parenting instructor such as myself. The more you get to be heard, the more you will be able to think clearly about listening to your baby crying in your arms.

I want to let you know how understandable it is to find it so hard – I imagine your feelings were never listened to when you were a baby. This is one of the reasons why it is so important for us to have our own feelings heard.

When do I listen to crying?

My baby was crying and unsettled after his feed. Is this the right way to do it or should you start with them calm and you telling them it's okay to cry?

Listening to him when his feelings are already bubbling up, when you believe that all his needs are met, and when you feel able to be with his healing-feelings, can be a helpful time to listen. Or you can offer your loving presence at any time and see if he has feelings to tell you. There is no 'right' or 'wrong' way here. Often, listening when we have the emotional spaciousness to be present with our baby's healing-feelings is one of the most helpful times to listen. The more we have our feelings heard, the more often we will have that emotional spaciousness, and the more likely that will also coincide with when our baby's feelings are naturally bubbling up!

Is the crying still helpful if I stop her crying before she has finished crying in my arms?

Every bit of listening you do will make a difference. See the next question and answer for more information about this.

Does my baby son need to finish a whole cry or a whole chunk of feelings?

Your baby will still get benefit from crying-in-arms if you stop him before he finishes expressing a whole chunk of feelings. He will still have experienced being heard and understood. He will have released some stress and tension from his body. Stopping him before he has finished doesn't take either of those away. However, you might not notice the same effect as if you listen to a whole chunk of his healing-feelings. Imagine you are sharing about your day with a friend and they stop you half way through. You might keep trying to share the story with them. Babies might keep trying to finish telling us about their experiences and to complete that whole process so they can move back into a calm state, or homeostasis. So, you might find, for example, that if you stop him from finishing expressing a whole chunk of feelings, and he goes to sleep, that he might wake up again soon afterwards, crying and ready to express more. Or you might feed him and then find he starts crying again a little while later. Understanding what is going on can make a huge difference!

When my daughter shows signs of having feelings but she avoids eye contact, shall I just move on or should I continue trying to help her feel safe to let those feelings out?

It's common for babies to avoid eye contact when they have feelings to express – she is probably avoiding connecting with you because when she sees the love in your eyes, this will help her connect with those feelings she's trying to suppress. When she's avoiding eye contact, she is probably communicating to you that she would love your presence and connection to help her feel and express her feelings. You might have experienced something similar if you've got feelings bubbling and you're with someone whom you feel safe with – you might avoid eye contact, and when you do make contact, you might then feel those feelings. Please note that when babies are in the middle of expressing their healing-feelings through crying with us, it is common for them to have their eyes closed. This isn't them avoiding connection; it's them being deeply present in their own experience and feelings. You may find that at times during the crying session she opens her eyes, looks at you, and then closes them again.

How can I hold my baby when he is crying so that I don't restrict his feelings but I'm holding him safely?

I invite you to explore and experiment with different positions. I used to love sitting on a chair with a pillow behind my back, and a stool under my feet, with my knees up, and my baby lying with their back along my thighs, facing me (there's a diagram of this at the back of the book). This way I could hold one of their hands with one of mine while their other hand moved around, and I could support them to move while also holding them safely. Some parents prefer crying-in-arms more like a traditional breastfeeding position, but this can also be harder for some babies to cry in, particularly if breastfeeding has become a *control pattern*. As long as your bodies are touching and they can see you if they need to, they are freely crying, and you are both comfortable, I invite you to trust that that's the way for you both.

Do I always need to hold my baby in my arms for crying to be healing? At what age does this change?

Before a baby is mobile, yes, they need to be in our arms, or have us lying next to them, offering touch, for them to feel the emotional safety for crying to be healing. Once they are mobile and can get to us, we can offer our loving presence and they might choose to not be in our arms while expressing their feelings. After this time, it's important to observe our baby and hold in mind the *balance of attention* so that we can be sure that they are experiencing enough closeness and emotional safety for the crying to be healing.

I can clearly see that my baby really needs to cry. What can I do help her do that?

I love your clarity, and your willingness to listen. That's often the first step, being clear that they do have feelings to tell us, and being willing to be present with them in the feelings. So we can offer our loving presence. We can hold them in our arms for a start, or if they're mobile, we can stay close with them. If they're in our arms we can simply sit still, connect with our own inner calmness, and let them know that we're here and listening. If they have feelings to share with us, those feelings will generally start coming out. If they are suppressing their feelings through things like thumb-sucking, we can move in with *attachment play*, such as also sucking our own thumb and making funny sounds and voices. You might find that she then takes her thumb out and starts to cry.

If she's crawling and is distracting herself with one thing after another, you could offer her a *Loving Limit*. For example, if they're wanting to crawl all around the house we might close a door, sit against the door of the room with them, and offer that *Loving Limit* if they are wanting to crawl away to distract themselves. "I see you want to go to another room, sweetheart, but I don't think that's the most helpful thing for you right now, and I'm here and I'm listening." You might find that the *Loving Limit* then helps her express the feelings she was trying to run away from. As always, this process requires us to remember that triangle of research – remembering the theory, listening to ourselves, and observing our baby.

When can I first start listening to crying-in-arms?

I gave birth a week ago to our second daughter. As I don't want to start breastfeeding when she has feelings to express like I did with my first child, I was wondering, at what age I can start doing the crying-in-arms?

I so hear that you want to differentiate between hunger and healing-feelings this time around. It is possible to start listening to feelings from birth, particularly with second-time motherhood and if you're confident with breastfeeding and building up your milk supply and if you feel comfortable and confident with crying-in-arms. I started listening to my son's feelings from birth and have supported other parents to do this too. As with all aspects of Aware Parenting, it's important to look at each mother and baby pair to discover when might be a helpful time to start listening to feelings. If you feel ready to listen, I invite you to do that. You might want to reach out for support from an Aware Parenting instructor or Aletha Solter while doing that.

Is it okay for me to cry when my baby is crying in my arms?

It's natural for our own feelings to bubble up when we are listening to our baby expressing their feelings in our arms. These might be our own unexpressed feelings from when we were a baby or a child. It could be that if our baby is healing from their birth experience, that we are also connecting in with our own feelings from that time. My rule of thumb is that if, while we're crying, we're also present with our baby, offering her eye contact and loving words that communicate that we are both safe and all is well, then us crying too can be a beautiful experience as we heal together. However, if we are immersed in our own feelings so deeply that we are hardly aware of our baby's presence, this can be a strong indication to get some emotional support from another adult. If we need to continue crying, then phoning a friend and sharing our feelings while still holding our crying baby in our arms, offering them loving words when we can, might be more helpful. In general, receiving more empathy time from our Listening Partner or Aware Parenting instructor can also help with this.

My baby has bigger feelings than other babies and is so intense when he's crying.

It can be so easy to think that big crying is unusual, or feel concerned or worried about the size and intensity of a baby's feelings, and if you are having those thoughts and feeling those feelings, I'm sending you so much love. If you have any concerns about his physical wellbeing, please get that checked out by a health professional. However, if you are confident that he is physically well and comfortable, I wonder if you find it reassuring to know that, given the opportunity, all babies have big and intense feelings.

All of the following can be symptoms of releasing accumulated uncomfortable feelings, stress and trauma:

- Back arching (often releasing birth-related feelings);
- Loud crying;
- Sweating;
- Being hot;
- Kicking legs and moving arms a lot;
- Looking more red;
- Crying for an hour or more.

And OF COURSE, it is always important to make sure that your baby isn't in physical pain.

The paradox is, the more familiar we are with healing-feelings and release crying, the more clearly we can differentiate that from a physical pain cry.

If a baby is in physical pain, the crying will generally be higher pitched.

If it is an emotional release, you will generally be able to stop the crying by feeding, distracting, and so on.

If your baby seems different, lethargic, or you are worried or concerned, then always TRUST your intuition and seek out support from your health practitioner,

I hardly ever reach the end of a crying cycle, as my baby cries for more than an hour.

At that point, I always offer her the breast or distract her in the baby carrier because the crying is intense for me and I am tired. What will happen if I always do this?

I really hear how intense the crying is for you and I'm sending you so much love. I'm also really celebrating how much crying-in-arms you are already being with. All of that listening will be making a big difference to how your daughter feels. However, you might be not seeing as much of a profound difference as is possible for both of you when babies get to complete a full crying cycle. You might also find that she starts developing *control patterns* such as thumb-sucking or breastfeeding. An alternative to offering the breast or putting her in the carrier would be to get more listening support for you, either before or during her crying-in-arms. If we are feeling tired after our baby cries, if often means that our own feelings have bubbled up. The more your feelings are heard, the less likely it is that you will feel tired when your baby cries with you. In addition, before turning to breastfeeding or distracting her with movement, helping yourself with your own feelings while you are holding her and she is continuing to cry will mean that she is freer to express her feelings and will be less likely to develop *control patterns*. That might even mean wearing earbuds or headphones. I talk more about the options and which are most and least helpful earlier on in the book.

Is it harmful if I do crying-in-arms while not being emotionally present?

I hear your concern and I'm sending you lots of love. We can really trust our babies here. Of course it is most optimal if we are deeply emotionally present while our baby is crying in our arms. However, as long as we are physically holding them, we can also trust that they will let us know if they're not feeling enough emotional presence for the crying to be healing – because they will dissociate, eg. through sucking their hand. If we are not emotionally present at times, our physical presence and loving intuition is likely to be enough for the crying to be healing. However, if we find that we are never emotionally present when our baby has healing-feelings to express, this is a loud invitation for us to ramp up the amount of listening we are receiving for our own needs and feelings.

Sleep

My baby is just fussy because his last nap was so short. I don't know if he has feelings to tell me.

In Aware Parenting, we generally see things the other way around – that they have short naps because they have unexpressed feelings. Those feelings are what is causing the 'fussiness' and those feelings are also waking them up from their nap, so they can express the feelings in our loving arms. Does this resonate with you?

How will my baby fall asleep? After breastfeeding and awake time, should I just hold him still in my arms?

No singing or movement? And if he starts crying, of course I listen to him. But is the baby supposed to just fall asleep in the arms afterwards, or how exactly does Aware Parenting recommend that a nap takes place? I only have experience with my baby being breastfed before naps and falling asleep that way.

Many people have never experienced a baby falling asleep in their arms after crying-in-arms, or if the baby has already expressed healing-feelings earlier, simply by lying in our arms and drifting off to sleep. Yes, in Aware Parenting, we don't need to do things to 'make' our baby relaxed – like jiggling, feeding to sleep or rocking. Instead, we can just be still and present and offer our warm words. If they have feelings to tell us, they will. For some babies, that might be a big chunk of feelings, others may only have a few to express. If they don't have any healing-feelings to express to us (which is less likely because most babies generally have feelings every day to express), they will simply fall asleep in our arms, feeling tired, connected and relaxed.

My baby will sleep for hours in the carrier but only for short periods when I put her in the bassinet. What can I do?

There are possibly two things going on here. One is that because a sense of closeness is a core need for babies and for them to be able to sleep restfully, being in the carrier is meeting those needs for her and the bassinet isn't. The other possibility is that movement is distracting your baby from feelings that are bubbling up. If you really want to put your baby in a bassinet for some or all of her naps, listening to as much of her feelings as you can *before* she goes to sleep will help her feel more relaxed in her body and is more likely to mean she can stay asleep while in a bassinet. Meeting her needs for both closeness and true relaxation will be most likely to lead to restful sleep.

If my baby does crying-in arms, this prolongs his awake time. Should I stop him from crying so he doesn't get overwhelmed and can sleep?

In Aware Parenting, we don't hold the idea of 'wake windows'. You can trust your baby. If he is crying in your arms when he is tired, this is helping him feel more relaxed, not more overwhelmed. The more relaxed he is, the more peacefully and restfully he will sleep.

Do I have to listen to my baby's feelings before sleep?

You don't have to do anything! You always get to choose! The aim of this book is to give you information to help you understand babies more, and in this instance, to understand the relationship between feelings and sleep. Once you know that all babies have healing-feelings to express, that pent-up feelings wake them up in the night, that babies have a natural relaxation and healing process of crying in our loving arms when they're tired, and that one of the easiest times for them to let out their feelings and heal from stress and trauma is when they are tired, you get to take that information and do whatever you want to do with it. You might love feeding to sleep and want to continue to do that, and I support you doing whatever you love. Experimenting with these ways that you are learning about might give you clarity about what you really want to do.

How do I know that my baby really isn't waking up hungry?

I so honour you wanting to make sure that you are meeting your baby's needs for nourishment. It's only your observations of your baby along with your understanding of Aware Parenting theory that will help you know whether or not your baby is hungry during the night. One way you could experiment with this is to put a lot of focus on meeting as many of his needs as you can, offering *attachment play* and listening to as many healing-feelings as you can, particularly before sleep. You might notice that, after an evening of some big and long intense crying-in-arms where your baby completes expressing a whole chunk of feelings, that they sleep for much longer periods that night, which will be direct evidence that the waking up could have been because of accumulated feelings rather than hunger. The more you experiment and observe, the more you will understand what is really going on for your baby.

I've started to listen to my baby's feelings in the night. Do I need the light on so he can see me?

I so acknowledge all that you're doing, listening to your baby's feelings. And yes, I do recommend a low light so that your baby can see you as well as feel your physical presence, either by being held or lying next to him. You might find that a red lamp or a salt lamp that doesn't contain blue light might support you to be able to see each other but not be stimulated by bright light.

I want to 'night wean' my baby because she is waking up so much at night.

I'm sending you love and so understand that you are wanting you both to get more sleep at night! There is no one set way to do this from an Aware Parenting perspective, so I invite you to listen in to how you would like to do it. Some parents don't want to be listening to feelings in the middle of the night, so they focus on listening to as many feelings as they can in the daytime, particularly before naps and evening sleep. The longer and more intense the cry that the baby gets to express in our arms, and the more she completes a whole crying cycle, the more relaxed she will be, and the less likely feelings will wake her up at night. Other parents are willing to listen to feelings at night too, in which case, you could calculate when you are confident that your baby is waking up and isn't hungry, and offer your loving presence to listen to her feelings then. After some big cries, you may find that she suddenly just starts sleeping for longer and longer stretches. Some parents plan for a few nights of lots of crying and find significant changes quickly with this approach. However, if she is still waking regularly, you might want to offer gradually longer periods between feeds during the day and also at night, so that her stomach also gets used to bigger feeds, less often. This can also help you more clearly differentiate between hunger and healing-feelings. As always, this is a nuanced process rather than a one-size-fits-all, so I invite you to take into account your observations of your baby and your own family set-up and capacity, and apply the theory and practice that!

I've started to wean my 18 month old baby at night but she is crying for two hours in the middle of the night.

I'm sending you so much love. Listening to two hours of crying in the middle of the night is a lot! I wonder if you find it helpful to remember that this crying is her catching up on expressing feelings that she has been holding in? Many parents find that listening to feelings in the daytime and evening is much easier than in the middle of the night. I wonder if you find that too? If so, my invitation would be to support her to express her feelings then. That might include watching out for signs that you are distracting her from her feelings, or that she is dissociating or suppressing her feelings, particularly before going to sleep in the evening. Doing plenty of *attachment play* in the evening can also support feelings to bubble up, and you might find that the play then turns into crying and raging. The more that your daughter expresses her feelings then, the less feelings she will need to express in the middle of the night.

Illness and physical discomfort

How can I tell if my baby is in physical pain? I worry about him.

If you ever feel concerned that your baby is in pain, I would always take that seriously. The more you practice crying-in-arms, the more you will be able to differentiate between when your baby is crying to release stress and when he is crying because he is in pain. One way to tell once your baby starts to sit up and get mobile, is when he has toppled over or bumped into something, and you can clearly hear the pain cry. That will help you get more clarity about what a pain cry sounds like.

Crying from physical pain pain is often more high pitched.

It can be very easy to confuse physical and emotional pain. For example, if a baby is kicking his legs a lot, or arching his back, we may think that he is in physical pain – but these actions can also both be ways that babies express and release emotional tension that was mobilised for the fight/flight response. Watching for other signs that might also point towards him being unwell or uncomfortable can also help – for example, if he seems listless, if his eyes look different, if he has a temperature, if he seems different in general, or if you just have a sense that something isn't as it usually is. You might intuit digestive pain if your baby always cries after being fed, while differentiating that from healing-feelings which they might try to express before you feed them, during feeding and after feeding.

If you ever feel worried, please listen to yourself.

If you can stop him from crying through feeding or rocking, that might give you information that it's less likely that he was in physical pain – because if he was, it's likely that those things wouldn't be enough to stop the pain. They can distract a baby from emotional pain but are less likely to be able to distract him from physical pain. However, dissociation can also numb physical pain too. But of course, if at any time you are worried, please seek professional help. And I invite you to trust that the more you practice this, at your own pace, in your own time, the more clearly, accurately and confidently you'll be able to read your baby's communications.

What about colic?

Some babies have uncomfortable stomachs and challenges with their digestion, including those caused by physical tension from birth trauma and microbiome issues such as from Caesarian births as well as food allergies and intolerances. If you suspect any of these things, please listen to yourself and reach out for support from a health practitioner experienced in these issues. Some parents find that modalities that release physical tension are helpful for babies who have physical discomfort from their birth experience.

And, in our culture we are often led to believe that crying indicates that something is physically amiss and to overlook the possibility that a baby is crying to release and heal from past stress or trauma.

And of course, we don't ever want to be holding our baby in our arms, listening to them crying, when there could be things we could do to help them feel more comfortable – while also not short-circuiting their healing process.

If you are concerned that your baby is physically uncomfortable because of their digestion, please listen to your intuition and visit a health professional for an assessment. I invite you to look more into what might be going on physiologically while also holding in mind that your baby might be experiencing the effects of stress or trauma.

I have spoken to many parents who have found physical therapies helpful for their babies. If you are breastfeeding, you might want to consider things like going on a breastfeeding diet, and testing to see whether it is making a difference by gradually, one by one, introducing the foods back into your diet and observing your baby. Again, it's all about observation!

If you had a Caesarean or have been on antibiotics and are breastfeeding, I invite you to look into information about the gut biome. If you think your baby might have food intolerances, please have that checked out. Other parents have shared with me that the following things have affected their child to experience what has been diagnosed as colic or silent reflux: mould in the environment, dairy, soy and other foods in their diet or in the breastmilk. Other parents have shared that they found that Elimination Communication helped their babies who previously seemed uncomfortable.

Challenges or trauma during or after birth can lead to digestive challenges. A combination of physical and emotional healing (both of which can happen through crying-in-arms) can help heal the trauma that is causing the digestive discomfort. Just like with adults, babies' physical and emotional worlds are completely interrelated. Their physical experience affects their feelings, and vice versa.

Pent-up feelings are related to physical tension and can lead to stomach aches and challenges with digestion. Digestive discomfort can lead to overwhelm and confusion. Crying-in-arms *can bring relief* to an uncomfortable digestive system for some babies. Therefore, a multifaceted approach can often be the most helpful.

Aware Parenting invites parents to differentiate between needs-feelings and healing-feelings, and to always check first whether a baby has underlying immediate needs before assuming that they are crying to heal.

You may also notice, that as you listen to crying-in-arms, your baby's symptoms reduce or disappear altogether. This is one very clear way of getting reassurance that accumulated healing-feelings and/or physical tension from stress or trauma were causing or contributing to the symptoms.

I would love to hear what the Aware Parenting perspective is on breastfeeding as 'soothing' for teething babies.

I find the answer to this one such a personal choice. Once you have taken action to reduce physical pain, e.g. with a teething ring or cold item to chew on, the next step is up to you. Some people prefer to listen to their baby's feelings, knowing that expressing the feelings such as confusion and overwhelm will also bring relief. Others prefer to feed the baby to reduce the discomfort that way. Often our choice will be affected by whether we prefer to have our feelings heard when we are sick and feeling physically uncomfortable or whether we prefer to do things to *not* feel the feelings and sensations.

Babies' physical and emotional sensations are so intertwined. Pent-up feelings are related to physical tension and can lead to tension in the mouth and jaw that is physically painful. Teething and other discomforts can help a baby connect with unexpressed uncomfortable feelings. And of course, when a baby feels physically uncomfortable, they don't have the cognitive skills to think, "I have a new tooth coming in," and so they may feel confused, frightened, overwhelmed or unsure – and those are healing-feelings they might need to express through crying-in-arms with us.

However, one thing I have noticed is that if people *do* choose to feed their baby to stop the crying during these times, that once the baby has finished teething, there will be an accumulation of the feelings that they didn't get to express at the time that are waiting to be expressed. This can often mean that the baby is then asking to be fed many extra times a day and at night. This is an opportunity, once you are sure they are physically comfortable again, to listen to any feelings that were being suppressed at the time of teething.

In our culture, we often believe that teething is incredibly painful for babies. And that may be the case for some babies. However, in talking to many parents over the years, I've found that in general, babies who regularly have opportunities to cry in arms don't seem to have much more than mild discomfort when teething. They may dribble, have a red cheek or two, be more clingy, wake up more at night, and cry a bit more than usual, but they don't show signs of strong pain. I've often wondered whether teething babies who haven't had chances for crying-in-arms much or at all, might use the opportunity of the mild discomfort to help them release other pent-up feelings.

I wonder if you've noticed something similar. For example, perhaps you've stubbed your toe two different times. One time you were relaxed and happy beforehand, and you had a small reaction to the toe-stubbing. But perhaps another time you had already been feeling frustrated and agitated, and after stubbing your toe, you made a big roar or burst into tears. In other words, sometimes mild discomfort can be a gateway to connecting with and releasing bigger accumulated uncomfortable feelings. The same can be the case with babies who fall over or bump into things once they become mobile. Sometimes, after falling over, they might have a big cry which seems much bigger than warranted by the fall. Again, this can be an opportunity to let out other feelings. These are all just my own personal observations and I support everyone to listen in to themselves, experiment, observe their baby, and come to their own conclusions!

What about sniffly noses, coughs and colds?

Each baby is different. For some babies, crying-in-arms can help mucous to flow more freely and to clear out blocked sinuses, which eases a baby's breathing. Crying-in-arms can also help to relieve any stress or fear that might be affecting a child's body to respond most helpfully to the symptoms.

However, with other babies, crying can increase hyperventilation, and thus increase mucous.

As always, I invite you to observe your own baby and make your decisions based on what you observe.

My own policy was that if my children as babies had coughs or mucous, I would generally offer less crying-in-arms opportunities. If they ever did cry in my arms when they had a sniffly nose or cough, I would make sure that they were fairly upright when they were crying, because lying down can increase hyperventilation. If the crying set off coughing, I would pause that crying-in-arms session.

Please listen to yourself, observe your baby, and make your own choices.

What happens if my baby cries more when I touch his head?

Babies who have had forceps, ventouse or medical procedures related to their head may cry more when we touch their heads. If your baby does that, then you might want to have a professional examine your baby or consider physical therapies to support any healing from the birthing process or time *in utero* and to eliminate any physical pain that might still be lingering.

You can also observe him. When he is crying-in-arms, you might feel inspired to gently touch his head in a certain way, and you might even remember certain aspects of his birth when you are doing it. You might want to ask him if you can touch his head, and you might want to talk about what happened to him during his birth. You might also want to do your own healing in relation to whatever happened. That will help him too. You might notice that he clearly moves through his birth experience with you touching his head and him crying more, and then after that crying-in-arms session, his posture has changed, he's more present and relaxed, and other observations that show you he's healed from more of his birth experience or time *in utero*.

My baby has a medical condition. Is it safe for her to heal through crying-in-arms?

If your baby has a medical condition, it is ***vital*** for you to ask your medical professional if it is safe for your baby to cry-in-arms. If it isn't, you could still focus on other elements of Aware Parenting, particularly attachment-style parenting and *attachment play* (if your medical professional has also said that *attachment play* is safe for your baby). I invite you to receive support from an experienced Aware Parenting instructor if your baby does have a medical condition, or with Aletha Solter herself.

In summary, it is so important to listen to your intuition in relation physical pain, and reach out for help if you feel concerned. It is also important to observe your baby, and through research and observation, work out what is really going on for them.

Nappy changes

How can nappy changes with my daughter be easier?

As with many caretaking activities, with nappy changes babies really benefit when we are present and gentle with our touch, when we explain what we are doing and why, and when we ask them to cooperate with us in the process. You might even find singing in a fun way can help the process be enjoyable for both of you! *Attachment play* can be helpful, such as some peek-a-boo with the nappy before you put it on her, or some contingency play, e.g. making a 'beep' sound whenever your baby touches your nose. Bringing in more fun and playfulness to the whole experience can be helpful for both parents and babies. Maybe you could put a nappy on your head and peer through the leg holes, or fly your baby to the place where you change her nappy. If you're changing her on the floor, you could roll around on the floor together and play some funny games first.

Some babies are reminded of birth trauma or early medical procedures when they are having their nappy changed. If you sense this is going on, you might lovingly listen to her feelings while having both of your hands on her body so she experiences the *balance of attention* for the crying to help her heal from the trauma.

As babies become more mobile, it's very common for them to not want to lie down for nappy changes. One way to meet their needs and our own is to support them to stand up and hold on to something as we change their nappy. You might want to change the type of nappies you are using to make this possible.

My baby always cries during nappy changes. I think he's remembering a medical procedure he had when he was lying down.

I'm sending love to you and your baby and invite you to trust your intuitive sense that lying him down for his nappy changes is helping him revisit the medical procedure he had. As I mentioned in the previous answer, please hold in mind the *balance of attention*, so you can be sure that although he is revisiting his birth, he's feeling a deep sense of emotional safety in the present. Depending on his age, you might want to bring in some *attachment play* to help him release some of the fear he probably felt during the procedure (but not to distract him from the crying). Over time, you will see if he is healing from the earlier trauma because he will be able to lie down without crying and without dissociating. I also recommend having a consultation with Aletha Solter herself or an Aware Parenting instructor to support you with this process.

I'm listening to their feelings. Why is this thing still happening?

I'm listening to my baby daughter's feelings, so why am I still seeing these things happening?

I have heard so many times over the years some version of, "I'm listening to their feelings, but my baby still ... [wakes up a lot ... sucks their thumb ... takes ages to go to sleep]." I'm going to explain what I think is going on here, which requires understanding of a few different things.

1. I think that all babies have feelings to tell us most days for about the first year.
2. Few of us grew up with Aware Parenting, or live around other families practicing Aware Parenting, and we don't live in a culture that supports Aware Parenting. At this point in time, as first-generation people practicing Aware Parenting in this culture, I don't think that anyone can listen to 100% of their baby's feelings.
3. The amount of crying each baby needs to do varies a lot, depending on their level of sensitivity, how much stress and

trauma they've experienced, the amount of crying-in-arms they've already done, and the amount and intensity of feelings that we're able to be present with.

4. Whatever percentage of their feelings we are not able to listen to, they will need to do something with those feelings. In other words, they will use a *control pattern* so they can suppress or dissociate from those feelings.

5. The more accumulated feelings they have, the more we will see that in the amount of time they engage in a *control pattern* and the amount of tension in their body. This will affect what else we observe in their behaviour, including how easily they go to sleep and how long they sleep.

6. When we understand what is going on, we can often listen to more of their feelings, which means that they need to dissociate or distract themselves from their feelings for less of the time.

In addition, sleep is often the most sensitive barometer of accumulated feelings, so if you've listened to, say, 45% of their feelings, you might still see them waking a lot, whereas if you listen to 60% for example, you might see that shift in terms of their sleep and night waking. Sleep often seems to be the place where unexpressed feelings are most clearly seen, which makes sense, doesn't it, when we realise how much true relaxation contributes to sound sleep!

Feeding

Quite often I don't know whether my baby is hungry or she has feelings to tell me. How can I tell the difference?

Differentiating hunger from healing-feelings is a deeply nuanced process which often requires close observation of a baby's movements and sounds, both before, during and after feeding. If you think from your baby's movements and sounds that she is hungry and you feed her, but she sucks really intermittently, or keeps coming on and off, or falls asleep almost straight away, it tells you she probably wasn't hungry. In this way, you can keep clarifying whether the cues you interpreted as hunger really were hunger cues or not. Having a journal or app where you can write notes for your observations can help with that clarification process. You might also find it helpful to know two other things: rooting is a reflex and doesn't necessarily indicate hunger, and babies' stomachs get bigger over time so they can take in more milk each feed and go longer in between feeds as they get older.

I'm finding it difficult to understand when our baby has feelings to tell us.

I tried doing crying-in-arms with my four-month-old but am struggling after a few nights and ended up feeding to sleep where she settles within minutes.

I so deeply acknowledge all that you're doing to differentiate between when your daughter is hungry and when she has feelings to tell you. There are a few different things to take into account when differentiating between hunger and what I like to call 'healing-feelings'.

In this book, I talk about the triangle of research, which is the combination of:

- your cognitive understanding of Aware Parenting theory and practice;
- your own internal resonance and intuition and sense-making;
- and your observation of your baby.

This is a nuanced process that develops over time and can often be helped by taking notes as you observe your baby.

Let's look at the cognitive understanding.

I wonder if you might like to read and re-read this book so you can really deeply understand the Aware Parenting understanding of food and feelings. In particular, you might like to take into account your baby's cues and behaviours both before, during and after you offer her the breast.

As you keep observing and making sense of things, you might notice certain things, such as: your baby can go longer in between feeds as her stomach gets bigger.

You'll be able to tell from her signals when she is hungry vs. when she has feelings. If she is feeding and sucks intermittently she probably isn't hungry. If she isn't interested in latching on she probably isn't hungry. If she falls asleep soon after starting feeding she probably isn't hungry.

As you observe and make notes of things like this, and as you observe the difference between how she is afterwards if you feed her when she has healing-feelings to express vs. listening to her feelings – in terms of things like eye contact, muscle tension or relaxation, ability to concentrate, and sleep (how relaxed she is during sleep, how long she sleeps for, etc.), you will gain clarity about what's really going on for her.

For each of us as parents, this is a nuanced journey, as each baby has different cues and we are different too. But you will gain reassurance from your own observations that you deeply understand what is truly going on for her and the actions you then want to take as a result.

Is breastfeeding 'for comfort' okay?

I don't see that there is an 'okay' or 'not okay', or a 'good' or 'bad', as that would be a judgement.

Instead, what each of us is invited to do as parents is to understand the difference between when a baby has immediate needs, such as hunger, and when they have feelings to express to heal from stress and trauma, and then to make our own decisions about how many healing-feelings we listen to.

This will be affected by how much stress we have in our own lives, how much we are able to be with our own feelings, how much trauma we experienced as babies and children, how much we have emotional support now, and how clearly we can differentiate between hunger (a need-feeling) and healing-feelings, as well as dissociation and. relaxation.

If we feed a baby when they need to cry, those feelings don't go away, but get suppressed. If that continues, it is likely to lead to an accumulation of feelings, which then is likely to lead to things like more frequent waking, more agitation during the daytime, taking longer to get to sleep, being more restless at night, waking up more at night, making less eye contact during the day, being less relaxed and 'melting' into our hugs less, and so on. Therefore it is more about understanding what is going on, and then listening compassionately to ourselves. We are also invited to then look at our own *control patterns*, particularly around food in this case, and how much we are able to differentiate between our own need for food and our healing-feelings.

I think that this approach understands the needs and feelings of babies and the genesis of control patterns more than any other parenting approach, and with that knowledge, invites us to be deeply compassionate with ourselves about what a huge ask it is for us to listen to our baby's feelings.

My baby has started biting me when he feeds. What can I do?

This is often a sign of accumulated feelings, although of course, there can be other things at play, such as teething. One thing we can do is aim to differentiate more between when our baby is hungry and when they have feelings to tell us and listen to the healing-feelings more often.

In the moment, when you sense your baby unlatching and about to bite, you could offer a *Loving Limit*, where you say no to the behaviour caused by feelings (in this case, the biting) and yes to the feelings that lie underneath it. So, you might do the minimum possible to stop the biting, for example gently putting your hand on his chin or forehead, and saying, "I'm not willing for you to bite, because it hurts, and I'm here and listening." If you get the *balance of attention*, he may then move into crying and raging, expressing the feelings that were causing the biting in the first place.

My baby twirls my hair or pinches my skin when she's feeding. I really don't like it.

I hear that you don't like it and I'm sending you lots of love. Her behaviour is probably a *control pattern* – a way she's suppressing her feelings. You might see it as a sign that she has feelings to express to you. You could move in with a *Loving Limit*, gently putting your hand on her hand and preventing the twirling or pinching but not moving her hand, so as to keep her close to the *balance of attention*. Then saying something like, "I'm not willing for you to (twirl my hair/pinch my skin), because I don't enjoy it, and I'm here and listening." You may find that she starts to cry, which is her expressing the feelings that she was trying to suppress. You can then stay with her and the feelings. Alternatively, you might want to offer her some *attachment play*, moving in playfully to stop her from doing those things in ways that facilitate healing through laughter, such as making your hand into a little shape and gently touching your baby's hand, making funny noises as you do, while noticing what brings laughter for your baby.

My baby is always 'cluster feeding'. He had a really long birth and ventouse and always cries in the car seat.

In Aware Parenting, we don't have the term 'cluster feeding' and instead, perceive a baby who is constantly feeding as a baby who probably has plenty of healing-feelings that they're trying to express and which the feeding is helping them mildly dissociate from. Given that your baby had a very long birth and ventouse and cries in the car seat – this indicates that the car-seat is also probably helping him revisit his birth and he's trying to heal from it. If the information you read in this book resonates with you, you might want to choose a time when you've already fed him plenty and you're confident that he's not hungry, and then simply hold him and listen to his feelings instead. You might find that the more of his feelings you listen to, the less he cries in the car-seat, because he is healing from his birth trauma and so the car-seat is no longer helping him connect with those feelings because they have been expressed. You may find that you want some support from an Aware Parenting instructor such as me or Aletha Solter herself.

My baby 'cluster feeds' every evening for hours and she is constantly spitting up milk. What is going on?

In Aware Parenting, we don't use the term 'cluster feeding'. Instead, we generally see this pattern as indicating that the baby has healing-feelings to express, and whenever they stop breastfeeding, those feelings bubble up to the surface. It sounds like this could be what's going on for your baby, and the spitting up might be because she is no longer hungry and is getting full of milk. However, to discover what is really going on, I invite you to reach out for support with both your health practitioner and an Aware Parenting instructor.

If my baby is crying or falling asleep while breastfeeding, how can I tell the difference between a tongue tie and healing-feelings?

Although there can be some similarities between symptoms of a tongue tie and signs that a baby has healing-feelings to express, such as thumb-sucking, or coming on and off the breast or falling asleep soon after getting on the breast, there are symptoms of a tongue tie which don't indicate healing-feelings, such as: challenges latching on, not being able to lift their tongue up past the middle of their mouth, little or no weight gain, feeding noisily, and dribbling and leaking milk around their mouth (and you might have sore nipples). I recommend the work of Alison Hazelbaker if you think your baby might have a tongue tie.

However, babies who do have a tongue tie might also feel more frustrated and have more feelings to express, because of the challenges of getting enough milk. If they have had a procedure for their tongue tie, they will probably also have healing-feelings to express to you afterwards. Your own nipple pain might also affect the breastfeeding relationship and connection, which they will probably have feelings to share with you about. If so, I invite you to receive extra support from a Listening Partner or Aware Parenting instructor.

How long should a nine-month-old baby go between feedings?

I try to distinguish between real hunger and feelings and it would be nice to know what applies to one aged nine months and over.

I love that you aim to distinguish between hunger and healing-feelings and so acknowledge all that you're doing in relation to that. As for the amount of time between feeds, each baby is so different and there are other factors involved here, including the size of the feed, whether or not the baby is eating 'solid' food, and how much other food they are taking in. Rather than generalising to all babies, I love to invite parents to know exactly how to observe their baby so that they can see when their baby is hungry and when they have healing-feelings to express. This process can also become a bit more complex once babies are this age, because they have often learnt from us to ask for feeding or food when they actually have feelings to express. Much of our own clarity comes down to observing how they are before, during and after feeding. For example, if they are showing agitation or crying when they are also clearly tired, that is more likely to be healing-feelings rather than hunger. If they seem to be hungry and you feed them but during and after that they show signs of agitation or dissociation, it may well be that they were needing to cry rather than they were hungry. If you make notes of these observations along with the length of time since the previous feed or food, you will gain clarity about approximately how long it might be until they get hungry again.

I've been trying to discern between hunger and healing-feelings but never get to give my son a full feed.

I've been counting the number of his sucks to work this out. I think I'm always feeding him before he actually gets hungry. What can I do?

I so acknowledge all that you're doing to discern the difference, and want to let you know that this can take some while. I invite you to keep observing him and making note of all that you're observing. Over time, I trust that you will become more and more clear. You might want to re-read the chapter in this book on feeding, and also the feeding chapter in *The Aware Baby*.

Thumb-sucking

I've done everything I can to listen to my baby's feelings. Why is she sucking her thumb?

I so acknowledge all that you've done to listen to your baby's feelings. There are a few key reasons why a baby might be sucking their thumb. 1. We repeatedly interpreted that our baby had a needs-feeling when they actually had a healing-feeling and gave them the message that their feelings weren't welcome. 2. We accurately understood that they had healing-feelings and offered our arms and listening, but were mildly dissociated ourselves and so they weren't receiving the quality of presence they needed to express their feelings to us. 3. We were busy or distracted when they needed to cry, eg. taking an older child to school each day and putting the baby in the carseat at the time where they have feelings to express. To support your baby to be more comfortable with expressing her healing-feelings to you, first I would suggest attending to these sources. If you are repeatedly feeding her or rocking her or distracting her when she needs to cry, I invite you to avoid doing those things and instead offer your loving presence. If you have some bubbling feelings or are mildly dissociated, I invite you to reach out for your own listening time. If you take them in the car every morning, are you able to offer them some calmness and presence in your arms before leaving, so they can express healing-feelings then? Once you've attended to the source, you might then want to read the next answer to what you can do in the moment when she is sucking her thumb.

Do I pull my baby's thumb out of his mouth to help him cry?

Since a baby who is sucking their thumb or fingers is communicating that at times they haven't experienced enough emotional presence for the *balance of attention* to express their feelings, it's important that we listen to that message and **don't pull their thumb out of their mouth** if we want to listen to their feelings. Instead, there are other factors that are vital to address. The first is making sure that there is enough emotional presence for them to be willing to express their feelings – that means checking in with ourselves and our own emotional state. Are we really willing to listen? Do we have a lot of big feelings sitting at the surface? Are our needs chronically unmet? Babies live in the sea of our emotional world, and it's not enough for us to just say that we are there to listen – we need to provide the emotional environment for them to really *feel* that.

If we *are* willing to listen to their feelings, the next step might be to offer *attachment play*, to support them in feeling more connected and even to release some lighter feelings through laughter. That could be putting our thumb in our mouth as we look at them and popping it out of our mouth with a big 'pop!' sound! Or we might use some contingency play, such as making a little sound when they make a noise or touch us. We might play peek-a-boo, inviting connection, and the release of any feelings they might have felt when we were unable to listen to their feelings. You might notice that your baby smiles or laughs and takes his thumb out of his mouth and then starts to cry.

What I have found useful is to have a policy that goes like this – *if they have already taken their thumb out themselves*, I gently put my thumb in the centre of their palm and, feeling the presence in my thumb, connect with their hand. I will offer a *Loving Limit*, gently preventing them from putting their thumb back in their mouth.

However, if they are desperately trying to put their thumb back in their mouth again, I would interpret that to mean that they are not feeling enough emotional safety to cry, and I would stop holding their thumb and go back to more *attachment play* to create more connection and more emotional safety. This is an ongoing process and can bring up lots of feelings for us; getting plenty of support ourselves is essential! I also invite you to read the next response, to the question about a dummy/pacifier, because although they are different (we gave them the dummy, but they chose their thumb themselves), many of the other elements of our response overlap.

Dummy / pacifier

Now I understand that a dummy is helping my daughter dissociate, I want to help her not have one anymore. Do I just stop giving it to her?

The answer to this question depends on lots of factors, and ideally, I invite you to have some consultations with an Aware Parenting instructor to support you with this. The longer the amount of time your baby has been using the dummy for, and the more stress or trauma she has experienced, the bigger the amount of feelings the dummy has been holding at bay and are likely to start tumbling out when you don't give her the dummy.

As always, the most important thing, if you are going to support your baby to stop using the dummy, is your own emotional presence and spaciousness. I invite you to receive lots of listening yourself first, especially if you gave your baby the dummy when she was crying a lot and you were feeling stressed, overwhelmed, frustrated or scared – any painful feeling, really, and particularly if she experienced birth trauma or early separation. Having your own feelings listened to about these things is vital if you are going to be able to listen to your baby's feelings from these experiences.

As always with any *control pattern*, I would recommend lots of connection and *attachment play* first. Then when you move to listening to the feelings, you might want to start off by not giving your baby a dummy at times when you have the emotional spaciousness to be able to listen to the crying and raging that the dummy has been holding in, first explaining to her what you are doing, which is particularly important if your baby is a bit older. As she expresses more feelings, she will need to use the dummy less and less to hold in the remaining feelings. Please hold in mind if you take away the dummy but don't provide the space for listening to feelings, your baby will need to find something else to do to suppress those feelings. I invite you to trust your baby's timing and go at a pace that is supportive for you both.

Why is a dummy different to thumb-sucking in Aware Parenting?

A dummy is something we have given to our baby to suppress their feelings when we didn't understand that they had healing-feelings to express or weren't able or willing to listen, whereas thumb-sucking is something they have found themselves to mildly dissociate when they don't feel the emotional safety to express their healing-feelings. Since we have given them the dummy because we weren't willing to listen, we can also choose to not give it to them and listen to their feelings that the dummy has been suppressing now that we are willing to listen. However, to pull a thumb out of a baby's mouth would not be taking into account their sense of whether there is enough emotional safety to express their feelings with us. Our role in this case is to do our own inner work so we can provide that emotional safety and presence. *Attachment play* can often be a part of helping babies to take their thumb out of their mouth when they have feelings to express.

Out and about and travelling

When we are busy, my baby doesn't cry. What's going on?

When we are busy, it's very common that a baby will be distracted from their feelings. You might notice signs of dissociation – a staring gaze or sucking their thumb, or they might just be very engaged, or even in a state of hyperarousal, looking intently at everything. It's very common for babies to try to express their feelings when they get home or when things get quiet – so if you find that when you come home, you are then feeding them much more often or jiggling and rocking them to prevent them from crying, this could indicate that they have feelings to express from the day they've just had.

What happens if my baby needs to cry when I'm out and about with him?

There are a couple of options here.

I'd love to share about what I did! If we were going out, I would offer them some 'Present Time' before we left, by holding them on my lap, being calm and present, and asking if they had any feeling to express to me, so that they could let out feelings beforehand, which meant that they had less feelings to express when we were out and they didn't generally need to cry then. However, my actions when out also depended on the setting. If I was at a mothers' group and I wanted to be a part of it, I knew that my own needs being met was important and that if they cried in the mothers' group the other mothers wouldn't be able to hear each other – so I would communicate to my baby that I saw that they were upset and had feelings to tell me, but that I was going to feed them rather than listen to their feelings for now, but that I would listen to their feelings when we got home. And I did that, I then put aside time to listen soon after getting home, again offering loving presence and calmness so they could express their feelings then.

In general, it is preferable to listen to feelings as a preventative if we are not going to be able to listen when we are out. This is because every time we do distract our babies from their feelings, we are telling them we're not willing to listen. That can make it harder and harder for them to express their feelings with us when we are able and willing to listen. It is also likely to lead to them developing control patterns so they don't express their feelings to us when we are ready and willing to listen.

You get to choose what you do, knowing that whenever you distract your baby, those feelings are still there, waiting to come out at another time.

> **We went on a plane and my baby didn't need to cry – she slept as long as I fed her, patted her, and held the dummy in her mouth.**

When we go travelling, babies will generally experience a lot of stimulation and will generally have a lot more feelings to express to us. At airports, they might experience lots of noise, people and objects that they don't understand. On a plane, they will also experience different sensations from the noise and the cabin air and pressure. Their ears might feel uncomfortable. Their eyes might feel dry. In combination with these sensory experiences, us sitting still for long periods often provides them with the exact *balance of attention* to catch up on a lot of crying. It's for this combination of reasons that babies will often cry a lot on planes, or otherwise, we will need to do a lot of things to them to stop them from their healing crying – whether that's feeding, jiggling, or giving them a dummy.

When I used to take my children from Australia to the UK, I used to do a few things to help us all. First, I would listen to as large a percentage of feelings as I could in the days and weeks beforehand, so they had fewer accumulated feelings. Second, I would listen to healing-feelings in the airports, such as in the bathroom or in a quiet place somewhere. I would also go into the toilet on the plane and listen to feelings there. When we arrived where we were going, I would listen to more feelings. And if I was staying with someone who wasn't comfortable with crying, I would find places to support my babies to cry in my arms – usually in a rented car parked somewhere I felt safe and comfortable.

But as always, you get to choose what you want to do. You might want to feed them lots or give them a dummy or do other things to distract them. However, please hold in mind that they are likely to have a lot of accumulated feelings and if you don't listen to those you are likely to see that reflected in their behaviour, such as taking them longer to go to sleep and waking up more frequently.

My baby daughter cries in the car seat. What can I do?

In Aware Parenting the key question is always: is the crying indicating an immediate need, or a need to release feelings from stressful or traumatic events? Let's go through the immediate need part first, as this is always the most important thing to check out initially.

Considering immediate needs:

To do whatever we can to meet our baby's needs in the car, there are a few things that we can do:
- Connection beforehand – spend time connecting with her before

going in the car. That might mean holding her, talking to her, telling her what is going to happen – that we are going to be going in the car, how long it will be for, and where we are going to.

- Connection during – I suggest doing whatever you can to be connected with her while you are in the car. If there are two adults in the car, I suggest that one of them sits in the back with the baby, with a hand on her chest or holding her hand or her leg. Alternatively, if you have an older child, perhaps you could ask them to hold your baby's hand. If there is only you and her in the car, having a little mirror so that she can see you, talking to her, and if it is safe and once you've turned the seat around to forward-facing, at moments when it is safe (eg. you have stopped the car) you put your hand to the back to touch her leg. All of these will create connection.

- Protection from overwhelm – the younger she is, the more likely it is that she will feel overwhelmed in the car. For a newborn or a baby in the first few months, there are a lot of new things to take in for her: being in a position where she isn't able to move; the different smell of the car; the sounds in the car; the noises of the wheels on the road; and the noises of other cars. I recommend doing whatever you can to limit stimulation for her the younger she is. As she gets older, she will be more able to understand the various elements of the experience and will find them less overwhelming.

- Autonomy and choice – being strapped in can sometimes be frustrating for babies, especially if the journey is a long one. Having an opportunity to move can really help. If she is older, you might suggest clapping games where she claps while you sing, so she is getting to choose about moving her hands.

Healing from stress and trauma:

I have found that many babies cry in the car seat not because of immediate needs, but because it provides the conditions to help crying to release healing-feelings, for the following reasons:

1. The containment of the car helps babies connect with feelings from their time *in utero*, during birth or during restraint while going through medical procedures. For example, babies who had a very long birthing experience. Remember the way that healing happens? When something in the present reminds us of something in the past that we haven't healed from, those feelings come up to be heard now. If the time *in utero* or the birth itself was stressful (or even if it wasn't – all babies have feelings related to birth), being in the car seat often helps provide the conditions for them to express these healing-feelings. If a baby has had any medical procedures where they were held still, car seats will also help them feel and express those feelings.

2. If we usually do things to stop the crying when we are home, and especially if those things are to do with our body, such as breastfeeding or jiggling or distraction, then those feelings will come up easily in the car seat when those usual distractions aren't available. Again, the reframe is that the baby is free to express the feelings that she isn't getting the opportunity to express at home.

3. There is the *balance of attention* – because not only is there the reminder of the past experience, there is actually the presence of us being there, being still, driving, which can also create a sense of emotional safety to help the feelings come.

Something to consider is that babies crying in the car seat (in the back seat, without anyone sitting next to them) isn't the most conducive to them experiencing their feelings being really heard, particularly if they are younger. The older they are, and the more they have experienced crying-in-arms at home, the more likely it will be healing for them to cry in the carseat.

So what can you do instead?

i. *You could listen to more crying-in-arms at home.* I have heard from so many parents, that when they started, or increased, crying-in-arms at home, their baby stopped crying in the car seat. If your baby is getting more of a chance to release at home, she will not need to do it so much in the car.

ii. *If there are two adults, you could have one of you sit in the back with your baby*, hold her hands, or put your hand on her, and/or hold her head or foot, and listen to the crying. Tell her that you are right there with her, listening. Your closeness, connection and empathy makes it a healing experience. The beauty of this is that it can also reassure you that the crying isn't indicating an immediate need for connection, because you are meeting that need.

iii. *If it's only you, you could stop the car and get in the back with her.* You could either just sit with her as above, or you could take her out. But I suggest avoiding distracting her. If you distract her or feed her when she isn't hungry, it will only push the feelings down a bit, and she is likely to start crying again when you start driving again. If you do take her out of her car seat, you could simply hold her (possibly in a different position to the usual feeding position if that suppresses her feelings) and listen to her healing-feelings.

iv. *You could make sure you listen to her feelings before you go out in the car.* I used to do this when my children were babies. It's particularly helpful if you are going to a mothers' group or somewhere where you are wanting to concentrate on having your own connection needs met with other parents. Offering her your loving presence before you go out means she will release and express a chunk of feelings and she is much less likely to need to cry to release in the car, or when you are out. You can then offer her *'Present Time'* when you get back too. Of course, if you are newer to Aware Parenting and she has accumulated feelings, she may have quite a bit to catch up on and thus might still cry in the car for a bit.

I have spoken to so many mothers whose lives have been changed through this understanding. Mothers who weren't going out anywhere in the first few months because their baby cried every time they got in the car. Mothers who were incredibly stressed about their baby crying in the car. Once they started listening to more crying in these various ways, all of that changed.

Please note: these suggestions depend on the age of your baby.

If your baby is a newborn or in the early months, it is likely to be traumatic for them to cry in a car seat in the back on their own.

However, if your baby is an older baby or toddler, crying in the car seat might still be beneficial even when there isn't a parent right next to them, especially if you regularly listen to their crying at home, so they have internalised that crying is safe and that you are with them when they are crying. You talking to them while they are crying, and when you stop at a red light, turning to make eye contact and physical contact from time to time, can be enough emotional safety for some older babies.

As with everything in Aware Parenting, this issue is nuanced and is a matter of discernment and observation. Only you can tell whether the crying is healing for them at any particular time.

I'd love to share Jamie's experience here. She says:

"My daughter was 12 weeks old and I had recently started having some sessions with an Aware Parenting instructor to help me through some of the challenges of having a second child. I was alone one morning

with my daughter and she had quite a lovely nap on my lap after breastfeeding. I started recording a voice message to my instructor to share some feelings (by this time my daughter was awake).

At the end of the message I added that my daughter had experienced some stress when we were on a longer drive – she had woken up and cried in her car seat for about 10 minutes while we reached the next service station. I was reflecting that she had become very upset in the car another time as well, and I thought that it may have been related to her birth. She was born after only two hours of labour, and for the second hour I was basically holding her in with my breath and position while we gathered ourselves and drove to the birth centre. I had a sense that she didn't enjoy being made to wait, particularly in the car!

Immediately after I recorded the message, she began to cry, which continued for five to 10 minutes while I held her, looked in her eyes and encouraged her to share. She then had another feed and sleep and was very relaxed.

My instructor later responded suggesting that I talk to my baby to say I know it must be difficult for her when she is made to wait in the car, and that if she has feelings to express that she is welcome to cry. I thought it was so profound that we had already done this – she had released feelings after hearing me reflect on that situation in my message!"

Other people

How can I respond to other people who don't understand this way of parenting and who have judgements or fears?

What I enjoy doing is modelling Aware Parenting with them – which often requires for us to receive empathy from someone else first so that we can go and offer the other person empathy. Then, if we can, to listen to their feelings. That might be saying things like, "I hear that you feel concerned when you see us doing xyz." Focusing on the needs they are valuing can help too – you might notice that underneath, they are wanting to value your needs or your baby's, but they just have very different ways of thinking that those needs will get met. For example, they might be concerned that if you co-sleep, your baby will never want to sleep in their own room. In that case, the underlying need or value might be for sleep for you and confidence for your baby. In that case, you could say something like, "Are you concerned when you think that we won't get any sleep and that they won't ever feel confident to sleep in their own room?" Connecting with shared needs and values can really help.

I also find it very helpful to hold in mind compassion for them, and the likelihood that two things are happening: 1. Their conditioning is being challenged, which can feel very uncomfortable; 2. When they see you holding your baby, co-sleeping or listening to their feelings, that it is helping them connect with deeply painful feelings from their own infancy.

Basically, the more compassion we receive for our feelings, the more likely it will be that we can see underneath their behaviour to the needs and feelings they are experiencing (just as with Aware Parenting and the way we are always aiming to see the needs and feelings that are causing our baby's behaviour).

Crying at different ages

At what age can I start listening to my baby's feelings?

You might want to start listening to your baby straight after birth – particularly if they have had a traumatic birth and seem ready to start expressing those feelings to you right from the beginning, and even more so if they have been affected physically by the birth. I helped my son heal from the way his fast birth was affecting the tension in his jaw and the painfulness of his latch by listening to his feelings three times in his first two days after birth.

However, most mothers (especially if this is the first time they have practiced Aware Parenting) prefer to wait for a week or two and to focus on building milk supply first. Many people find listening to the feelings of a newborn particularly hard, so you might want to wait for longer, bearing in mind that they will by then also have accumulated feelings and possibly *control patterns* in place that will affect the process.

If you already have an older child with whom you are already practicing Aware Parenting and you confidently breastfed last time, you might feel confident to listen to your baby's feelings right from their birth. Similarly, if you you are bottlefeeding.

Our baby is 11 months old and I'm finding it physically difficult to listen to his feelings.

When I hold him in my arms, he rolls over and tries to crawl away. I keep bringing him back into my arms and he crawls away again. I find it physically very difficult to do this for very long.

I'm sending so much love to all the feelings that you feel when he is crying – and I wonder if you have a Listening Partner with whom you can share all your beautiful feelings with? I want to remind you that having our own feelings heard is vital if we are to be able to listen to our baby's feelings.

Also, at around 9, 10 or 11 months, when a baby becomes more mobile, crying changes from crying-in-arms to what I call a *crying dance*. This is a subtle and nuanced way of staying connected with our baby and supporting them to cry by finding the *balance of attention*. I talked in more detail about this process earlier on in the book if you want to find out more.

More than one child

How can I listen to my baby daughter crying in my arms if I have more than one child?

I'm sending you lots of love and compassion and want to remind you that we are meant to live in community, where many people are looking after children. And, it is still possible in this culture to find ways for everyone to get their needs met. I'd love to share my experience again here.

My children never went to school or daycare and their dad had a 9-5 job when my son was born, so I was with both of them for the majority of the time. I set up an environment so that I could listen to hours of my baby son crying every day while also being with my daughter, responding to her needs, and chatting with her. For the first four months that was in our bedroom – I set up two big comfy chairs, one for her and one for me. I had big bottles of water and lots of snacks, and lots of activities for her to do – activity books, weaving, craft, etc. It was such a beautiful time of simply being together.

Every family is in a different situation and has different needs and preferences. I wonder if you might like to change anything about your home environment so you could listen to your daughter's feelings while also attending to your older child? I'm so willing for you to find ways for you to all get your needs met!

Help with practicing Aware Parenting with a baby and a toddler with only one adult.

What can I do when my husband is at work and both of them need focused attention at once? Attending to one means the other becomes more jealous or is left to cry unsupported. The toddler's big cry distresses the baby or stops the baby from completing her cry release and the supported cry of the baby makes the toddler more frustrated!

First of all, I want to send you so much love and compassion. I really hear how hard it is, and want to acknowledge that we really aren't meant to parent in nuclear families or for one parent to be alone with one or more children for hours. Here are a few suggestions – I wonder if any resonate for you?

1. When your husband is home, I invite you both to maximise each being with one child and one baby, and listening to as many feelings as possible then.
2. Setting up the environment – this can make a huge difference. I had two really comfy chairs set up next to each other with loads of activities, drinks and snacks. That way we can listen to our baby crying-in-arms as much as possible while also interacting with the other child.
3. Giving one empathy when the other one is crying, and trusting that this is all part of their ongoing relationship. For example, saying to the baby, "I'm here with you too, I see how you're feeling," and to the toddler, "I'm not going to feed the baby, sweetheart. I'm listening to her feelings. And I'm also here with you. I love you. I'm here with both of you."
4. Setting up the environment so there are ways to be with both of them when they are both crying at the same time eg. a mattress on the floor with lots of cushions.
5. You and your partner maximising listening to your toddler's feelings so that the hitting etc. decreases and disappears – I've found that this can make a huge difference when there is a small age gap like this and can influence the sibling relationship and overall ease of parenting hugely.

Do any of those resonate? Big love to you.

Birth trauma and other forms of trauma

How can I help my baby heal from birth trauma?

Babies innately know how to heal from birth trauma. Your baby will naturally search for opportunities to do this. Any time they are crying in your arms when all their needs are met, they might be healing from birth trauma. If you find yourself remembering the birth while they are crying, it's likely that they are revisiting that experience and are healing from it. You also might find that they get in particular positions that they were in during birthing, or will push with their feet, or push their head into particular situations that replicate their birth or that they didn't get to experience that they need for completion of the birthing process. They might put their arms in particular positions that they were in during their birth. You might feel called to put your hands underneath their feet so they can feel the power of getting to push, or to gently place your hand on their head in a way that helps them revisit their birth in a safe way. They might arch their back as part of the healing process. They might want to turn during crying-in-arms, in which case you can support them with completing that process. Getting support to heal from your own experiences of the birth, if you're their biological mother, will help you be more able to support their natural wisdom in being able to heal, and having the guidance of an Aware Parenting instructor who is experienced with this can make a big difference too.

If you share about their birth with a listener, I invite you to observe your baby too – you will probably notice him making particular movements and communicating in various ways. Babies understand so much more than we realise.

My baby was premature. When can I start helping her heal from stress and trauma?

First of all, I am sending you so much love. I understand from personal experience what a huge thing you both have been through.

In the early days, your focus will be on helping your baby physically, including helping her gain weight. If there were any physical issues from her prematurity, you will probably want to gain reassurance from your paediatrician that it is safe for her to cry in your loving arms. As always, please listen to your own intuition here, and observe your baby's cues for when she calls out to have her feelings heard.

One of the key things to start with will be giving her (and you) reparative experiences, particularly in relation to closeness and agency, as she probably experienced separation and powerlessness. For closeness, I would recommend as much skin-to-skin contact as possible, and as much closeness as possible for as long as possible, which means carrying and co-sleeping and avoiding prams, strollers and cots if your paediatrician gives you the go-ahead that those actions are safe for her. In your touch, I invite you to be deeply present in your body. She probably experienced a lot of touch which wasn't present and tender and may be starving for that kind of deep connected presence.

As for agency, asking her for her willingness before you do things to her, and waiting for her response, can be one of the ways you help give her a sense of agency, compared to where she would often have experienced having things done to her that she didn't want. I would also recommend talking to her and telling her what's happening, so that she has information and her needs for respect are met.

As for her feelings, before it is safe for you to start listening to her crying in your arms, or when you are able to listen but aren't able to listen to them all (because she will probably have A LOT of feelings to tell you and a lot of stress and trauma to heal from), I invite you to mirror her feelings. "Are you feeling scared/sad/frustrated, sweetheart? I'm right here, I'm listening." When she crinkles up her eyebrows and shows you that she is scared or confused or overwhelmed, I invite you to reflect that back to her. When she is dissociating, which you will be able to tell from her staring eyes, let her know that you understand what is going on for her. "I see that you're holding in feelings, sweetheart. I'm here with you. I understand."

When you do start listening to feelings, go gently for both of you and keep listening in to her and to yourself about the pacing. She is likely to have a lot of feelings over a long period. It's likely that your own feelings will bubble up and that you will need to cry too. Make sure you receive lots of listening too and be really tender with both of you.

What I'd love to share from my experience of healing from being in an incubator is, even if a baby is not yet ready for crying-in-arms to heal from their experience, that here are the things that little baby me would have LOVED:

- Being given clear information about what was going on.
- Having my feelings honoured and mirrored even if I didn't get to cry in arms while in the hospital, eg. "I imagine you're feeling scared/confused/overwhelmed/sad/powerless/frustrated, sweetheart. I understand. When we go home, I will listen to all of your feelings."
- I would have wanted my parents to advocate for me and not leave me alone in the hospital, and to do whatever it took for that to happen and for one of them to be with me at all times.
- To touch me and hold me AS MUCH as possible.
- To stand in their power as my parents and not to be overpowered by the medical system.
- To have lots and lots of their feelings heard so that they could be calm and present with me, and to listen to my feelings when I was strong and healthy enough to cry in loving arms to heal.

I'm so willing for you to receive all the Aware Parenting support you need, for your baby to heal from her early experiences, and for you two to develop a deep bond with each other.

My baby was adopted. How can I practice Aware Parenting with him?

I love that you are wanting to support your baby with all that he has been through. It is normal for a baby who has been adopted to have a lot of big feelings to express. All the aspects of Aware Parenting are relevant, but I particularly recommend receiving support from an Aware Parenting instructor or Aletha Solter herself, because it's important that the healing process is attended to in a gentle way, focusing on the *balance of attention*, to avoid the baby becoming traumatised. The attachment-style part of Aware Parenting will be particularly important as part of creating the emotional safety for healing to happen.

My baby has been through major trauma. Can I listen to her feelings to help her heal from it?

If your baby has experienced major trauma, it's important to receive Aware Parenting professional help to make sure that you are going slowly and that nothing you are doing is re-traumatising them. However, you can certainly offer attachment-style parenting and *attachment play,* which are even more important than usual after major trauma.

CHAPTER TWELVE

Quick reference guide

When you're unsure of what to do, here are some questions you could ask yourself and actions you might take.

1. Does my baby have an immediate need, or do they have healing-feelings to express?
2. Do I feel calm and present enough to listen to their healing-feelings? If not, what do I need to be able to help myself feel calm and present?
3a. Shall I offer just connection, *attachment play* or invite them to cry with me?
3b. (Once your baby is mobile) To support my baby to cry, do I need to just stay close and present with them, do the *crying dance* or offer *Loving Limits*, or *holding*?
4. Keeping in mind the *balance of attention* – is there enough emotional safety and enough of a reminder for them to revisit the stress or trauma without reliving it?
5. Being willing to stay connected with myself during the process.
6. Observe them afterwards. Are they feeling relaxed and present, or are they dissociated?

1. Does my baby have an immediate need, or do they have feelings to express?

The first and most important question! How do we answer it!? Through observation. One of the main ways we can discern is to do what we think will meet the need, and then observe our baby afterwards. For example, if we think that they need closeness, then we pick them up. If we think they are hungry, then we feed them. Then we can observe them. If they were expressing an immediate need, and if we did meet that need, then they will show us.

How?

Closeness

Closeness is different from other needs, because to express feelings in a healing way our babies *always* need to be very close with us. If they *only* need closeness, and we pick them up, they will feel relaxed in their body, they will make eye contact, and they will melt into our bodies in a connected way.

If they *also* need to express healing-feelings, then they will show us by starting to cry, often at first in a quieter way, but gradually, if we stay present and connected with them, without jiggling or rocking or feeding, then they will start crying more.

If we pick them up and they stop crying but they are tense and avoid eye contact, it's likely that they are dissociated rather than relaxed, which suggests that they might have some healing-feelings to express to us.

Hunger

If we think they are hungry, we can feed them. But again, we need to observe them to see if they really are hungry or whether they have uncomfortable feelings to express. If they are agitated while feeding, if they push off, if they suck intermittently, if they fall asleep very soon after starting to feed, if they are tense and moving a lot, then it is possible that they have healing-feelings to express rather than they are hungry.

And we can find that out by continuing to be with them and to observe them. If after about half an hour, we are present with them, and hold them, and they start to cry in our arms, then it is likely that they do have uncomfortable feelings to express.

All immediate needs

If we have checked out their immediate needs – we are holding them; they have been fed recently; they have a clean nappy; there isn't anything causing discomfort; and we are holding them and are present with them without moving, jiggling, and distracting – and then they start to cry, it is very likely that they have feelings to express to us. We can simply be present with them and listen.

However, if they always cry after feeding (and not before and during, which could be healing-feelings), or their cry is high-pitched or unusual, or you have a sense that there is something going on for them physiologically, like digestive issues, please always listen to yourself and get these things checked out by a health professional. Food intolerances, gut microbiome challenges and other issues might be causing discomfort, so please always listen to yourself.

If your baby generally cries in the evening, or when they are tired, that is very likely to indicate that there isn't anything amiss physiologically, and that they are simply trying to express healing-feelings before going to sleep.

Being an emotional detective like this can help you discern what is really going on for your baby.

2. Do I feel calm and present enough to listen to their feelings? If not, what do I need to be able to help myself feel calm and present?

This is such an important question! Even if your baby definitely has healing-feelings to express, Aware Parenting is *also* about your feelings and needs. If your baby *isn't crying* yet, and you think about listening to your baby crying in your arms when all their needs are met, and you feel exhausted or overwhelmed or resentful or angry or scared or deeply sad, then it is probably preferable for you to not invite them to cry with you for now.

Why do I suggest *not* to invite your baby to express their feelings if you are feeling big feelings or have an empty needs cup? Because babies live in a feeling world. If you are saying that you are willing to listen, but emotionally are not really in a space to listen, they will pick up on that. Helping them trust their own sense of what is going on means being congruent with how you really feel and what you are offering them. It is more helpful, if you notice that your needs cup is empty or you are full up with feelings such as agitation, fear, frustration, anger or dissociation, to then give that top priority. Making arrangements to fill your needs cup and talking with a compassionate adult is important so that you can help yourself. In that way, you will be able to help your baby more.

What about if your needs cup is a bit empty, or you have just a few upset feelings? I trust that you will gauge for yourself if you have enough to start to listen to them. Even if you start listening to a chunk of feelings but then start feeling big feelings yourself, or start feeling exhausted, you can tell your baby, stay with them, and do what you can to meet your own needs, trusting that they will also do what they need to do. Listening to yourself and how much emotional spaciousness you have is so important!

However, if they are *already* crying and you don't feel calm or present, I invite you to return to the list of options from Aletha Solter, earlier on in the book.

3a. Shall I offer just connection, *attachment play* or invite them to cry with me?

If you sense your baby has healing-feelings to express, connection is always the first thing to offer. Through us becoming present in our bodies, and offering body contact, presence, eye contact and a warm tone, and inviting connection with our baby, they will show us what they need next. If, when we offer those things, they start to cry, and we've already ascertained from above that they need to express feelings, then we can simply be present with them and listen lovingly.

If, when we offer connection and support and our presence, our baby starts sucking their thumb or avoiding connection or crawling away (if they're mobile), or asking for breastmilk or the bottle (and they've recently had some), what can we do then?

The first thing to remember is that we've ascertained that their needs are met. They are close with us, we've checked all their needs, and they've been recently fed.

If they're moving towards a *control pattern* (e.g. sucking their thumb, asking to be fed if they have been recently fed, sucking on a dummy, clutching on to something, distracting themselves), then often *attachment play* can help.

Attachment play means bringing in warmth and laughter to what our baby is doing. So, if she is sucking her thumb, we might ask to suck it too, or we might suck our own thumb and make big slurpy noises and pull it out of our mouth with a big pop! We might trace our fingers up her arm and then pretend to be surprised to see her thumb in her mouth. We might play some peek-a-boo. Bringing warm love and gentle laughter to whatever they are doing to hold in healing-feelings can help bring release. Laughter releases lighter feelings and can pave the way for crying if needed.

If they have a dummy or pacifier, we can play similar *attachment play* games. We could get another dummy for ourselves and do funny things with it – pretending to put it in our ear, or making big slurping sounds, or pretending that it keeps falling out of our mouth.

Attachment play is a powerful way to bring connection and warmth to places where our baby is feeling some mild dissociation. Remember that dissociation is akin to freeze. We can see connection plus *attachment play* that brings warmth to the freeze, melting it into healing-feelings that flow out through tears.

3b. (Once your baby is mobile) ~ If my baby is indicating that they need to cry, do I need to offer *Loving Limits*, the *crying dance* or *holding*?

If your baby is mobile, and they are clearly needing to express healing-feelings, and when you come close, they start to move away, then the question is: how can you help them stay connected with themselves by you maintaining the *balance of attention* to help them release those feelings?

When your baby becomes mobile, Aware Parenting changes, and crying-in-arms changes to the *crying dance*, where staying connected and using *attachment play* and *Loving Limits* become more important. It's vital that *holding* is only a small part of the Aware Parenting practice, and only after *attachment play* or *Loving Limits* or the *crying dance*, and only if your baby is hitting or biting or about to hurt herself or someone else.

We can use *Loving Limits* when we see that our baby needs more to help them feel safe enough to cry and also to have something to push up against. For example, you could offer a *Loving Limit* if they have learnt to move to distract themselves from their feelings and are doing everything they can to keep moving away from being connected with you, from themselves and from their feelings.

For example, imagine you have been observing your baby all morning and she clearly has feelings bubbling (because whatever you do to meet her needs, she is still agitated). When you connect in with her, she is doing everything to avoid connection with herself and you. Imagine she is trying to go outside as part of disconnecting and avoiding. In this case you might offer a *Loving Limit*, such as, "I see that you want to go outside. And I'm not going to open the door now because I don't think that's the most helpful thing for you right now. I'm right here with you. I'm listening."

With any *Loving Limit*, we are offering it with absolute love, gentleness, no harshness, no disconnection in any way. We are simply pairing love and empathy with a limit.

That might be, "I see you want boobie now, and I'll give you some soon, but not right now. I'm here, and I'm listening. I don't think you're hungry and I would love to hear what is really going on for you, sweetheart."

Loving Limits are all about finding the *balance of attention* so that our baby can express the feelings that are bubbling.

What about the *crying dance*? The *crying dance* is all about staying close to the *balance of attention*. When we are clear that she has uncomfortable healing-feelings to express, we can stay close, following them, keeping connected and offering our love and presence.

Holding is when we choose to hold our baby when we are clear that she needs to release and is hitting, biting or head-butting. *Holding* is a powerful practice and just about every parent has questions about it. If you ever feel angry, resentful, scared or unsure, I would suggest NOT using *holding*.

Some babies do appear to need some *holding* as well as *attachment play*, *Loving Limits* and the *crying dance*, especially if the birth was traumatic or long, or if there were early separations. But it is a nuanced and advanced practice, so if you are called to use *holding*, I suggest receiving support from an Aware Parenting instructor or Aletha Solter herself. I also invite you to read the section on *holding* earlier in the book, where I talk about this in more detail.

4. Keeping in mind the *balance of attention*

The *balance of attention* is key to ensuring that laughter or crying are healing. This is essential so that a baby feels emotionally safe in the present while being able to revisit the past. On one hand is our closeness, warmth, offering eye contact, etc. and on the other hand is supporting them to revisit the past thought whatever is helping our baby connect with their feelings. In order to help our baby express those uncomfortable feelings and heal from stress or trauma, it's important that we are bearing in mind the *balance of attention*. "Am I providing enough closeness, warmth and presence?" "Am I helping them with what they need to connect with their feelings?" The more experienced you get, the more you will play with the *balance of attention* to help your baby express their uncomfortable feelings.

5. Staying connected with yourself during the process

This is so important! In order to deeply connect with your baby, it's important to stay deeply connected with yourself. Staying compassionately connected with yourself while you are helping your baby express their healing-feelings, doing *attachment play*, listening to crying-in-arms, offering *Loving Limits*, doing the *crying dance* or *holding* is vital. If you start dissociating, I invite you to bring yourself back by connecting with your breathing, the sensations in your body, and the exact things you can see – such as the freckles on your baby's face or their eyelashes or the play of light on their skin. If you start getting frustrated, resentful, scared, upset or sad, I invite you to check in with what you need and what the most helpful thing is for you in the moment, which might include reaching out for emotional support while continuing to hold your baby while they are crying.

6. Observing them afterwards

This is such an important part of the process. It is only through observing them that you will gain reassurance that *attachment play* and listening to crying is helping them. When you see that they are more relaxed, more connected, make more eye contact, are more engaged, and so on, it will help you have reassurance that this is helpful for them. If you stop them in the middle of a cry, you might find that they start to cry more readily next time. Often, when our baby gets the sense that we are really listening, they will want to share more of their feelings with us, and might start crying more often, which is another element to consider in our observations.

MARION ROSE, PHD

CHAPTER THIRTEEN

Conclusions

What a journey this has been for you and me both! I wonder how you are feeling now?

Some of the beautiful effects of Aware Parenting are: helping our babies sleep and be securely attached; it means that Dads or non-breastfeeding Mums can do bedtimes as much as breastfeeding Mums; it means that parents have effective and compassionate ways to respond to challenges... and it means so much more too!

Aware Parenting is about the relationship that you are forming with your child. The way you respond to them now becomes the bedrock for the whole of your relationship and as well as the foundation of your child's psyche.

The way you respond to your baby's needs will profoundly influence the way that she responds to her needs.

The way you respond to his feelings will deeply affect the way he responds to his feelings.

The way you talk to her will profoundly influence her own internal dialogue.

The more he gets to express his feelings, the more he will feel comfortable with his own feelings and will be able to feel those feelings when he is older.

If you feed her she is hungry and stop when she is full, she will know when to eat and when to stop eating.

If you feed him when he is hungry and listen to him when he is upset, he will know the difference between hunger and upset feelings in his body.

The bigger the range of feelings you can mirror and be with, the bigger the range of feelings she will be able to be present with within herself.

The more you respond to him with empathy, the more he will learn to respond to himself and others with empathy.

The more you can hear her sadness, frustration and confusion, the more she will come to you and tell you about those feelings when she is an older child and a teenager.

The higher the percentage of his feelings he gets to express and release, the more your baby will be connected to, and express, his true self.

The more you support her to cry-in-arms, the more she will stay connected with her innate capacity to heal from stress and trauma through crying, with a sense of loving support to do that.

The more of his feelings he gets to express and release the more aware, present and relaxed he will be. The longer he will be able to concentrate. The more he will be connected with his true nature to connect, cooperate and contribute. The more restfully he will sleep. The more peacefully he will feed. The more gentle and caring he will be with you, other children, and animals.

Aware Parenting has incredibly profound implications for your child's psyche, and the relationship between you. This is something that can be clearly observed.

If I look at a baby or a toddler or a three year old, I can tell how many of his feelings he gets to express, how he holds his feelings in, and how his parents probably hold their feelings in. A toddler whose feelings are regularly heard and whose needs are met looks very different to a toddler who doesn't get the opportunity to express feelings and release stress and tension. These are palpable and observable differences.

> *Self-Compassion Moment*
> And again, I want to remind you, if you are feeing concerned or sad or frustrated when you remember what you have or haven't done, that it is never too late to listen to your baby's feelings, and that he can reconnect with his feelings.

Rachael, an Aware Parenting instructor in New Zealand, sums up the long-term effects and power of Aware Parenting:

"My introduction to Aware Parenting came in parts and I didn't start parenting in this way until my daughter was about six months old. When my daughter was three months old, my circumstances led to us needing to move country. In the process of packing up our things, there was a time of about three to four days where my daughter's bassinet was not available and the only sleeping option was for us to co-sleep. I knew nothing supportive about co-sleeping. All I knew was how 'dangerous' it was. I was terrified and scared that I would somehow harm my baby. I was fortunate to know that one of my friends co-slept with both of her children and so I asked her, "How do I do this without harming my baby?" She beautifully and delicately guided me towards safely co-sleeping with my daughter as well as supporting all my feelings that came bubbling up. And once I started to co-sleep, I never wanted to do sleeping any other way, and we haven't. It felt so natural, connected, close and supportive. I really felt how much this met my daughter's need for closeness and safety.

The same friend who supported me with co-sleeping, also offered the invitation to become empathy partners. I did not know at the time that my friend was actually also an Aware Parenting instructor! How lucky was I!! I had never heard of empathy partnerships or Listening Partnerships before. As I learnt more about it, I felt so deeply connected to supporting my friend in this way, learning how to listen non-judgementally, and to offer unconditional love and acceptance. And this was all reciprocated; having my feelings heard, valued, acknowledged and unconditionally loved. What an incredible gift to give and receive.

It was through the Listening Partnership that my friend offered the invitation to look into Aware Parenting. I jumped onto this! I researched, read, listened, read some more, ordered books and signed up for some of Marion's courses. Everything I could possibly do while being a new mum to a young baby.

One of the most important things for me as a new parent was to reduce my daughter's need for therapy later in life. I had no idea how to do that, or where to find it or what I needed to do to make that a reality. I longed to have a relationship with my daughter that felt deeply connected, trusting, supportive and nourishing. I longed to be the person she chose to come to, when big feelings came up for her, when life felt hard, when things were not working out the way she had hoped, to be the person she trusted most in her life and knew that I would always be there... unconditionally.

I found that in Aware Parenting.

This parenting philosophy so deeply runs through my heart, that it extends beyond just parenting. The relationship between my own Mum and me has become so much more connected and has deepened to a level that I never thought was possible. The way in which I see all of life stems from an Aware Parenting philosophy. I am so grateful for the gift that Aletha Solter has offered and for those who have continued to share Aware Parenting in the world."

I'm so grateful to you for reading this book and I'm sending love to you and your baby. If what you read resonated with you, I invite you to read this book again, as this material is deep and nuanced. You will probably find that you take in different information each time you read it.

I so appreciate all that you are doing in your parenting, and I'm so glad that you're here.

So much love,

Marion

xoxox

ACKNOWLEDGEMENTS

I am incredibly grateful to Aletha Solter, PhD, the founder of The Aware Parenting Institute, for Aware Parenting, which has transformed my life and the lives of those in my family in beautiful and powerful ways. I'm so appreciative of all of her books, particularly *The Aware Baby*, which helped me understand babies in a way that I didn't even know was possible. So many thanks go to Aletha for editing this book you are reading now and making helpful suggestions. If you enjoyed *The Emotional Life of Babies* and want to learn more about all the aspects of Aware Parenting, I highly recommend reading *The Aware Baby* and all of Aletha's other books. You can find them on her website: **www.awareparenting.com**

I so deeply appreciate my book publishing consultant, Julie Postance, without whom this book wouldn't be in your hands, and to Sophie White, for the beautiful typesetting and cover editing.

Thank you so much to everyone who read and edited the book, with particular thanks to my editors Belynda Smith and Jenny Exall as well as Joss Goulden. I'm so grateful to everyone who was a beta reader, including Eirini Anagnostopoulou, Terri Nicholson, Ana Haberfield, Stephanie Heartfield, Kim Rigter, Sheryl Stoller, Georgie Bancroft, Thalia Ellis, Rebecca Thums, Sarah Pannekoeke, Clare and Brittany.

So much gratitude goes to Michael, the father of my children, for many things: the photo of our son on the cover; editing the photo of me on the back cover; being willing to trust and join with my initial calling to practice Aware Parenting all those years ago; the parenting journey we've been on; and many hours of brainstorming the title of the book together as well as the description of the book on the back cover.

I'm also grateful to all the people who offered ideas, information and suggestions, including many of my friends on Facebook, and my

Marion's books support team, with a special mention to Clare-Louise Brumley, Maru Rojas and Feyza Celik.

I also so deeply appreciate all the parents of babies I have mentored over the years, and all that I learnt from them. Thank you so very much to each and every one of you for sharing your journey with me.

I'm thankful beyond words to my daughter and son, who taught me to deeply understand babies and children. I adore these two beings.

Lastly, the person without whom none of this would be possible, my lovely Mum. Thank you for all you've done to support us to heal from our rocky start together, those long weeks being separated. I'm so grateful for your unconditional love and support, for your editing and proofreading expertise and for all you've done to support me to be here now, writing this book. I love you.

GLOSSARY

Aware Parenting Terminology

Attachment play

Nine specific kinds of play between parents and children as described in Aletha Solter's book *Attachment Play*. This type of play creates connection, elicits cooperation, and supports babies and children to both prepare for, and heal from, stressful or traumatic events.

Balance of attention

A state in which a baby feels emotionally safe while being reminded of a trauma. A *balance of attention* is necessary for emotional release and healing to occur (crying, play, laughter, etc.). I used to call this 'the sweet spot'.

Classical Attachment Parenting

This term refers to the original attachment parenting paradigm, which was first described by William and Martha Sears. The Aware Parenting version of attachment parenting has several key differences from this original version. (This term was created by me and has been adopted by Aletha Solter.)

Control pattern

Repetitive or compulsive behaviours which are usually acquired during infancy and childhood to suppress crying and strong emotions. A typical *control pattern* is thumb-sucking. *Control patterns* can put babies and children into states of mild dissociation. They are also called emotional suppression habits and self-soothing behaviours. I used to call these 'repression mechanisms'.

Crying-in-arms approach

The practice of holding babies while they cry (after all their needs are met) while communicating love, empathy and reassurance.

Dissociation

An unbalanced state that temporarily numbs feelings and produces passivity but doesn't reduce stress. This is also known as the freeze response.

Emotional release

Any behaviour which helps restore homeostasis by releasing tension from the nervous system that was acquired during stressful or traumatic experiences. Forms of emotional release in babies include crying, raging, trembling, laughter, certain kinds of therapeutic play, and body movements. These are also called healing mechanisms and tension-release processes and are often shortened to the term, 'release'.

Loving Limits

These are the combination of a verbal or physical limit paired with empathy to create a pretext for a baby to cry to release pent-up stress. *Loving Limits* say no to a behaviour or a baby's request and yes to the underlying feelings causing the behaviour. (This term was developed by me and adopted by Aletha Solter.) We may offer a *Loving Limit* in response to a baby's behaviour, such as if they are hitting or biting. We might also offer a *Loving Limit* in response to a baby's requests, such as if they are asking for the breast and we don't think that they are hungry. As Aletha Solter says, in this second situation, this is essentially a limit on our own behaviour.

Suppression

This is when babies (or children or adults) stop the natural healing mechanisms such as crying and raging, often with the use of *control patterns*.

Marion's Terminology

Crying dance

This is a nuanced process where we stay close and connected with mobile babies who have healing-feelings to express, especially if they are trying to move away to distract themselves from their feelings. The *crying dance* is one way that we help create the *balance of attention*.

Disconnected Domination Culture

The culture that has been firmly in place since industrialisation and has spread around the world through colonisation, but has its roots thousands of years before. The core tenet of disconnection is disconnecting babies from families, and disconnecting us from our bodies, feelings, wisdom, nature, seasons and traditions. From that disconnection comes domination – force, coercion, guilt, should and have-to, power-over and authoritarianism. This is a Marion Method term.

Emotional shepherd-dog

When we are staying close to our mobile baby to help maintain the *balance of attention* so that they can continue to laugh or cry to release healing-feelings.

Emotional sticks

These are ways we learn to judge or shame ourselves in The Disconnected Domination Culture. Examples of *emotional sticks* include guilt and shame and all other forms of self-judgement. This is a Marion Method term.

Healing-feelings

Feelings that are caused by stress or trauma and when expressed through crying and raging with vigorous movement in loving arms or with loving support, help a baby release that stress or trauma and move back into homeostasis.

Needs-feelings

Feelings that are caused by immediate needs in the present moment and which go away when the need is met.

Research triangle of Aware Parenting

A triangle between your cognitive understanding of Aware Parenting theory and practice, your own internal resonance, intuition, sense-making and conclusions, and your observation of your baby.

Terminology and concepts NOT used in Aware Parenting

'Cluster feeding'

In Aware Parenting, a baby's desire to regularly feed more often at a certain time of day is generally seen as an indication of accumulated stress and a need to express healing-feelings.

'Sleep regressions'

More frequent awakenings can be caused by things like illness, teething, a developmental leap where babies feel more frustrated, and so have more feelings to express, and thus will wake up more if they are not getting to express those feelings in our loving arms.

In Aware Parenting, frequent night waking in later months is generally seen as either indicating an unmet need, such as for closeness or some other physical discomfort, an indication of accumulated painful feelings that aren't getting to come out in the day or evening, or a correlation to similarly-spaced feedings during the daytime.

'Overtired'

In Aware Parenting, a baby who is tired and connected but isn't going to sleep, and who is crying and arching their back isn't 'overtired' but is utilising their innate healing and relaxation response to release stress and trauma from their body before sleep.

'Sleep window'

In Aware Parenting, babies are most able to sleep when they feel sleepy, connected and relaxed. As parents, we can observe their tiredness cues, offer closeness, and support them to feel relaxed through crying in our loving arms. Thus we do not need to be concerned about missing a specific moment when babies would presumably fall asleep more easily.

'Fighting sleep'

In Aware Parenting, rather than fighting sleep, we see that parents are more often fighting a baby's natural processes to feel relaxed enough to sleep, often through crying in loving arms. Babies need to feel tired, connected and relaxed to be able to sleep peacefully and restfully.

'Settling to sleep'

Rather than settling, we are aiming to help a baby feel deeply relaxed through meeting their connection needs and listening to any feelings that they need to express.

Terminology and concepts used differently in Aware Parenting compared to other approaches

Weaning

In Aware Parenting, the term weaning might still be used, but is a gradual process based on both the mother's needs and the baby's needs and may include listening to the baby's healing-feelings.

Breastfeeding on demand

In Aware Parenting, this term does not mean feeding babies whenever they are agitated or crying. Instead, it means carefully observing babies and identifying their hunger cues and feeding them based on those nuanced observations so that we are feeding them when they are hungry.

RECOMMENDED READING AND RESOURCES

Books by Aletha Solter

Attachment Play: How to Solve Children's Behavior Problems with Play, Laughter and Connection

Cooperative and Connected: Helping Children Flourish without Punishments or Rewards

Healing Your Traumatized Child: A Parent's Guide to Children's Natural Recovery Processes

Raising Drug-Free Kids: 100 Tips for Parents

Tears and Tantrums: What to Do when Babies and Children Cry

The Aware Baby

For more information: **www.awareparenting.com/books.htm**

Aletha Solter's Aware Parenting Institute Website: **www.awareparenting.com**

Books by Marion Rose

I'm Here and I'm Listening: Empathic and empowering responses to needs, feelings, and behaviours with Aware Parenting

Raising Resilient and Compassionate Children: A parent's guide to understanding behaviour, feelings, and relationships (Co-authored with Lael Stone)

Sound Sleep and Secure Attachment with Aware Parenting

The Emotional Life of Babies: Find closeness, presence, and sleep for you and your baby with this compassionate approach to crying

Marion Rose's website: **www.marionrose.net**

Aware Parenting Courses by Marion Rose, PhD
https://marionrose.net/aware-parenting-courses/

Podcasts by Marion Rose, PhD

The Aware Parenting Podcast
This was co-hosted with Lael Stone until episode 124.

https://podcasts.apple.com/au/podcast/the-aware-parenting-podcast/id1455772681

The Aware Parenting and Natural Learning Podcast
This is co-hosted with Joss Goulden.

https://podcasts.apple.com/au/podcast/the-aware-parenting-and-natural-learning-podcast/id1643837590

I also have a non-Aware Parenting Podcast, *The Psychospiritual Podcast*.

https://podcasts.apple.com/au/podcast/the-psychospiritual-podcast/id1344385341

Aware Parenting Community

The Aware Parenting (based on the work of Aletha Solter, PhD) Facebook group: This is a free Facebook group facilitated by a team of Aware Parenting instructors.

Further Reading

Leboyer, Frederick. *Birth Without Violence*.

Motha, Gowri. *The Gentle Birth Method*.

Verny, Thomas and Weintraub, Pamela. *Nurturing the Unborn Child*.

Verny, Thomas and Weintraub, Pamela. *Tomorrow's Baby*.

Wirth, Frederick. *Prenatal Parenting*.

The Calm Birth Method: **https://calmbirth.com.au/**

YOUR NOTES AND OBSERVATIONS OF YOUR BABY

I invite you to use this space to make notes as you observe your baby.

Eye contact / presence in eyes:

_____

_____

_____

_____

_____

Facial expressions and tension around the eyes and mouth:

_____

_____

_____

_____

_____

_____

Vocalisations (agitated or calm):

_____
_____
_____
_____
_____
_____
_____
_____

General agitation / calmness:

_____
_____
_____
_____
_____
_____
_____
_____

Muscle relaxation / tension:

_____

_____

_____

_____

_____

Number of night wakings:

_____

_____

_____

_____

_____

Movement during sleep:

_____

_____

_____

_____

_____

Other:

DIAGRAM OF THE CRYING-IN-ARMS POSITION I PREFERRED

WAYS YOU CAN WORK WITH ME

If you enjoyed this book, and would like to work with me, here are some of the ways you can do that.

Articles on my website:
https://marionrose.net/articles/

Free Aware Parenting Courses:
https://marionrose.net/aware-parenting-courses/#free-intro-courses

Aware Parenting Courses:
https://marionrose.net/aware-parenting-courses/#specific-topics

Aware Parenting Instructor Mentoring Training:
https://marionrose.net/aware-parenting-courses/#aware-parenting-instructor-mentoring-course

1-1 Mentoring: You can find more at:
https://marionrose.net/mentoring/

IF YOU ENJOYED THIS BOOK

If you enjoyed this book, I'm so glad! I would love for Aware Parenting to spread to even more parents and I wonder if you are willing to consider letting others know about this book as part of that. Here are some ways you can do so.

Please share your review on Amazon – it helps people see if this book might be for them.

Please leave a review on Goodreads.

Are you willing to tell your friends about it via your blog, podcast or YouTube channel, or on Facebook, Instagram, X (formerly known as Twitter), Pinterest or Linkedin? If so, please use the hashtag: #theemotionallifeofbabies. Are you willing to mention it to your friends and family members or colleagues?

I so appreciate your support!

MARION ROSE, PHD

AUTHOR CONTACT PAGE

Email:
marion@marionrose.net

Website:
https://marionrose.net/

Instagram:
@_marion_rose_
@awareparenting
@theawareparentingpodcast

Facebook:
https://www.facebook.com/MarionRosePhD

www.ingramcontent.com/pod-product-compliance
Lightning Source LLC
Chambersburg PA
CBHW020313010526
44107CB00054B/1824